FIFTY YEARS OF SERVICE

FIFTY YEARS OF SERVICE TO WEST TEXAS AGRICULTURE: A HISTORY OF TEXAS TECH UNIVERSITY'S COLLEGE OF AGRICULTURAL SCIENCES 1925-1975

Donald E. Green

Texas Tech Press, Lubbock, Texas

1977

Library of Congress Catalog Card Number: 77-21214

Texas Tech Press, Lubbock, Texas 79409, U.S.A.

Printed in the United States of America

ISBN (hardcover): 978-0-89672-056-6
ISBN (paperback): 978-1-68283-299-8

CONTENTS

PREFACE

The history of American agriculture has been approached from a variety of vantage points. Some historians have viewed American farmers as dissatisfied elements of society who have made significant contributions toward political and social reform through such agricultural organizations as the Grange, the Farmers Alliance and the Populist Party. Still others have discovered that much can be learned about the roots of American mores and values by studying the history of rural society. Still other historians have studied the development of agriculture in a particular region or state or in terms of one certain crop or product. Biographies of agricultural leaders have illuminated the roles played by various individuals, while the histories of various government agricultural programs have helped us to understand the political origins and socioeconomic ramifications of such endeavors. Some have written of agricultural technology and its impact upon national and regional economic development. Yet another route is through studies of the relationship of science to agriculture resulting in the rise of agricultural colleges and experiment stations. Still another emphasis may be found by studying the relationship between agriculture and the use of natural resources and the impact of that relationship upon the environment.

In this work, I have attempted yet another approach. I have tried to write not only an internal history of the Texas Tech University College of Agricultural Sciences, but more significantly, of the relationship between the institution and the region of West Texas, particularly of the High Plains subregion surrounding "Tech." Because the Texas High Plains through its extensive irrigated agriculture is one of the richest farming areas in the western United States, it is tempting to overstate the impact which Tech has had on the region. In my mind there is little doubt that the institution furnished valuable leadership and expertise in such developments as cotton and grain production, certified seed production, dairying, dairy manufactures, and the livestock industry. This is not to say that other institutions such as Texas A&M University and its Texas Agricultural Experiment Station through such sub-stations as Lubbock, Spur, and Chillicothe have not also exerted influences on West Texas agriculture, but the feeling of High Plainsmen that Texas Tech was "their" institution coupled with the relative isolation of the High Plains-Panhandle from the rest of the state and Texas

A&M forged a kind of grass-roots relationship between the College of Agricultural Sciences and the regional agricultural interests.

The central theme of this book is that relationship. The agricultural staff at Tech not only furnished expertise and acted as catalyst, but was led by the needs and aspirations of the region as well. That is, the College of Agricultural Sciences not only influenced but was influenced by West Texas. W. L. Stangel, the first head of the Animal Husbandry Department and later Dean, began promoting the concept that the High Plains' production of grain sorghums held a vast potential for the development of a feedlot industry as early as 1925 when a local farmer asked him to work out a feed ration for one of the first feedlot operations in the region. Texas Tech's dairy furnished a model for that embryonic West Texas industry while Kenneth M. Renner's Dairy Manufactures Department furnished expertise for new emerging dairy plants all over the Southwest.

As in any preface, an author must express a debt of gratitude to those without whom the work could not have been written. In a very real sense, a writer or historian is one who simply combines the resources provided by others into something that is (or should be) coherent and readable. I am indebted to many for those resources. First, and foremost, is Dean Anson R. Bertrand and the staff of the College of Agricultural Sciences who not only provided me with financial aid, but gave me a completely free hand in access to file materials as well as in my writing and interpretations. Although the first draft was read by the College's Semi-Centennial Committee (composed of Anson R. Bertrand, William F. Bennett, Walter Grub, George O. Elle, Billy G. Freeman, John Hunter, Chester Jaynes, and Thomas A. Musiak), which found some factual errors and made suggestions, most of which I agreed with and have used, the final draft is mine. Any errors of fact or interpretation are my responsibility, and not that of Texas Tech University or its College of Agricultural Sciences. Although I deeply appreciate the opportunity afforded me by Texas Tech to do this study, I also feel very deeply that my ultimate responsibility as a historian must be to get as close to the truth as humanly possible in order to produce a work which will stand the test of time. Library shelves contain many dusty institutional histories which were not only "authorized" by those institutions, but made "official" as well. In other words, the final contents were not really those of the historian, but rather were ultimately selected, approved and made official by the institution. Such works usually have little more than sentimental value and in time are read, if at all, only by the descendants of people mentioned in the books or by historians who want to demonstrate to their graduate students the worthlessness, on the whole, of such efforts. My most sincere wish is that when some historian fifty years from now is given a free hand by Texas Tech to write its centennial history, this book will prove to be of some value. All direct quotations from letters, *etc.*, have been left unrevised. Consequently the errors of grammar, spelling, *etc.*, as well as minor errors of identification (*i.e.*, initials, exact current title of the rapidly changing College of Agriculture, *etc.*) are preserved in the text.

The author has abbreviated frequently cited primary sources located in the Southwest Collection of Texas Tech University. The following are the sources and their abbreviations: Texas Tech University School of Agriculture Papers, Dean's Files—TTSAP, DF; Texas Tech University School of Agriculture Papers, W. L. Stangel Files—TTSAP, WLS; Texas Tech University School of Agriculture Papers, Animal Husbandry Department Files—TTSAP, AH. In addition, papers still in the possession of the College of Agricultural Sciences (Dean's Files) have been abbreviated to DF, TTCAS. The separate W. L. Stangel Papers in the Southwest Collection have not been abbreviated.

Because most of the correspondence cited in the footnotes originated on the Texas Tech campus or in Lubbock, the author has taken the liberty of putting the place of origin for each letter in the citations *only* if the letter was written at some place other than Lubbock. In other words, the reader may assume that all letters were written from Lubbock unless otherwise stated.

I am a continual debtor to my very good friends, Director R. Sylvan Dunn, Archivist David Murrah, and the rest of the staff of the Southwest Collection of Texas Tech University who not only furnished me with their massive collection of materials on the College of Agriculture-Agricultural Sciences, but also provided the most pleasant environment any researcher could wish. Many histories of higher education have been lacking in primary source materials because no adequate facilities for the preservation of those materials have existed. Consequently, those valuable letters, memoranda and reports have often been lost. But because of the pioneering work of W. C. Holden, Seymour V. Connor, and Sylvan Dunn in establishing and expanding the Southwest Collection, Texas Tech has excellent institutional archives within the Collection.

Thanks are also in order to the staff of the College of Agricultural Sciences, both active and retired, for providing me with reports, information, interviews, conversation and encouragement. Among that number are W. L. Stangel, Fred Harbaugh, Arthur W. Young, Bill Bennett, Ralph Durham, Donald Ashdown, James Osborn, and especially to my fellow native Collingsworth Countian, J. H. Baumgardner, who was the first to interest me in this project.

Finally, a special note of appreciation must be given to three lovely women: Pat Hensley, Dean Anson Bertrand's secretary, who took much time from her own heavy workload to gather materials for me; Rita McGinnis, a most extraordinary typist who possesses the unusual knack of being able to read my scribbling; and my wife, Ozella, who has managed to endure my love for history these past twenty years.

Donald E. Green
Edmond, Oklahoma
February 14, 1976

FIFTY YEARS OF SERVICE

INTRODUCTION: THE FIRST ONE HUNDRED YEARS OF AGRICULTURAL EDUCATION IN THE UNITED STATES

When Texas Technological College first opened its doors in 1925, agricultural education was approximately one hundred years old. The Tech College of Agriculture was built upon that hundred years of development and experience. In order to understand the foundation upon which it was erected, it is necessary to trace the development of agriculture as a science and field of formalized learning.

Agricultural education originated with the concept of agriculture as a science, and scientific agriculture began with the work of innovative gentlemen-farmers of eighteenth-century England and Western Europe. These men were products of that intellectual period called The Enlightenment or The Age of Reason that emphasized a rational rather than traditional approach in all matters in order to bring man into harmony with nature. This age gave the world such thinkers as Adam Smith, whose *Wealth of Nations* expounded the theory of the marketplace as the regulator of a "natural" economic system, and Benjamin Franklin, whose discoveries of the nature of electricity paved the way for the work of Edison in the next century. The Enlightenment also gave the world the first group of scientific farmers, knowledgeable members of the upper classes such as Thomas Coke, Lord Townsend and Robert Bakewell. Eager to increase production of wool, meat, and crops, each had his own experimental farm. Bakewell improved his strains of horses and cattle through selective breeding. Townsend was the best known of those Norfolk farmers who introduced the raising of turnips for livestock forage. Coke experimented with agriculture on a broad spectrum ranging from the use of new grain drills, to improved strains of crops, to the increased production of wool in his famous Southdown flock.

Farmers such as Coke experimented in hit-and-miss fashion. Before the beginning of the nineteenth century, there was no scientific agriculture within the framework of workable theories. Those who achieved desirable results in animal breeding knew nothing of genetics. Agriculturists in Norfolk who worked marl and clay into their sandy soil in much the same way that deep-breaking is now used to improve certain varieties of soils possessed little knowledge of chemistry. As early as 1757, however, an English physician named Francis Home wrote that agriculture was dependent upon "Chymistry," and implied that a better knowledge of that science could form a basis for a more productive agriculture. Half a century later the Briton, Humphrey Davy, began the studies which culminated in his pioneer book of 1813, *Elements of Agricultural Chemistry*.[1]

American gentlemen-farmers were also influenced by The Enlightenment. Both George Washington and Thomas Jefferson drew upon experiments of their English and French counterparts to improve their farms. Washington changed Mount Vernon from a one-crop tobacco plantation to a diversified farm and even designed an experimental, though unsuccessful, iron plow. When the Spanish emissary to the United States presented a valued gift to Washington, it was appropriately an exceptional Spanish jackass. Jefferson, on the slopes of his beloved Monticello, was perhaps the first North American to use contour plowing.[2]

By the beginning of the nineteenth century, this interest in improved agriculture was manifested in a number of ways. Agricultural societies patterned after those of England were organized in virtually every state. In 1784, the South Carolina Agricultural Society was founded. Similar organizations sprang up in Pennsylvania, New York and Massachusetts within the next few years. By 1852, three hundred agricultural societies were actively promoting concepts of improved farming. Not least in importance was the appearance of county fairs, many of which were supported by state and local government. One of the early boosters was Elkanah Watson of Albany, New York. Watson helped organize the Berkshire County Agricultural Fair in 1810 as a means of displaying his superior breeds of livestock, such as his purebred Merino sheep, and other farm products. A number of new agricultural journals such as *The Cultivator* served to publicize the new knowledge. And a number of states aided farming by undertaking soil surveys, offering bounties for better strains of crops and methods for the treatment of plant and animal diseases, establishing quarantines and in numerous other ways. The federal government was also active in promoting better agriculture. The Secretary of the Treasury asked the nation's consuls throughout the world in 1827 to begin collecting seeds, plants, and animals which might be of use to American agriculture. For the next few decades thousands of specimens were imported from Latin

1. Roland E. Prothero (Lord Ernle), *English Farming: Past and Present* (4th ed.; London: Longmans, Green, 1927), 148-223. Paul H. Johnstone, "Old Ideals Versus New Ideas in Farm Life," pp. 112-114 in *Farmers in a Changing World*, United States Department of Agriculture Yearbook, 1940 (Washington, D.C.: Government Printing Office, 1940).
2. *Ibid.*, 114.

America, Africa and Asia, including the Lima bean, alfalfa, soybeans, the purple Chile potato (crossed with domestic varieties to produce a disease resistant strain), fescue, grain sorghums, Mexican upland cotton, and numerous breeds of Asian chickens.[3]

Still another outgrowth of the movement for improved agriculture was the introduction of formal instruction in agricultural subjects in a few private colleges in the 1820's—the first faltering steps of agricultural education. Robert H. Gardiner, founder of the Gardiner Lyceum of Maine in 1821, was keenly interested in the advancement of agriculture. He provided leadership for a number of agricultural societies, imported improved herds of beef animals, and built a model farm. His school established a professorship of agriculture in 1824, but was forced to close in 1832 due to lack of funds. Other agricultural institutions founded during this early period included the Agricultural Seminary at Derby, Connecticut (1824), the Boston Asylum and Farm School (1832), designed for educating indigent boys, and the Cream Hill Agricultural School of West Cornwall, Connecticut (1845). Most of the early schools were apprenticeship institutions in which students learned their farming through supervised work in the fields.

The most important early school to teach agriculture was the Rensselaer Institute of Troy, New York. Stephen Van Rensselaer, heir to a huge old Dutch estate of more than 3,000 farms on the upper Hudson River, founded the institution in 1824. By 1850, the school had become known as Rensselaer Polytechnic Institute. Its departments of agriculture and engineering supplied a rapidly expanding nation with scores of engineers and pioneer agricultural scientists. Before the Civil War its graduates could be found working in virtually every area of scientific agriculture from state geological surveys to early state agricultural experiment stations to staff positions in the early state-supported agricultural colleges.[4]

The interest in agricultural education was merely one branch of a broad democratic impulse which emerged in the 1820's. A frontier aristocrat from Tennessee named Andrew Jackson emerged as the symbol of the movement. The new forces of democracy brought forth a number of reforms. Older states such as Virginia, Massachusetts and New York were forced by a militant majority to rewrite their constitutions in order to end or liberalize their property qualifi-

3. *Ibid.*, 114-116. Henry David *et al.*, eds., *The Economic History of the United States*, vol. 3, *The Farmer's Age: Agriculture, 1815-1860*, ed. Paul W. Gates (New York: Harper and Row, 1960), 295-357.

4. Alfred Charles True, *A History of Agricultural Education in the United States, 1785-1925* (Washington, D.C.: Government Printing Office, 1929), 35-43.

cations for voting and holding office. To old aristocrats such as John Randolph of Virginia, "King Numbers" (democracy) appeared to be in the saddle of government.

"King Numbers," which sent Jackson, Henry Clay, Abraham Lincoln and others of their homespun kind to Washington, was not the proletariat propertyless masses which Karl Marx saw in Europe. Although American mechanics and laborers from eastern cities were part of the movement, the great majority of voters were farmers—farmers who demanded not only changes in government but changes in other institutions as well.

One of the most far reaching changes occurred in education. By the 1820's, American education above the primary grades was still dominated by a curriculum devoted almost exclusively to Latin, Greek, and mathematics, designed to produce cultured sons for the wealthy minority. Leaders of the new democracy reacted against classical education and by the 1840's were demanding a more practical, useful curriculum for the children of the many. Characteristic of the reformers were Francis Wayland and Henry P. Tappan who disagreed on the means toward accomplishing that goal. Tappan, who became president of the University of Michigan in 1852, favored the approach of German higher education in advocating an exclusively academic or liberal arts curriculum for all. Wayland, on the other hand, wanted to combine academic and vocational education in a single institution responsive to the demands of the people.[5]

The land-grant college movement served not only to materialize Wayland's dream, but proved to be the most significant tool of all for the cause of agricultural education. As early as 1819, Simeon DeWitt, Surveyor-General of New York, advocated establishing "The Agricultural College of the State of New York." Alarmed over the trend of sons of the country gentry entering the law profession, DeWitt's objective was to provide young gentlemen with training in agriculture in order to keep them on the land.[6] Agrarians such as Edmund Ruffin of Virginia espoused the cause of agricultural education for the purpose of ushering improved agriculture into his native state in hopes of restoring the fertility of its depleted soils. John P. Norton, influenced by the work of tax-supported experimental farms in Europe, wanted the states to establish collegiate agricultural programs united with experiment stations. In 1848, Norton began a two-month short course for farmers at Yale in which he com-

5. For an excellent analysis of the forces which produced the land-grant college movement see Winton U. Solberg, *The University of Illinois, 1867-1894: An Intellectual and Cultural History* (Urbana: University of Illinois Press, 1968), 22-58.

6. Morris Bishop, *A History of Cornell* (Ithaca: Cornell University Press, 1962), 52-53.

bined scientific theory with farming practices. The famed Sheffield Scientific School of Yale grew out of the teaching and research in agriculture led by Norton and his colleagues. In the 1850's, state tax-supported colleges were chartered for the primary purpose of teaching agriculture in New York (1853), Pennsylvania (1854), Michigan (1855), and Maryland (1856).[7]

It was a Massachusetts-born reformer from Illinois who directed the agricultural education movement toward badly needed support by the federal government. Jonathan B. Turner, a Congregational minister, embraced many causes during his life: abolitionism, spiritualism, monetary reform, universal law, and universal education, to name only a few. He also carried on experiments in horticulture, agronomy and entomology. In the process he introduced the Osage Orange (bois d'arc) into Illinois for fencing purposes. But Turner became best known as a crusader for establishing colleges to teach agricultural and industrial skills. He believed that "Almighty God was not mistaken when he put the first man in the garden instead of the academy, and made his own son a carpenter instead of a Rabbi."[8] In March of 1852, the *Prairie Farmer* of Chicago carried a letter from Turner in which he counseled farmers to press their congressmen and senators to enact a law which would appropriate public lands to build "Industrial Education" institutions.[9]

The movement grew rapidly in Illinois, thanks in no small way to Turner. In 1853, the Illinois General Assembly instructed its congressmen and senators to bring the matter before Congress. Consequently, on March 20, 1854, Senator James Shields and Congressman Elihu B. Washburne introduced resolutions to establish land-grant "industrial universities."[10]

Getting that kind of bill through Congress awaited the skill of Congressman Justin S. Morrill of Vermont. Morrill became a member of the House of Representatives in 1855. The next year he attended a meeting of the United States Agricultural Society and listened to a discussion of the Illinois proposal. On December 14, 1857, he introduced his "bill donating public lands to the several States and Territories which may provide colleges for the benefit of agriculture and the mechanic arts." Unfortunately, the sectional struggle between North and South sucked the bill into its battleground.

7. Solberg, *The University of Illinois*, 38-40. For a detailed account of variations in the movement for agricultural education in one important state, see Donald B. Marti, "The Purposes of Agricultural Education: Ideas and Projects in New York State, 1819-1865," *Agricultural History*, 45 (October 1971): 271-283.

8. Quoted in Solberg, *The University of Illinois*, 42.

9. *Ibid.*, 40-47.

10. *Ibid.*, 53.

Southern leaders such as Howell Cobb of Alabama and Jefferson Davis of Mississippi opposed it on grounds that it was an unconstitutional enlargement of federal power. Morrill responded that the federal government had passed laws to protect commerce, grant lands to railroads, provide for military education, and protect the rights of inventors and writers, but had refused to aid the farmers and mechanics who made up four-fifths of the nation's population. In a sectional vote the bill barely squeaked by both houses only to be vetoed by President Buchanan on February 26, 1859.[11]

After the inauguration of Lincoln and the beginning of the Civil War, Morrill introduced a modified bill to a favorable Congress now shorn of hostile southerners. The bill passed both Houses by substantial margins and Lincoln signed the College Land Grant Act into law on July 2, 1862. According to its provisions, each state was entitled to a thirty thousand-acre grant from the public domain for each senator and representative as of 1860. The lands were to be selected and sold by the states. Proceeds were to be invested and the income used to establish colleges in which the primary objective would be "to teach such branches of learning as are related to agriculture and the mechanic arts," but should not exclude "other scientific and classical studies, and including military tactics." Under this authority, the federal government ultimately granted a total of 17,430,000 acres to the states.[12]

Morrill did not intend for the new institutions to be simply vocational schools. Like Francis Wayland earlier in the century, the Vermont senator wanted to integrate vocational and liberal studies into a single institution. In 1888, some twenty-six years after the passage of the act, Morrill stated: "The fundamental idea was to offer an opportunity in every State for a liberal and larger education to larger numbers, not merely to those destined to sedentary professions, but to those much needing higher instruction for the world's business, for the industrial pursuits and professions of life."[13]

In little more than two months after Lincoln signed the bill, Iowa became the first state to use the law. By 1871, thirty-six states were in one stage or another of implementing the provisions of the subsidy. A few, such as Rhode Island and New Hampshire, embodied the subject matter into curriculums of existing institutions at first. The majority, however, used the money to create new institutions such as Iowa State, Rutgers, Cornell, Penn State, University of Illi-

11. True, *A History of Agricultural Education in the United States*, 94-104. Solberg, *The University of Illinois*, 54-56.
12. *Ibid.*, 57. True, *A History of Agricultural Education in the United States*, 104-106.
13. *Ibid.*, 106-109.

nois, University of Nebraska, and the numerous A&M colleges. Some, like California and Wisconsin, added departments and schools of agriculture and engineering to their already existing state universities.[14]

Federal funding for agricultural education proved to be less of a struggle than establishing worthwhile programs of agriculture in the new land-grant institutions. Scientific agriculture was still in its infancy, no standards for agricultural education existed, and the nation had only a few agricultural scientists capable of molding such programs. At Wisconsin, a school of agriculture was not established until 1867. That same year, William W. Daniells left his instructorship at Michigan Agricultural College to become Wisconsin's new professor and established a three-year curriculum made up of courses, for the most part, in general science. Agriculture had become a four-year course by 1875 with more specialized courses the last two years in animal husbandry, breeding, history of agriculture, plants, and chemistry of soils. But the program failed to attract many students. Daniells earned his keep primarily by teaching chemistry in the college of arts. In 1878, the first student received his degree in agriculture. A number of years passed before another graduated.[15]

The president of Cornell, Andrew D. White, wanted to mold his agricultural department primarily into one devoted to research and experimentation. Educating agricultural leaders would be secondary. White hired Henry H. McCandless to head the department. McCandless, a Briton from an Irish agricultural school, appeared to have the research credentials. But he knew next to nothing of the needs of American agriculture. One local farmer who met McCandless said of him: "Yew kin depend on't, he ain't a-goin to do nothin'; he don't know nothin' about corn, and he don't want to know nothin' about corn; and he don't believe in punkins!" By 1873 the program had only seven students.[16]

In some of the new institutions, things were even worse. At Illinois the few students in agriculture performed required daily work on the college farm and attended class only to hear an inadequately trained instructor read from a book.[17] The first professor at California embellished his cosmic general lecture on agriculture with observations on growing fruit in the Garden of Eden, then described grain culture under Joseph and Ramses II in Egypt. Students in later

14. *Ibid.*, 116-118.

15. Merle Curti and Vernon Carstensen, *The University of Wisconsin, 1848-1925: A History* (Madison: University of Wisconsin Press, 1949), 1:461-464.

16. Bishop, *A History of Cornell*, 157.

17. Solberg, *The University of Illinois*, 105.

years recalled that when the instructor reached the subject of growing cabbages in the Rome of Cincinnatus, most of the class was asleep.[18] Texas A&M, established in 1876, hired as its first head (and only teacher) of the department of agriculture a man named C. P. B. Martin, a Doctor of Divinity! According to one member of the first class at A&M, "The only thing agricultural about the college was the grass on the campus." The departmental farm at the University of Wisconsin was valued chiefly as a local source of firewood.[19]

A kind of vicious circle existed. A good program was impossible without adequately trained agricultural scientists and teachers. And yet excellent programs of instruction and research were required to turn out adequately trained personnel. To make matters even worse, programs with only a sprinkling of students were difficult to justify to legislatures for increased appropriations.

Still other problems retarded the growth in numbers of students. Many farmers were not yet convinced of the value of "book-learning" for their sons. Farming had always been steeped in a mixture of mythology and practical agricultural methods which sons had learned by working alongside fathers. Thus even those who manured their fields persisted in planting and harvesting their crops, as well as breeding and butchering their animals, by the phases of the moon. The new programs in agriculture required nothing less than a revolution in farmers's attitudes, although the groundwork for this change had already been laid in the earlier part of the century by agricultural journals, fairs, and societies preaching the necessity for improvement. Moreover, the new departments of agriculture were handicapped by lack of support on the campuses themselves. Professors of traditional academe, for the most part, looked upon agriculture as vocational training unworthy of the university's basic objective of developing the mind.[20]

Still another factor which retarded the development of agricultural education was the depressed state of American agriculture from the early 1870's to about 1900, which made it less attractive to farm youths who, in turn, flocked to towns and cities for opportunity and employment. Agricultural overproduction caused by the rapid plowing-up of the Great Plains and the increased productivity ushered in by horse-drawn riding implements coupled with a steady

18. Verne A. Stadtman, *The University of California, 1868-1968* (New York: McGraw-Hill, 1970), 143-144.

19. George Sessions Perry, *The Story of Texas A and M* (New York: McGraw-Hill, 1951), 59-60, 62. Curti and Carstensen, *The University of Wisconsin*, 1:466.

20. *Ibid.*, 464. Earl W. Hayter, *The Troubled Farmer* (DeKalb: Northern Illinois University Press, 1968), 4-8.

appreciation (deflation) of the American dollar meant low prices for farm commodities. These trends occurred at the same time that American farmers were moving away from subsistence farming toward more cash-crop operations.

The social implications of the depression were as disastrous as the economic impact. The farmer in an earlier age of Thomas Jefferson and Andrew Jackson had been stereotyped as the sturdy, independent yeoman who had left his plow to defend his country at Lexington and Concord in 1775. He was often characterized as the mortar which held together the framework of American society. Jefferson's well-known belief that if God ever had a people, they were the tillers of the soil has been often quoted. By 1880, a new stereotype emerged. He was now the ignorant hayseed who could do nothing but farm. Farmers struck back by organizing themselves into political and social groups such as The Grange and the Farmers Alliance. This new militant voice of agriculture demanded government regulation of railroad rates, schemes for holding commodities from markets, anti-monopoly legislation, a graduated income tax and other such innovations.

The new militancy also demanded a voice in agricultural education. In response to demands of the Wisconsin Society of Agriculture, the governor appointed a farmer to the Board of Regents of the University of Wisconsin in 1878. Farmers even tried unsuccessfully to get a bill through the Wisconsin legislature in 1883 to create a separate college of agriculture.[21] Boards of regents were forced to bring in capable professors who, in turn, formed viable relationships with their farmer constituencies. William A. Henry was such a person. When he came to the University of Wisconsin in 1880 as the new professor of agriculture, he "found no correspondence, nothing that connected the farmers with the agricultural department."[22] Henry set about to change all that by working closely with various farm leaders and agricultural organizations. The Wisconsin Dairy Association and The Grange readily supported him in such work as establishing a state experiment station. A year after he arrived Henry reported to the Wisconsin Agricultural Society that he was receiving from three to ten letters a day from farmers.[23]

21. Curti and Carstensen, *The University of Wisconsin*, 1:470-471.

22. *Ibid.*, footnote on p. 466.

23. *Ibid.* For an incisive look into the work of the new "entrepreneur-scientists," see Charles E. Rosenberg, "Science, Technology, and Economic Growth: The Case of the Agricultural Experiment Station Scientist, 1875-1914," *Agricultural History*, 45 (January 1971): 6-13.

At Cornell improvements began when Isaac P. Roberts was hired from Iowa State College as dean in 1874. Symbolic of the sad state of affairs was the condition of the college farm. Roberts saw "ten milch cows that had among them only twenty-two milkable teats." He threatened to resign unless the regents voted money immediately to improve the farm. The new dean got his money and within the next few years succeeded in making the farm into an important research facility. He introduced alfalfa and a number of new crops. He got rid of the old tubercular dairy herd and brought in a prize herd of Holstein-Friesian cattle. Incidentally, that step greatly irritated the most influential member of his board, Alonzo B. Cornell, son of the institution's namesake, because Cornell owned a competitive herd of prize milking Shorthorns. Roberts also constructed the second silo in America and introduced courses and research in poultry husbandry.[24]

The same year that Cornell hired Isaac Roberts, Eugene W. Hilgard came to the University of California from Michigan State. Born in Germany, reared in the United States but educated in European universities, Hilgard was one of the most experienced agricultural scientists in the nation. By 1873 he had already published a pioneer work on soils in Mississippi while serving as a professor at the University of Mississippi. Hilgard met regularly with farmers to discuss their problems, taking care to keep scientific terms and jargon from his conversation while alluding to his boyhood on an Illinois farm. In 1878 he began the experiments in viticulture which aided the development of California's giant wine industry.[25]

The number of students in agriculture did not grow in the 1880's, but through adequate funding for research the new agricultural scientists were developing a body of material to teach. When Isaac Roberts later recalled his tenure at Iowa State in the early 1870's, he remarked: "I might as well [have] looked for cranberries on the Rocky Mountains as for material for teaching agriculture in that library."[26] That summed up the lack of printed matter on scientific agriculture. The situation was not entirely without advantage, however, because teachers like Roberts were forced to use laboratory methods, rather than lectures, for teaching. This, in turn, induced more research.[27]

With only a small number of students and a growing staff in the 1880's, Dean Henry made Wisconsin a model for significant research

24. Bishop, *A History of Cornell*, 158-159.
25. Stadtman, *The University of California*, 144-146, 148.
26. True, *A History of Agricultural Education in the United States*, 155.
27. *Ibid.*

in agriculture. Henry himself paved the way in his livestock feeding experiments by demonstrating that chemical analysis alone was insufficient to account for feeding results, thus opening the road for future nutrition research in both animals and humans. His *Feeds and Feeding*, published in 1898, remained the standard for a couple of decades. Emmett S. Goff, the horticulturist, contributed an important theory on the formation of fruit tree flower buds. But it was Stephen M. Babcock who was most responsible for bringing fame to Wisconsin. Babcock devised his famous test for determining the butterfat content of milk in 1890, thus giving the dairy industry for the first time an adequate standard for measuring the quality of milk. Babcock also established new standards and methods for pasteurization and cheese-making. It is impossible to measure the economic impact of Babcock's work upon the emerging Wisconsin dairy industry.[28]

The lack of students in the 1880's also gave the schools of agriculture the opportunity to provide a more direct service to actual farmers in the inauguration of "short courses" dealing with practical farming problems. Although some schools, such as Kansas State, had been providing one or two-day symposiums for farmers since the 1860's, few conducted them until the middle 1880's. Even then, it was the constituency which was primarily responsible for the innovation.

At Wisconsin, Dean Henry at first opposed and later accepted the move by the board of regents to begin such courses. Called Farmers Institutes, the first one in Wisconsin was conducted over a two-day period in the fall of 1885. Attendance ranged from 200 to 400 and included farm leaders, politicians and university personnel. Enthusiasm for the work grew rapidly among farmers. Eighty-one were conducted at Wisconsin during the winter of 1887-88. Fifty thousand farmers attended the proceedings. In an article appearing in *Harpers* in 1888, Charles Dudley Warner wrote: "The distinguishing thing . . . about the State University [University of Wisconsin] is its vital connection with the farmers and agricultural interests. . . . I know of no other State where a like system of popular instruction on a vital and universal interest of the State, directed by the highest educational authority, is so perfectly organized and carried on with such unity of purpose and detail of administration; no other in which the farmer is brought systematically into such direct relations to the University." Frederick Jackson Turner, at that time a young historian at the University of Wisconsin, stated in 1892 that the great

28. Curti and Carstensen, *The University of Wisconsin*, 1:374-395.

improvements in agriculture then in evidence in the state such as the movement away from growing grain cash crops to dairying and horticulture, could be attributed to the work of the Institutes.[29]

Farmers Institutes constituted the first direct, sustained service of agricultural colleges for farmers. Aided by federal funds appropriated by the Second Morrill Act of 1890, more programs were established. Illinois introduced a "free short course" in the winter of 1892-93. Cornell began a ten-week short course in the 1890's. Commonly called "short-horns," these rustic rural participants at Cornell in their ill-fitting clothes became campus fixtures. In 1912-13 there were 597 "short-horns" enrolled.[30] In contrast to the low enrollments in the regular programs, the short courses were well attended throughout the country and no doubt did a great deal to make agricultural education more acceptable to farmers. The University of California alone had 20,000 in its Institutes in 1901. Rapid growth of short courses was a mixed blessing. Dean Hilgard complained in 1902 that the demands of the Institutes upon his staff were so great that he and his colleagues were spending far too much time away from classes and research. But the next year the California legislature indicated its continued support by appropriating money to hire assistants and some outside lecturers.[31]

Public acceptance of agricultural education made much headway toward the end of the century as a number of important developments strengthened the movement. A "convention of friends of agricultural education" met at Chicago in 1871. Representatives of twelve agricultural and land-grant institutions attended. One of its resolutions advocated the establishment of experiment stations in every state. Another showed a desire to found some kind of permanent national organization for institutions of agricultural education and research.[32]

Other nationwide meetings followed in later years at Washington. One result was the Hatch Act of 1887 which authorized federal funds for building and maintaining an agricultural experiment station in every state. The federal government followed the lead of the states in this respect. In 1875, Connecticut had created an experiment station. Within the next ten years, sixteen more states provided for similar facilities. All except three were located at or near their

29. C. Clyde Jones, "An Agricultural College's Response to a Changing World," *Agricultural History*, 42 (October 1968):287. True, *A History of Agricultural Education in the United States*, 119. Curti and Carstensen, *The University of Wisconsin*, 1:712-714.

30. True, *A History of Agricultural Education in the United States*, 199-200. Solberg, *The University of Illinois*, 345. Bishop, *A History of Cornell*, 312-313.

31. *Ibid.*, 312. Stadtman, *The University of California*, 149.

32. True, *A History of Agricultural Education in the United States*, 192-194.

land-grant institutions, and all suffered from lack of adequate financing. Just prior to the Washington meeting of 1883, Seaman A. Knapp of Iowa State College drafted a bill to appropriate federal funds for experiment stations. Iowa congressmen introduced the bill into Congress in 1882 and 1883. But it was not until 1887 that the so-called Hatch Act became law.[33]

Another result was the establishment of the Association of American Agricultural Colleges and Experiment Stations (AAACES) in 1887. In subsequent years the AAACES set up a committee to study agricultural college curricula. This committee reported in 1896: "There exists at present in this country no standards for instruction in agriculture." After examining programs in a number of European schools, the committee proposed this standard division of areas within the curriculum: agronomy, zootechny or animal industry, agrotechny or agricultural technology (e.g. dairying, sugar-making), rural engineering, and rural economy or farm management. In a later report the committee stated: "One radical defect of agricultural instruction thus far has been that so much of the teaching of agricultural subjects has been done in a disjointed way by experts in different branches of science. The student has therefore often not had the subject . . . presented to him as a connected whole with related parts." The report ended with a plea for schools of agriculture to develop uniform courses of instruction to show vital relationships such as those of plant to soil and of animal to plant.[34] Although some of the nomenclature (e.g. zootechny) was discarded, subjects such as agronomy, animal husbandry, horticulture, agricultural engineering, etc., became standardized.

Near the turn of the century, the agricultural education movement was aided by perhaps the most important factor of all—growing support by the agricultural community. In adjusting to the demands of an emerging industrial society with its growing technology, farmers became more aware of advantages in keeping abreast of the latest developments in agricultural science. Much credit for this is due to an early Secretary of Agriculture named James Wilson, himself an agricultural scientist who had taught at Iowa State and been director of its experiment station. Wilson became Secretary in 1897 and served in that post for sixteen years. Under his leadership the Department of Agriculture became a national clearinghouse for agricultural experimentation and dissemination of information. Much of the success of Wilson's approach was due to the "professionaliza-

33. *Ibid.*, 203-210.
34. *Ibid.*, 216-219.

tion" of agricultural scientists such as Wilson, Henry and Hilgard as well as the growing popularity of agricultural magazines which, like the many bulletins issued by Wilson's Department, spread the gospel of progressive farming throughout the rural countryside. The shift in attitudes was apparent. A southern farm journal noted in 1903 that there had been a change in the feelings of farmers toward agricultural colleges within the last twenty years and "now all progressive farmers look to the agricultural colleges for help."[35]

The period from 1900 to 1925 was primarily one of consolidating gains made in agricultural education. Curricula were expanded, impressive buildings sprang up, and expenditures for research, primarily in cooperation with the experiment stations, became commonplace. The number of students grew dramatically. Cornell, for example, had 1,704 students in the college of agriculture for 1915-16. Between 1909 and 1914, Wisconsin built three major buildings—the Stock Pavilion, Horticulture Hall and Agricultural Chemistry. Perhaps typical, but more spectacular than most, was the progress at Cornell. When Liberty Hyde Bailey became Director of the College of Agriculture in 1903, its buildings were valued at $60,000, and a staff of nine taught twenty-five courses. When Bailey retired in 1913, the college had buildings valued at $1,250,000, and an overall staff of 129.[36]

The improved state of agriculture itself favored the development of the agricultural schools during this period. Due to growing demands for agricultural products by a rapidly expanding urban population, it was a period of unprecedented rises in prices for agricultural commodities and farm land values. In later years farmers would call this their "golden age." Intervention of World War I further increased demand for agricultural products. During that international conflict the price of wheat shot above $2.50 per bushel and cotton rose to 37 cents per pound.[37]

A few significant new developments occurred in the expansion of curriculum. Traditionally, agricultural research and education had emphasized greater efficiency in production. Soon after the turn of the century, however, many agricultural educators became interested in the quality of rural life, marketing, the cost of production in

35. N. James Wilson, "The Farmers' Search for Order, 1880-1910," Ph.D. dissertation. University of Oklahoma, 1974, pp. 172-173. *Progressive Farmer*, 28 (November 10, 1903):2; quoted in Wilson, 173.

36. Bishop, *A History of Cornell*, 374. Curti and Carstensen, *The University of Wisconsin*, 1:407.

37. Gilbert C. Fite, "The Farmers' Dilemma, 1919-1929," pp. 67-69 in *Change and Continuity in Twentieth Century America, The 1920's*, edited by John Braeman (Columbus: Ohio State University Press, 1968).

relation to price, and the more efficient management of farms. The most important manifestation of this concern was the Country Life Movement.

The Country Life Movement was led by agricultural reformers rather than by grass-roots farmers.[38] It attracted the attention of President Theodore Roosevelt who in 1908 established the temporary Commission on Country Life to investigate and make recommendations on measures to improve the quality of rural life. A number of prominent staff members of agricultural colleges served on the blue ribbon panel. These included Eugene Davenport, Dean of the College of Agriculture, University of Illinois; Benjamin H. Hibbard, agricultural economist from the University of Wisconsin; Kenyon L. Butterfield, President of the Massachusetts State College of Agriculture; and the chairman, Liberty Hyde Bailey, Director of the College of Agriculture of Cornell. Other prominent members included Seaman A. Knapp, author of the Hatch Act, who was emerging at this time as the pioneer of cooperative demonstration (county extension) work; Henry C. Wallace, editor of *Wallace's Farmer*; Clarence Poe, editor of the *Progressive Farmer*; and Charles Barrett, President of the Farmers' Union.[39] Although many farmers questioned the work of the Commission, and it failed to halt the movement from farm to city, there is no doubt that its report on the causes of the farm exodus produced several important results such as the organization of the American Farm Bureau Federation, rural school consolidation, the Smith-Lever Act (1914) which provided federal funds for county extension service, and the Smith-Hughes Act (1917) which subsidized public school courses in agriculture and home economics.[40]

In higher agricultural education, the movement produced new programs in agricultural economics, farm management, and rural sociology. The Report of the Country Life Commission stressed, among other matters, the use of economic and social surveys of farm conditions as a prerequisite for solving farm problems. This, in turn, supported the growth of two new areas—agricultural economics and rural sociology. The pioneer in this work at Cornell was George F. Warren who completed an agricultural survey of Tompkins County, New York in 1911, which served as a model for future surveys. As early as 1903, Henry C. Taylor, a member of the political economy department of Wisconsin, began offering a course in agricultural

38. William L. Bowers, *The Country Life Movement in America, 1900-1920* (Port Washington, New York: Kennikat Press, 1974), 15-44.
39. *Ibid.*, 25, 160-164.
40. *Ibid.*, 128-134.

economics and two years later published the first textbook on the subject. He moved to the College of Agriculture in 1909 and created one of the best departments of agricultural economics in the nation. Taylor also brought the pioneer rural sociologist Charles J. Galpin into his department.[41] These new disciplines became even more important in the 1920's when agriculture emerged from the war into another depression destined to last for the next two decades.

When the cornerstone for the Administration Building of Texas Tech was laid in 1924, a hundred years had passed since the establishment of Rensselaer Institute. The first century of experience had been difficult, but aided by such forces as the land-grant college movement and the leadership of men such as Eugene Hilgard and William A. Henry, agricultural education became an accepted part of the American scene by 1924. It was no longer in its youth when Tech was founded, but neither was it fully mature. There were few really first-rate programs, and even fewer advanced graduate programs such as those at Wisconsin and Cornell. Agricultural education was in its adolescence and still having growing pains when Tech opened its doors.

41. *Ibid.*, 86-88. Curti and Carstensen, *The University of Wisconsin*, 1:420-424. George F. Warren, "The Origin and Development of Farm Economics in the United States," *Journal of Farm Economics*, 14 (January 1932):2-9.

LAYING THE FOUNDATIONS

The development of Texas Tech University's College of Agricultural Sciences has been inextricably interwoven with the history and agricultural interests of West Texas. Before 1900, the region had largely been the home of cattle ranches whose names are now part of the romance of the American West—Matador, Spur, XIT, 6666, LS, T-Anchor, JA, LX, the Spade, IOA, the Lazy S, to name only a few. But after the turn of the century when prices for farm commodities and farm land moved upward, cattlemen began to plat their holdings into quarter-sections and sell them to farmers eager to plow up cheap but rich virgin soil free of weeds and insect pests. The movement of farmers into the region accelerated after 1920 as East and Central Texas farmers fled from the Mexican boll weevil. When W. E. Halsell put his 70,000-acre Lamb County "Sod House" pasture on the market in 1923, he sold 50,000 acres within nine months. Between 1920 and 1930, the population of Lubbock County increased from 11,096 to 39,104, and Hale County went from 10,104 to 20,189. The number of farms in the Panhandle expanded 70.6 per cent during the decade.[42]

Even before the region of Texas beyond the 100th meridian had as many as 5,000 farmers, R. D. Gage, state senator from Pecos, introduced a bill in the Texas legislature in 1896 to set aside 50,000 acres of land in the area in order to establish a "West Texas Agricultural and Mechanical College" from its revenues. The bill was defeated but the idea remained alive as various legislators introduced similar measures in later years. A. J. Baker of San Angelo was author of another bill soon after the turn of the century. J. J. Dillard of Lubbock sponsored still another West Texas A&M bill in 1911. Although the bill failed to pass, Dillard did help to secure that same year a substation of the Texas Agricultural Experiment Station for Lubbock.[43]

42. Garry Lynn Nall, "Agricultural History of the Texas Panhandle, 1880-1965," Ph.D. dissertation, University of Oklahoma, 1972, pp. 133-135. A. M. Hove, "The Transformation of Texas' South Plains," *The Earth* (Chicago), 20 (July 1924):18, 20. U.S. Department of Commerce, Bureau of the Census, *Fourteenth Census of the United States, 1920: State Compendium, Texas* (Washington, D.C.: Government Printing Office, 1925), 13-16; *Fifteenth Census of the United States, 1930: Population* (Washington, D.C.: Government Printing Office, 1931), 1:1058-1062.

43. Gilbert C. Fite, *The Farmers Frontier, 1865-1900* (New York: Holt, Rinehart and Winston, 1966), 200. Clifford L. Gibbs, "The Establishment of Texas Technological College," M.A. thesis, Texas Technological College, 1939, pp. 7-8.

State colleges and universities are products of political processes. The population of West Texas, growing in political strength as well as numbers, continued to press the proposition before the legislature at a time when Texas was creating colleges to satisfy virtually every local interest. In 1899 the state had only four institutions of higher learning (the University of Texas, Texas A&M College, Sam Houston State College, and Prairie View A&M College for blacks). But the number grew rapidly in the first two decades of the century with the founding of Southwest Texas State (1899), North Texas State (1901), College of Industrial Arts for Women (1902), West Texas State (1910), Texas College of Mines (1913), Texas A&I (1917), East Texas State (1917), and Sul Ross (1920).[44]

Believing that a West Texas agricultural college would aid the economic and cultural growth of their region, it was the townsmen rather than the farmers who assumed the leadership to create the institution. In late 1915, the editor of the *Fort Worth Record* demanded that the state establish a college in the region, but failed to specify the type of institution he had in mind. Porter A. Whaley, secretary of the Board of City Development of Amarillo, wrote to a number of commercial clubs and chambers of commerce throughout West Texas in March, 1916, suggesting that representatives of the towns get together and work toward establishing the proposed college. Whaley, who had come from South Carolina, had been influenced by the positive role Clemson had played in the rural economy of that state. Subsequently, delegates from fifty towns and twelve counties gathered in Sweetwater on April 6, 1916, and formed the West Texas A&M College Campaign Association. Porter Whaley was named treasurer and campaign manager of the organization. About $3,000 was raised during the summer and Whaley directed a well-planned publicity campaign. When the state Democratic Convention opened in Houston later that year, Thomas F. Hodge, of Sweetwater, secretary of the Association, and Homer D. Wade, who worked for S. M. Swenson and Sons, owners of the Spur Ranch, succeeded in getting a plank for the college in the platform. A bill to create the institution, providing $750,000 initially, was passed by the legislature in 1917, and the controversial governor Jim Ferguson signed the bill into law. Ferguson appointed a committee of five, including himself, Lieutenant Governor W. P. Hobby, Commissioner of Agriculture Fred W. Davis, Speaker of the House W. S. Fuller, and Superintendent of Public Instruction W. F. Doughty to select

44. Seymour V. Connor, *Texas: A History* (New York: Thomas Y. Crowell, 1971), 322.

the site for the college. Ferguson announced that the vote for the site was Abilene, 3; Snyder, 1; Amarillo, 1. But the entire proceeding was called into question when two of the committee announced that they had voted for Snyder. The legislature met in special session in the summer of 1917 as a whirlwind of controversy surged around Jim Ferguson on other matters as well. Consequently, the legislature repealed the West Texas A&M Act and set about to impeach Ferguson for his various sins.[45]

The movement was far from dead. The West Texas Chamber of Commerce (WTCC) sprang out of the Association the next year and in February 1919, Porter A. Whaley, then secretary of the Wichita Falls Chamber of Commerce, became manager of the new WTCC. The WTCC continued to carry out the program of publicity and lobbied for establishing the college. Among those enlisted in the cause was the influential *Fort Worth Star-Telegram.* A second bill which would have made the college a branch of Texas A&M was passed by the legislature in 1921 but vetoed by Governor Pat M. Neff. The governor later said he did so because the meager $50,000 appropriation to create the college was an insult to West Texas. But an obvious reason was that the state Democratic convention had previously turned down the proposal. West Texas reacted to the veto with bitterness. Some newspapers came out in favor of making West Texas into a separate state. But the *Fort Worth Star-Telegram* simply demanded "justice for West Texas."[46]

Pat Neff was renominated for governor by the Democratic Party convention in 1922. Far from being unsympathetic to the movement to create the college, he told Homer D. Wade, "legislative manager" (lobbyist) for the WTCC: "Get a plank in the platform if you want that A&M College." Wade and Whaley subsequently led the successful fight to get the plank in the Democratic Party platform. The way was now clear for the battle in the new legislature.[47]

Led by the WTCC, friends of the proposal held a rally in Fort Worth to present a united front, but separate bills were introduced in the legislature in January, 1923. In the senate, W. H. Bledsoe of Lubbock co-authored a bill with R. M. Chitwood of Sweetwater to

45. Hamilton Wright, *The Winning of the West Texas College* (Amarillo: privately printed, 1926), 5-9. Homer Dale Wade, *Establishment of Texas Technological College* (Lubbock: Texas Tech Press, 1956), 3-28. The most comprehensive account of the founding of Texas Tech is found in Jane Gilmore Rushing and Kline A. Nall, *Evolution of a University: Texas Tech's First Fifty Years* (Austin: Madrona Press, 1975), 1-25.

46. Wright, *The Winning of the West Texas College*, 10-16. Wade, *Establishment of Texas Technological College*, 44-45, 57-58. Rushing and Nall, *Evolution of a University*, 7-8.

47. Wright, *The Winning of the West Texas College*, 16-17.

place the new college under the Texas A&M Board. But representative R. A. Baldwin of Slaton vowed to accept nothing less than a completely independent board. Differences over the amount to be appropriated and other matters cracked the united front. In the meantime, L. A. Carpenter of Dallas introduced a bill in the house to create a "College of Technology and Textile Engineering."

In desperation, Porter Whaley arranged a conference among the factional leaders. On the morning of January 25, 1923, a small group including Bledsoe, Chitwood, Baldwin and Carpenter sat in the reception room of the senate and for two hours worked on a compromise. In the final bill, Carpenter contributed the name of Texas Technological College and Baldwin provided the separate board. The bill passed both houses. When Neff signed it on the morning of February 10, he turned to its sponsors and said, "Gentlemen, I look upon this act . . . as one of the greatest accomplishments of my administration as Governor of Texas."[48]

The bill creating Texas Tech provided that the institution was "particularly to give instruction in technological, manufacturing, and agricultural pursuits and domestic husbandry and home economics."[49] A five-member board was charged with locating the site for the college and thirty-seven towns and cities west of the ninety-eighth meridian submitted location proposals. The site-board was composed of blind S. B. Cowell, chairman, who was also the Chairman of the State Board of Control; F. M. Braley, President of Texas College of Industrial Arts; S. M. N. Marrs, State Superintendent of Education; W. B. Bizzell, President of Texas A&M; and William S. Sutton, Acting President of the University of Texas. From July 14 through August 7, 1923, the board toured the competing towns which had submitted briefs outlining their advantages for Tech's location. For three weeks the group was dined, entertained, and subjected to speeches upon speeches. The Committee deliberated the better part of two days in a Fort Worth hotel before announcing on August 8 that Lubbock was its choice.[50]

Lubbock in 1924 was unimpressive to any outside observer who happened to stray into town. The census of 1920 had counted 4,051 people but the "city" claimed to have 10,000 in 1924. Cut off from the northeast by Yellowhouse Canyon, the town on the flat terrain was surrounded by native grass and new cotton fields. Only thirty-four

48. Wade, *Establishment of Texas Technological College*, 64-103.

49. Lawrence L. Graves, "Education, Welfare, and Recreation," p. 520 in *A History of Lubbock*, edited by Lawrence L. Graves (Lubbock: West Texas Museum Association, 1962).

50. Wade, *Establishment of Texas Technological College*, 149-159. Rushing and Nall, *Evolution of a University*, 19-20.

years old with a recently constructed water and sewage system, the town had been incorporated only since 1909. Its population consisted primarily of merchants and professional people. Its economy was predominately agricultural, divided between a declining cattle ranch industry crippled by the low prices of the 1920's and an emerging farm industry producing primarily boll weevil-free cotton, grain sorghums for livestock forage, and some wheat. Lubbock was the geographic center of this growing agricultural economy on the South Plains. Between 1910 and 1925 the number of cattle on the South Plains decreased 40 per cent while the number of farms grew from 7,258 to 16,891. The brief submitted by Lubbock stressed the recent development of the region and called it "the coming agricultural section of Texas."[51]

The Board of Directors appointed by Governor Neff chose Paul W. Horn, President of Southwestern University of Georgetown, Texas, as the first President of Tech in November 1923. Early the next year, he and members of the Board toured several technological and agricultural schools including Iowa State, Auburn and Georgia Tech looking for ideas to incorporate in the new institution to be built on the 2,000-acre campus on the west side of Lubbock.[52]

President Horn interpreted the charter to mean that Tech was to be primarily, but not exclusively, a vocational institution. Although the Board originally divided the school into four "colleges" (changed to "schools" before Tech opened its doors)—Engineering, Liberal Arts, Household Economics and Agriculture—which served to emphasize a gulf between "academic" and "vocational" subjects, Horn showed an interest in breaking down artificial divisions of learning.[53]

It was symbolic that a bale of cotton from a Lubbock gin was used for the speakers' podium when the ceremonies to lay the cornerstone of the Administration Building were conducted on Armistice Day, 1924.[54] In accordance with the wishes of Tech's "founding fathers" who had worked hard to establish a "West Texas A&M," from the beginning agriculture constituted an important emphasis. Indeed, the School of Agriculture was that part of Tech which most closely related to the majority of the constituency of the region. Even the primary thrust of the School of Engineering with its Textile Engi-

51. Roy Sylvan Dunn, "Agriculture Builds a City," pp. 255-256, 262-263 in *A History of Lubbock.*

52. Graves, "Education, Welfare, and Recreation," 523-525.

53. Ruth Horn Andrews, *The First Thirty Years: A History of Texas Technological College, 1925-1955* (Lubbock: Texas Tech Press, 1956), 14-15.

54. *Ibid.*, 10.

neering Department bore a direct relationship to the agriculture of West Texas.

Horn recognized this importance when he offered the position of Dean of the School of Agriculture to Arthur H. Leidigh in April, 1925. At the time, Leidigh was assistant director of the Texas Agricultural Experiment Station, a position he had held since 1923. Born at Hutchinson, Kansas, in 1880, he held a B.S. degree from Kansas State (1902) and M.S. from Texas A&M (1923). He first came to the Texas Panhandle in 1903 to work as an agronomist with the U. S. Department of Agriculture experiment station at Channing in the Office of Grain Investigations. He returned to Kansas to farm from 1908 to 1911. From 1911 to 1913, Leidigh taught agronomy at Kansas State. Then in 1913 he went to the Texas Agricultural Experiment Station as agronomist and became assistant director. His specialty was small grains. "My particular contribution to agriculture," he wrote Horn, " . . . consists in the development of the western limit of the wheat belt in the Texas Panhandle, together with a study of methods of growing wheat in that region; the impetus given to the use of milo in the upper Panhandle, western Oklahoma and southwestern Kansas, during the five years I worked in the Texas Panhandle; the specific selection and introduction of Sunrise kafir, Dawn kafir, and Acme broom corn." In 1925, he was working on rust-proof varieties of wheat suited for Texas. He counted among his friends F. D. Farrel, acting President of Kansas State, B. Youngblood, Director of the Texas Agricultural Experiment Station, and William M. Jardine, the U. S. Secretary of Agriculture. Included among his former students were R. E. Karper, Superintendent of the Texas Agriculture Experiment Substation at Lubbock and Harry L. Kent, President of New Mexico A&M.[55]

Leidigh had two tasks at hand—assembling a faculty and establishing a new agricultural program. Even before he left College Station, Leidigh chose his staff. Early in May, he made offers to W. L. Stangel and C. H. Mahoney. Both accepted. Charles H. Mahoney would teach horticulture. He was 24 years old, a native of Douglas, Arizona who held a B.S. in horticulture from the University of Arizona (1923) and would receive his M.S. from Texas A&M in June 1925. He was experienced in irrigation and fruit farming. At "A&M" he did research in cotton plant breeding. Leidigh believed he would

55. A. H. Leidigh, College Station, March 31, 1925, to P. W. Horn, Texas Tech University School of Agriculture Papers, Dean's Files, Southwest Collection, Texas Tech. Hereafter cited as TTSAP, DF. Neil Casey Fine, "A. H. Leidigh," pp. 122-124 in *Builders of the Southwest*, edited by Seymour V. Connor (Lubbock: Southwest Collection of Texas Tech, 1959). A. H. Leidigh, College Station, April 21, 1925, to P. W. Horn, TTSAP, DF.

be a valuable resource not only in working with cotton in West Texas but also in "beautifying the campus." Incidentally, Mahoney would plant the first trees on campus in February, 1926.[56]

W. L. (Wenzel Louis) Stangel, commonly called "Runt" by his friends, was more experienced than the younger Mahoney. Born in 1899 in Wisconsin but reared in Fort Worth, he graduated from Texas A&M in 1915 with a major in animal husbandry. The next year he received his M.S. degree from the University of Missouri. From 1916 to 1925 he was a member of the Animal Husbandry Department at Texas A&M. He worked primarily in livestock judging. In 1919, he coached the Texas A&M team into First Place at the International Livestock Exposition in Chicago. For that accomplishment, Stangel was promoted to full professor. Leidigh and Horn agreed in offering the job to Stangel that he could continue his many livestock judging activities. To round out the small staff, young F. I. Dahlberg with a B.S. from Texas A&M was hired as superintendent of the college farm in the fall of 1925.[57]

Leidigh's objective was to build a balanced, flexible program in agriculture. Mahoney was to handle horticulture and cotton, Stangel would put together the animal husbandry offerings and Leidigh would be responsible for agronomy, especially small grains. Their fields corresponded to the needs of West Texas agriculture. The first college bulletin announced: "Special attention will be given to arid and semi-arid farming, and such subjects as are especially adapted to the work of that portion of Texas in which the College is located." The Dean wrote to his friend William Jardine, Secretary of Agriculture, "Candidly, I have great hopes that this college will point the way for a more liberal and less 'cut and dryed' type of education in agriculture." At the same time he confided that its future development "will be complicated by our lack of being an integral part of the land-grant college system."[58]

Indeed, as Leidigh would be reminded again and again, the fact that Tech was not a land-grant institution would prove to be one of the most formidable obstacles in the development of the School of Agriculture. Cut off from federal funds and direct access to the the Texas State Experiment Station, it had to rely primarily upon

56. A. H. Leidigh, College Station, May 5, 1925, to P. W. Horn; Leidigh, January 18, 1926, to Horn, TTSAP, DF. The place of origin for all letters cited is Lubbock unless otherwise stated.

57. *Ibid.* Neil Casey Fine, "W. L. Stangel," pp. 235-236 in *Builders of the Southwest.* A. H. Leidigh, October 14, 1925, to P. W. Horn, TTSAP, DF.

58. A. H. Leidigh, November 19, 1925, to William M. Jardine, Secretary of Agriculture, TTSAP, DF. *Bulletin of Texas Technological College*, vol. 1, no. 1 (1925).

its own resources and the resources of the region. This, in turn, greatly influenced the development of the College.

Texas Tech officially opened its doors in September, 1925 during the beginning of an unusually wet fall season. On September 13, 2.4 inches of rain fell in thirty minutes, collapsing the flat roof of the Lubbock post office. When the first faculty meeting convened two days later, President Horn announced that some staff members were absent because of high water on roads leading into Lubbock.[59] To the new professors of agriculture, the region did not appear dry and barren. Playa lakes were full, pastures were green, unharvested cotton fields were soggy, and the dirt streets of Lubbock were at times impassable.

Agriculture had two buildings completed when Tech opened its first term—the Livestock Judging Pavilion and the Dairy Barn, but no classroom building. Classes and offices were located in the Home Economics Building. Chaos was the only certainty those first days. In later years Marvin T. Warlick, the superintendent of buildings and grounds and temporary farm superintendent, recalled: "my life was never secure. Irate professors without offices, Miss West [the librarian] without bookshelves, Miss Weeks [Dean of Home Economics] with a horde of sweating football players storming her 'sacred home' [the Home Economics Building]."[60]

With no livestock, no laboratories, and little furniture, faculty members were thrown back upon their own individual resources at first. W. L. Stangel utilized a treadle sewing machine for his desk, and at the first meeting of his introductory animal husbandry class, he required the students to bring lengths of rope and showed them how to make an animal halter. At the second class meeting, Stangel located a sick Hereford cow in a back yard and passed the time pointing out the animal's deficiencies "from the tip of her nose to the tip of her tail." C. H. Mahoney built two window boxes over a steam radiator for use in his plant propagation class.[61]

Of the 914 students who registered for the first semester, 60 were enrolled in the School of Agriculture. Among their accomplishments that year, the Aggies formed the first student club at Tech—the Agriculture Club. Six courses were offered—three in animal husbandry, two in horticulture, and one two-semester course in agro-

59. Andrews, *The First Thirty Years*, 18-19.

60. Marvin T. Warlick, Eugene, Oregon, February 11, 1938, to Mrs. A. H. Leidigh, Arthur H. Leidigh Papers, Southwest Collection, Texas Tech.

61. Personal interview with W. L. Stangel, March 7, 1973, by David Murrah at Lubbock, Southwest Collection. *Texas Techsan*, 3 (December 1952):6. Andrews, *The First Thirty Years*, 23-24, 104.

nomy. Courses in animal husbandry were market types, classes and breeds of livestock, dairying, and farm poultry. Horticulture offerings were plant propagation and principles of fruit growing. The agronomy course was fundamentals of crop production.[62]

One of the most pressing needs was for animals and equipment for the program. Some animals such as the gray Percheron mares "Maude" and "Blue" and a few Southdown sheep were purchased by the college. Of more immediate importance, however, were the animals and equipment donated to the institution. The service rendered in this regard by Clifford B. Jones was immeasurable. Jones was manager of the Spur Farm Lands, past President of the West Texas Chamber of Commerce, active promoter of the West Texas A&M College scheme, and now a member of the first Board of Directors of Tech. Leidigh and Stangel did not hesitate to call upon him for assistance. In February 1926, the Dean sent lists of needed machinery and livestock to Jones, including a grain drill, planter, power sprayer, five-ton scale, double-disc riding plow, "one-row sled go-devil cultivator," hay baler, gasoline tractor, and other implements. The success of Jones in obtaining many of these items is seen in the gift of a Fordson tractor valued at $580, obtained through a dealer at Spur in March, 1926. By June the Ford dealer in Lubbock offered to loan the School of Agriculture any implement in his stock.[63]

A number of donors gave prize cattle to start Tech's foundation herds of Herefords and Holsteins in the spring of 1926. John Orr and A. E. Flowers of Dallas each donated a Holstein bull calf. John Gist of Odessa gave two Hereford heifers. Tom Ivey of Lubbock and Henry Wilkerson of Hereford gave an Anxiety Hereford heifer from their herd. And R. V. Colbert and Sons of Stamford contributed a Hereford cow which had won First Prize at the Fort Worth Fat Stock Show in 1925 and 1926. Some generous cattle breeders appeared to be motivated by more than their interest in agricultural education. Such gifts usually received a great deal of publicity in West Texas newspapers—publicity which was expected by the breeders of prize herds. For example, one Hereford contributor wrote to Stangel: "P. S. We are writing Mr. Clifford B. Jones today in reference to his giving this matter some publicity . . . and would

62. *Ibid.*, 21, 104.

63. C. B. Jones, Spur, Texas, February 16, 1926, to A. H. Leidigh; A. H. Leidigh, February 17, 1926, to C. B. Jones; A. H. Leidigh, June 4, 1926, to R. M. Chitwood, *Plains Journal* (Lubbock), April 11, 1926, clipping file, TTSAP, DF. Personal interview with W. L. Stangel.

be glad [if] you would get in communication with him and arrange to give this matter all the publicity possible."[64]

The primary emphasis of Animal Husbandry was livestock judging. Judging, of course, relied upon these prize herds for training teams as well as for laboratory instruction in livestock selection and feeding. The first judging contest entered by a Tech team was the Fort Worth Intercollegiate Contest in 1927. The next year, a Tech team competed in the International Livestock Exposition in Chicago, and placed a respectable eighth among twenty-three teams.[65]

From the beginning the School of Agriculture had a close relationship with the agriculture of West Texas, especially that of the High Plains. At the time Tech was established, the spread of cheap cotton production to the Plains was the talk of the cotton belt. By 1927, the region west of the Mississippi was producing 60 per cent of the cotton in the United States and the percentage was growing. Moreover, the cost of producing cotton decreased in direct ratio to its spread westward. Whereas South Carolina required 143 man-hours and 71 horse-hours per acre of cotton, West Texas required only 40 man-hours and 46 horse-hours.[66]

The region was not only free of the boll weevil and most noxious weeds at that time, but its farmers demonstrated an aggressive, innovative spirit. Innovation and adaptation of industrial technology to the unique demands of a semiarid environment had long been hallmarks of pioneers on the Great Plains.[67] That process did not slacken in the twentieth century. Fifteen years before Tech was established, High Plainsmen began adapting pump irrigation technology from the humid Gulf Coast rice belt and the far western fruit farms.[68]

Like folklore, it is impossible to establish inventors and dates for most farmers' innovations. When a farmer got an idea to improve his machinery, he took the idea to his local blacksmith. The smith produced the item and if the neighbors liked the thing, they copied the idea (a supreme compliment to the original innovator). Thus, there appeared in the region the open-end planter drag, knives on "go-

64. A. H. Leidigh, June 4, 1926, to R. M. Chitwood; T. R. Colbert, Stamford, Texas, June 23, 1926, to W. L. Stangel; *Dallas Morning News*, April 10, 1926, clipping file, TTSAP, DF.

65. W. L. Stangel, January 14, 1939, to Millard Cope, Texas Tech School of Agriculture Papers, W. L. Stangel Files. Hereafter cited as TTSAP, WLS. *Plains Journal* (Lubbock), April 11, 1926, clipping file, TTSAP, DF. Andrews, *The First Thirty Years*, 110-111.

66. Victor H. Schoffelmayer, "Southwest has 64 Per Cent of U.S. Cotton Acreage and 60 Per Cent of Whole Crop," *Dallas Morning News*, January 2, 1927, section 2, p. 1, clipping file, TTSAP, DF.

67. Walter Prescott Webb, *The Great Plains* (New York: Ginn & Company, 1931).

68. Donald E. Green, *Land of the Underground Rain: Irrigation on the Texas High Plains, 1910-1970* (Austin: University of Texas Press, 1973), 38-61.

devils" and cultivators, and later such implements as the chisel-plow, the packer (made from an old car, it was simply driven up and down freshly planted rows of cotton or grain in order to press the seed into the moist subsoil), the press-wheel which replaced the packer, the revolving toothed "sand fighter," and many others.[69] When farmers in the early 1930's began to replace their Model T Fords with the more powerful Model A and the Chevrolet, they designed a cheap trailer, put hitches on their cars, and discarded their horse-drawn wagons. A visitor from Central Texas wrote to Leidigh: "While visiting in Lubbock some months ago I noticed the farmers using a large low hung trailer on two wheels . . . behind their cars. They seemed to be able to haul most everything transportable, from some pigs to a team of heavy horses. Could you furnish me with a plan . . . to make one of these trailers?" The Dean responded: "I will say that this general region is said to be the center of the automobile trailer use in the United States. . . . Most of the trailers are built on abandoned Ford automobile parts. I am enclosing a rough sketch herewith."[70]

The innovation which interested most farmers both in and out of the region in the mid-1920's was the cotton sled. Cotton had long resisted mechanization. While wheat was being harvested with the combine-harvester pulled by the wheatland-type tractor on the Great Plains, cotton was still being picked by hand. The sled first appeared in the Lubbock area in 1914 when cotton was selling for a nickel a pound and cotton culture was in its infancy on the High Plains. A few farmers took picket fence slats, nailed them into V-shapes and attached them to the front of small, horse-drawn wooden sleds. By 1927 the most common type had long steel fingers on the front to strip the cotton stalks although some still had a V-shaped wooden slot which extended into the front of the sled. While a driver handled the team, another worker forked cotton to the back. It was estimated that a bale of cotton could be sled-harvested for $2 while a hand-pulled bale cost the farmer $13. Two Lubbock inventors were reported to be working on a two-row cotton harvester equipped with fingers on revolving cylinders in 1927.[71]

69. Observations of author and personal interview with Arthur W. Young, May 27, 1975, by author at Lubbock, Southwest Collection.

70. W. F. Hofmann, Carrollton, Texas, August 16, 1933, to A. H. Leidigh; Leidigh, August 23, 1933, to W. F. Hofmann, TTSAP, DF. The author's father, Lewis Green, was said to have been one of the first farmers in the Lutie community of Collingsworth County, Texas, to pull such a trailer behind his Model A Ford in the fall of 1935.

71. " 'Sled' Cotton on the Plains," *Dallas Morning News*, January 2, 1927, section 2, p. 1. Much of the information for this article was supplied by Leidigh.

Cotton sledding was big news in 1927 and the *Wall Street Journal* published an article, probably picked up from a feature in the *Dallas Morning News* of January 2. Leidigh was quoted in both articles as saying "mechanical pickers . . . are here to stay." The National Bureau of Economic Research and a cotton planter from Mississippi wrote inquiries about the sled. After asking for information, the Mississippian remarked: "It looks as if you fellows are going to make us produce cheap cotton or no cotton at all." As in the case of the trailer, Leidigh had no plans to share with the planter but promised to try to obtain a set.[72] Tech had no budget for research or services for its constituency.

In spite of its lack of resources, Leidigh and his small staff contributed various services to regional farmers from their crowded schedules and often on their own time. The Dean confided to Horn in early 1926: "I plan to build up a service in the way of Farmers' Institute work, research work, and newspaper publicity. . . . I plan to do this by competing with such existing agencies as are supposed to cover this territory but which do not do so. . . . All of such work will be directly of instructional value to our students and much of it absolutely necessary."[73]

Although the State Extension Service had county agents in the area, they often did not have the immediate expertise on special problems because they were generalists. And it required time to get the answers from faraway Texas A&M. Indeed, New Mexico A&M was nearer to Lubbock than Texas's own land-grant college, and Oklahoma A&M was about the same distance as College Station. Moreover, the staff at Texas A&M, like that at Tech, was already overworked and often not well acquainted with the immediate needs of West Texas farmers. For example, when it became clear to Leidigh in 1928 that the 36 to 38-inch traditional cotton crop rows were too narrow to harvest with tractor-pulled sleds, he asked an agricultural engineer at A&M what he thought about moving to a 40 to 42-inch row. The engineer refused to commit himself to any row width and concluded, "The last word in mechanical harvesting has not yet been written."[74] It was evident that the Dean saw the coming trend in widening row width occasioned by mechanical harvesting with tractor power because the 40-inch row became the

72. *Ibid.* Harry Jerome, Washington, D.C., August 29, 1927, to Texas Tech; A. H. Leidigh, October 13, 1927, to Harry Jerome; J. T. Thomas, Jr., Cruger, Mississippi, January 25, 1927, to Texas Technological College; A. H. Leidigh, February 3, 1927, to J. T. Thomas, Jr., TTSAP, DF.

73. A. H. Leidigh, February 2, 1926, to P. W. Horn, TTSAP, DF.

74. A. H. Leidigh, February 21, 1928, to Daniel Scoats; Daniel Scoats, College Station, February 29, 1928, to A. H. Leidigh, TTSAP, DF.

standard on the Plains. In another case involving the inspection of seed wheat in Hansford County for the county agent in 1926, a work which Leidigh had started while still connected to the Experiment Station, the Texas Agricultural Experiment Station was too short-handed to carry through with the work, much to the consternation of the Dean, who wrote, "It has been my understanding that you folks there in A&M are trying to give service to the farmers in west Texas, and I was assured that the work I started last year would be carried out."[75]

Farmers found that the agricultural staff was readily accessible either by letter or by simply strolling into their cramped offices. No reasonable request for service was turned down. In July, 1926, one farmer asked Leidigh to identify a new kind of weed on the Plains. Weed seed was introduced to the Plains in a number of ways: in impure crop seed, in hog and cattle feed (many weeds first sprang up around the edges of hog wallows), and by the railroad boxcars which carried seed to the region. Leidigh was unfamiliar with this particular pod and sent the seed directly to an expert at the Texas Agricultural Experiment Station for identification. Word came back that the plant was "*Helianthus ciliatus* or blue-weed." The Dean not only advised farmers on methods for controlling what became a common weed pest, but when bindweed, also a new weed, sprang up along the Santa Fe tracks, he did not hesitate to ask the railroad to keep the weed from spreading. The manager of the 18,000-acre Price Brothers Wheat Farms of Kress asked Leidigh if one could double-crop wheat and grain sorghums. The Dean replied that it was risky but worth trying. W. L. Stangel received numerous letters from farmers, vocational agriculture teachers and public school students asking all kinds of questions. Letters from students whose teachers had suggested reports on agricultural topics were both humorous and time consuming to answer. Queries ranged from those such as, "Will you please tell me what breed of cattle is best for beef?" to "Please send me all the information about stock raising. Do they have many of cows? How many hogs do they have? Answer promptly."[76]

75. A. H. Leidigh, June 7, 1926, to R. E. Karper; R. E. Karper, College Station, June 11, 1926, to A. H. Leidigh, TTSAP, DF.

76. H. J. Reinhard, College Station, July 12, 1926, to A. H. Leidigh; A. H. Leidigh, April 17, 1929, to M. B. Lee; M. B. Lee, Levelland, April 5, 1929, to A. H. Leidigh; H. C. Kuthe, Kress, Texas, June 13, 1929, to Division of Agriculture; A. H. Leidigh, June 15, 1929, to H. C. Kuthe; H. C. Kuthe, Kress, July 3, 1929, to A. H. Leidigh, TTSAP, DF. W. L. Stangel, May 25, 1928, to Bob Allen; Bob Allen, Leander, Texas, May 11, 1928, to W. L. Stangel; W. D. McElroy, White Deer, Texas, June 20, 1929, to W. L. Stangel; W. L. Stangel, June 24, 1929, to W. D. McElroy; Charles Cowart, Jr., Lockney, March 19, 1927, to

The traditional "short course" long associated with agricultural colleges was yet another area of service to regional farmers. The College announced in the fall of 1925 that a short course would be available to farmers in the winter of 1926. The next one was held on January 29-30, 1928.[77]

The short course held February 3-5, 1930, was of particular interest to farmers distressed over steadily declining prices for their crops. Subject for the first day was Agricultural Cooperative Marketing which many agricultural experts in the twenties believed would solve the market glut. Morning speeches of the first day included, "History and Development of Marketing in the Panhandle" and "Cooperative Efforts for the Development of the Agriculture of the Panhandle Plains." In the afternoon, Carl Williams of the Federal Farm Board spoke about the work of his organization. Still other speeches dealing specifically with the cooperative marketing of cotton and wheat were delivered.[78]

Primary thrust of the federal government's farm policy in the twenties was the cooperative movement. The Capper-Volstead Act of 1922 exempted farmers' "co-ops" from antitrust regulations. In 1926 Congress created the Division of Cooperative Marketing within the U. S. Department of Agriculture, and the Hoover Administration sponsored a law passed by Congress in 1929 to establish the Federal Farm Board. The Farm Board was authorized to loan $500 million to producers' cooperatives and to create federal "stabilization" corporations to buy and pull commodities off the open market. President Hoover appointed Alex Legge, President of International Harvester, to be chairman of the organization.[79]

West Texas farmers showed more than a passing interest in the cooperative movement. The Texas Wheat Growers Association was founded in December, 1921 at Amarillo. By 1926 the Association had 4600 members.[80] Mayor George M. Whitson of Spearman said at a meeting of the West Texas Chamber of Commerce in 1928: "The solution of the farm problem is economic rather than political. The farmers must help themselves through cooperation." But as the farm crisis worsened and prices for commodities plunged down-

Agricultural Department; W. L. Stangel, March 26, 1927, to Charles Cowart, Jr.; O. D. Woffoed, Lockney, March 24, 1927, to Agricultural Department; W. L. Stangel, April 2, 1927, to O. D. Woffoed, TTSAP, WLS.

77. *Bulletin of Texas Technological College*, vol. 1, no. 4 (1925):13. A. H. Leidigh, July 8, 1927, to W. L. Huckabay, TTSAP, DF.

78. A. H. Leidigh, December 19, 1929, to Clifford B. Jones, TTSAP, DF.

79. Address by Alexander Legge to U.S. Chamber of Commerce, April 30, 1930, pp. 143-153 in *Agricultural Thought in the Twentieth Century*, edited by George McGovern (Indianapolis: Bobbs-Merrill, 1967).

80. Nall, "Agricultural History of the Texas Panhandle," 125-126.

ward, enthusiasm for the Farm Board waned from interest to downright hostility. By 1930, wheat farmers around Spearman believed that "the Farm Board is . . . bunk."[81]

Arthur Leidigh was not overly enthusiastic about the creation of the Farm Board. As he said, "It may help it and it can't make it worse." Once it became law he wanted to "do everything possible within reasonable limits to assist the . . . Board in its general program in this part of the country." Working with Clifford Jones, who was skeptical about the Board accomplishing much, Leidigh helped word a lukewarm resolution of the WTCC supporting the Farm Board in 1930 in spite of its declining popularity.[82]

Throughout the twenties, W. L. Stangel's contributions to Tech and West Texas agriculture were many. He was very active in promoting local junior livestock judging contests. In April, 1926, he supervised the first high school judging contest in West Texas on the Tech campus. By 1928, the annual contests were attracting twenty-eight teams from as many schools. He helped establish similar shows within the next few years in several counties and was the most popular livestock judge in the region.[83]

Stangel's most important work in these early years was probably in the promotion of the dairy industry in West Texas. Tech led the way by establishing its own model dairy. Even before Stangel moved permanently to Lubbock in 1925, he picked the location for the Dairy Barn. An early 1925 college bulletin announced: "This first year some spare room will be available in the barn. The space will be assigned to approved students who can care for not to exceed three dairy cows of their own at their own expense." In the spring of 1926, thirteen freshmen students were allowed to bring their cows to the campus. Obviously, Tech could not allow students to bring as many cows as they sometimes wished. A prospective student from Bowie, Texas, who wished to transfer from Texas A&M, wanted to bring his twenty-one registered Jerseys. "You may use my herd for the official college herd," he wrote.[84]

81. Quoted in mimeographed report of West Texas Chamber of Commerce field meetings October 16-17, 1928, in West Texas Chamber of Commerce folder, TTSAP, DF. Nall, "Agricultural History of the Texas Panhandle," 161.

82. C. B. Jones, Spur, Texas, May 12, 1930, to A. H. Leidigh; A. H. Leidigh, May 19, 1930, to C. B. Jones, TTSAP, DF.

83. W. L. Stangel, January 14, 1939, to Millard Cope; *Plains Journal* (Lubbock), April 11, 1926, clipping file, TTSAP, WLS. "What Agriculture at Texas Technological College Offers You," *Bulletin of Texas Technological College*, vol. 4, no. 3 (July 1928):11.

84. *Bulletin of Texas Technological College*, vol. 1, no. 2 (1925), 14. Personal interview with W. L. Stangel, Lubbock, Texas, March 7, 1973, by David Murrah, Southwest Collection. W. L. Stangel, February 27, 1929, to L. R. Neel, TTSAP, WLS. Norman E. Heath, Bowie, Texas, September 14, 1925, to Business Manager of Texas Tech, TTSAP, DF.

The boys sold their milk wholesale for a short time to a dairy in Lubbock for thirty cents per gallon. When the dairy stopped buying the milk, the students found a market only for their sweet cream. At Stangel's suggestion and with his assistance, the boys formed their own retail cooperative—the Student Dairy Association. They borrowed money to buy an old delivery truck and some other equipment and elected officers. By the fall of 1927, Raleigh C. Middleton, who would later become Farm Superintendent, was elected president. Other officers that year included J. M. Kirksey, vice president; Guy Stark, secretary-treasurer; and Raymond C. Reed, bookkeeper. Dressed in white uniforms, two students delivered the milk, one operated the milkroom, one cleaned buckets and utensils in the washroom, four milked the cows by hand, one did the feeding, and still another took care of janitorial chores. But student turnover in the organization produced an unstable labor force for the retail trade. The Department of Dairy Manufactures was established in the fall of 1927. The Student Dairy Association went out of the retail business that year, and thereafter sold its milk directly to the Department.[85]

At first there were more applicants than could be accommodated. The college limited the total number of cows to 20. When Stangel was forced to turn down a request in 1927, he counseled, "Do not let the matter of getting two cows into the barn keep you from obtaining a college education." To another student who thought he could completely meet his expenses through his animal's profits, he wrote, "It will be impossible for you to make your way through college with one cow."[86]

Students were required to pay for the feed and also to contribute work in caring for the College dairy herd. Occasionally, one did not pull his load, but this appeared to be an exception. Stangel wrote to one father that, "Continued neglect on the part of your son . . . in the care of the two cows . . . forces me to give you the facts." Because the student was neglecting either to feed or milk the animals, Stangel warned, "If he does not brace up and meet us halfway the next few days I will be forced to ask him to withdraw his cows."[87]

Andrews, (*The First Thirty Years*, 116) states that there were six "charter members" of the Student Dairy Association, but Stangel in 1929 wrote that there had originally been thirteen members. (W. L. Stangel, February 27, 1929, to L. R. Neel, Editor of the *Southern Agriculturist*, TTSAP, WLS.)

85. *Ibid.* Virgil E. Hobby, "Texas Tech Students' Dairy Association," *The Plains Progress* (Lubbock), November 17, 1927, p. 1, W. L. Stangel Papers, clippings.

86. W. L. Stangel, August 25, 1927, to Earl Bavousett; W. L. Stangel, August 27, 1927, to L. D. Brooks, TTSAP, WLS.

87. W. L. Stangel, November 22, 1928, to H. A. Blevins, TTSAP, WLS.

The Association proved to be a boon for the students. For the eleven-month period from November, 1926, to October, 1927, Raymond C. Reed netted an average of $65.49 per month on the production of his two Holsteins. A sampling of three other students who had two cows apiece showed that even in the least profitable month of the year they made from $26.40 to $31.02 each.[88]

In the farm depression of the 1920's, small herds of dairy cattle became lifesavers to the farmers of West Texas. Many families milked as many as fifteen to twenty cows, mostly Jerseys. They sold the cream to the local "creamery" and fed the skim milk from their hand-turned separators to their hogs. The "cream check" commonly provided the food, clothing and few items of luxury the family purchased. The production of cream made West Texas by the middle 1920's an exporter of butter. Mistletoe Creameries of Amarillo informed Dean Leidigh that in addition to meeting the local demands for butter, the company was selling its product in Oklahoma, New Mexico, Arizona, and to other points in Texas. The emphasis on milk production on the family farm was reflected at Tech where the single course in dairying in January, 1926, was completely full.[89]

To aid the development of the fledgling West Texas industry, Stangel wrote to an expert at the University of Wisconsin in early 1927 asking for "methods that you found most successful in your state in establishing the dairy industry." The professor encouraged Stangel to use organization, public meetings, demonstrations, cow testing associations, and herd improvement records to promote the endeavor. Working with local service clubs such as the Kiwanis and chambers of commerce, Stangel helped establish the Texas Panhandle-Plains Dairy Show Association in 1927. When it held its first show at Plainview, March 26, 1928, he served as manager, a position he continued to occupy for a number of years.[90]

West Texas farmers had much to learn about dairying. The question asked Stangel most often was: "I want to know if there is any feed that makes milk richer." Stangel usually responded with information about feeding a balanced ration of grain sorghum heads, wheat bran, cotton seed meal, and roughage, but went on to inform the farmer that "richness of milk is not fed into the cows but bred into them." Indeed, "Runt" Stangel's interest in dairying was not pri-

88. W. L. Stangel, February 27, 1929, to L. R. Neel, TTSAP, WLS.

89. George T. Mazzard, Amarillo, November 29, 1926, to A. H. Leidigh; A. H. Leidigh, January 18, 1926, to P. W. Horn, TTSAP, DF.

90. W. L. Stangel, February 3, 1927, to George C. Humphrey; George C. Humphrey, Madison, Wisconsin, February 7, 1927, to W. L. Stangel, TTSAP, WLS. Maury Hopkins, Plainview, March 26, 1928, to A. H. Leidigh, TTSAP, DF.

marily in producing more milk through balanced rations; it was in the production of richer milk through selective breeding.[91]

Better milch cows was not the only area of dairying which interested Stangel. He realized that "we cannot have a satisfactory market without dairy manufacturing plants." In 1927 the new Department of Dairy Products and Manufactures (later changed to Department of Dairy Manufactures) was created and Kenneth M. Renner was hired as head. Born in Iowa, Renner received the B.S. from Iowa State and his M.S. from Kansas State, where he served as instructor in dairy husbandry at the time he accepted the Tech position. Renner began the Department with a small separator, a cooler which was not much larger, and an equally diminutive bottler. He not only set about to train men for managerial positions in dairy manufacturing concerns, but also opened a retail dairy to sell products to both the Tech cafeteria and the townspeople. The horse-drawn delivery wagons became familiar sights around town. By 1929, Renner still had no permanent dairy manufactures building and no appropriation other than his salary of $2,700. He was purchasing equipment and financing the operation from the profits of his enterprise, located in a small addition to the Dairy Barn.[92]

Renner's lack of permanent quarters for Dairy Manufactures was symptomatic of a problem affecting the entire School of Agriculture. Building expansion was modest at best. Charles H. Mahoney's Department of Horticulture relied upon a greenhouse rented from the Glenn Floral Company until late 1927. Construction on the department's own greenhouse started in October, 1927, at about the same time that the lease on the Glenn structure expired, leaving Mahoney without adequate laboratory space for a time. When completed, the new greenhouse, a modest twenty-five by seventy-five feet, was adequate for the time. The most important addition was the new one-story stucco Agricultural Building. The staff moved out of the lower floor of the Home Economics Building and into the new quarters in 1927. Like the greenhouse, it was adequate for the time being.[93]

The faculty and the curriculum expanded much more rapidly than the buildings. Ray C. Mowery, a teacher of vocational agriculture in Lubbock before the establishment of Tech, was hired in 1927 to teach animal husbandry and coach the livestock judging teams. As

91. Woodrow B. Denton, Littlefield, December 22, 1927, to Texas Tech; W. L. Stangel, January 7, 1928, to Woodrow B. Denton; R. B. Davis, Brownfield, June 11, 1928, to W. L. Stangel; W. L. Stangel, June 14, 1928, to R. B. Davis, TTSAP, WLS.

92. Andrews, *The First Thirty Years*, 116-117. A. H. Leidigh, July 22, 1929, to P. W. Horn, TTSAP, DF.

93. Charles H. Mahoney, October 24, 1927, to A. H. Leidigh, TTSAP, DF. Andrews, *The First Thirty Years*, 112-114.

an old friend of Stangel, the relationship extended back to Mowery's A&M days when the latter was his teacher and livestock judging coach. Born in Illinois and reared in Houston, Ray Mowery had received a B.S. from Texas A&M in 1921, and his M.S. from Iowa State in 1926.

Another new member of Animal Husbandry was "Doc" Fred G. Harbaugh, the departmental veterinarian. Harbaugh, a native of Chicago, received both the B.S. and D.V.M. degrees from Iowa State. Stangel hired Harbaugh in 1927. His first responsibility was to take care of the health of the College's herds, and to teach courses in livestock diseases and meat processing. But farmers beat a continuous trail to his office for advice about their own animals' problems.

Other changes in faculty in 1927 included the addition of agronomist Hershel M. Bell and Leander D. Howell, an agricultural economist. Howell came to Tech to head the new Department of Agricultural Economics and Farm Management, but resigned after only one year. F. I. Dahlberg resigned as Farm Superintendent that year to attend graduate school at the University of Wisconsin and later went to Texas A&M where he became professor of animal husbandry.

Dean Leidigh hired John Orval Ellsworth in 1928 to replace Howell. Ellsworth was well qualified to carve out the new program in agricultural economics. He had grown up in Idaho, gotten his B.S. from Utah A&M (Utah State) and returned to his home state to become a county agent. In the early twenties he went to Cornell where he received his M.S. and Ph.D. (1926). His specialties consisted of marketing, farm management and the use of statistical methods in agricultural analyses. At the time of his appointment, Ellsworth was on the staff of Oklahoma A&M.[94]

A number of problems plagued the School of Agriculture in its beginnings. Classes were often crowded and the faculty was overworked. Stangel, for example, was teaching nine hours plus three laboratory sections, and Leidigh admitted that his load of nine hours of lecture courses and four sections of laboratories "slows up my other work." Large class loads produced frustration for the staff. Leidigh noted that his faculty members were not able to keep abreast of the current literature and research within their respective fields. "All three of us are complaining that the long period of high

94. *Ibid.*, 104, 110, 120. A. H. Leidigh, May 5, 1926, to P. W. Horn; A. H. Leidigh, May 21, 1928, to P. W. Horn, TTSAP, DF. *Bulletin of Texas Technological College*, vol. 11, no. 4 (1935) for dates of faculty employment. Personal interview with Fred G. Harbaugh, Lubbock, May 29, 1973, by David Murrah, Southwest Collection. *Lubbock Avalanche-Journal*, August 18, 1940, p. 6.

pressure work has reduced our reading. This is the most adequate index of an overload." Moreover, although their "service to farmers" was "rapidly increasing. We are not meeting the demand."[95]

Another thorny issue was that of orienting prospective students in the region toward Tech rather than traditional Texas A&M. This was difficult to accomplish because almost all the county agents, and most of the vocational agriculture teachers were products of and oriented toward A&M. The lack of equipment and the crowded facilities at Tech undoubtedly slowed down the growth in numbers of agricultural students the first few years. Leidigh received word that some high school teachers and county agents in the region, while advising students in other areas of study to attend Tech, were telling those interested in agriculture, as well as engineering, to go elsewhere.[96]

The lack of a coordinated campaign to publicize Tech's offerings was also an adverse factor. Leidigh received word in 1929 that some high school students at Lockney, in neighboring Floyd County "did not know that agriculture was taught at Texas Tech." The Dean complained to President Horn about the need for a public information campaign. But with the institution's facilities already strained to the breaking point, Horn responded that if the legislature did not increase the appropriations for Tech "We may be in the position of needing less publicity and less enrollment next year rather than more."[97]

Finally, the lack of a certificate-granting vocational agriculture program for teachers undoubtedly limited enrollment. Leidigh believed that if the "certificate" had been offered in the 1928-29 school year, the School of Agriculture would have had more than 200 students instead of the 150 enrolled. Before Tech could offer the teaching certificate, the program had to be approved by the state vocational agriculture board composed of members from the only three colleges in the state which already offered the certificate. Leidigh stood knocking at this door until the early 1930's.[98]

The Dean was also disheartened by 1929 about the low salaries some of his best people were saddled with. Mahoney was making $3,000 per year and Renner's salary was $2,700, in spite of the Dean's efforts to raise them.[99] Similar problems were commonplace

95. A. H. Leidigh, January 18, 1926, to P. W. Horn, TTSAP, DF.

96. *Ibid.*; A. H. Leidigh, June 24, 1925, to P. W. Horn; A. H. Leidigh, July 1, 1929, to P. W. Horn; P. W. Horn, July 5, 1929, to A. H. Leidigh, TTSAP, DF.

97. *Ibid.*

98. A. H. Leidigh, July 22, 1929, to P. W. Horn, TTSAP, DF.

99. *Ibid.*

elsewhere on campus as Tech struggled to make ends meet with its small legislative appropriation.

Beginnings for any major educational institution are always chockfull of difficulty. The Tech School of Agriculture was no exception. The lack of adequate teaching facilities, low salaries, inadequate appropriations, overcrowded classrooms and overloaded professors were all part of the scene. Unlike earlier agricultural colleges, the faculty did not have to labor against farmers' prejudice against "book-learning." But at the same time, like the earlier institutions, the School had to establish itself firmly as a permanent institution serving both students and farmer-constituents. With its stable and capable faculty, the institution planted solid foundations during its first five years. When the Great Deparession and Dust Bowl emerged in the next decade, Leidigh and his faculty were ready for the challenge.

HARD TIMES AND PROGRESS

The stock market, already vastly inflated by speculative pressures and reflecting a downturn of economic indicators, began its infamous plunge in the fall of 1929. Sharply rising unemployment, falling profits, an increase in bankruptcies, and the appearance of "soup lines" were manifestations of the hard times descending upon the nation as the Texas Tech School of Agriculture entered the 1930's. In Lubbock, a "shack town" of the itinerant unemployed sprang up in the northeastern part of town, and three children were reported to have starved to death in 1930. City officials turned a plot of ground on the city hall lot into a turnip patch for relief purposes in the fall of 1931. A Tech professor, the controversial John C. Granbery whom the Board fired in 1932, got the local Ministerial Association to promote a day for a citywide fast. The participants contributed a total of $610 from their food budget to the cause. And religious organizations, especially the Salvation Army, provided food, clothing and even shelter to many of the needy.[100]

Farmers who had been in their own depression since 1920, saw prices for their crops and livestock decline even more. Wheat dropped from ninety-four cents a bushel in 1929 to thirty-three cents by 1932. Cotton fell from sixteen cents to a nickel a pound during the same period. And beef cattle plunged from $8.00 per hundredweight to $3.10 from 1929 to 1933.[101] An old friend of W. L. Stangel who had been a cattleman wrote to him from Clarendon in 1932: "I'm broke and looking for a job and when I say broke I'm not using any figure of speech or nothing. I mean just plain broke." After observing that one of their old Texas A&M classmates now worked for the Reconstruction Finance Corporation after losing both his bank and a job with a fertilizer company, he pleaded: "If by any chance you know of anything—be it ever so humble—down there or anywhere else, for God's sake say a good word for me."[102]

The drouth on the Southern Plains in evidence by 1934 added to an already intolerable situation. An official of the Levelland Chamber of Commerce predicted in the late summer of 1934 that "this county will not gin over 3000 bales [of] cotton [and] our feed crop is virtually a failure. Our normal farm income totals about

100. Merton L. Dillon, "Religion in Lubbock," pp. 483-484, in *A History of Lubbock*.

101. Garry Lynn Nall, "Agricultural History of the Texas Panhandle," Ph.D. dissertation, University of Oklahoma, 1972, pp. 155-156.

102. Louis E. Holloway, Clarendon, Texas, May 10, 1932, to W. L. Stangel, TTSAP, WLS.

$2,000,000. This year including Government benefit payments, our visible income will not exceed $600,000."[103] One county agent reported in 1932 that "a condition of near poverty is found on farms in Randall County. . . . Three short crop years have hurt Randall County farmers a great deal more than the low prices for their products."[104] Hickman Price, owner of the 23,000-acre Price Brothers Farm in Hale and Swisher Counties went bankrupt in 1932. He had left an executive position with Fox Movie News in California in the late 1920's to apply his business talents to wheat farming. He set out to demonstrate that profits could be made in growing cheap wheat if one applied economies of scale and produced in great volume. But like W. J. Casey, the "Corn King" of Dallam County who abandoned some 9,000 acres, Price's bankruptcy showed only that big single-crop farmers took bigger losses.[105]

Decline of the economy caused falling revenues for government. And lower revenues brought a decrease in appropriations for state institutions. From its establishment, Texas Tech had never been adequately funded. The number of students grew more rapidly than the college budget. Like the piney-woods hog of the south, Tech had been "fed" only enough to keep it "tame," but not enough to improve its looks much. In 1930, things turned from bad to worse when state appropriations for the College were cut by $37,500. At the same time, enrollment from 1929 to 1931 suffered only a temporary decline from 2,353 to 2,155 before resuming its upward climb.[106]

The School of Agriculture, however, dropped in enrollment only one year, 1932. The number of students then increased 10 per cent the next year. By 1934, Agriculture's enrollment of 263 was larger than that of twenty other schools of agriculture throughout the nation, including Auburn, Colorado A&M, Arizona University, New Mexico A&M, Utah A&M, and the University of Tennessee. Yet Tech with its faculty of twelve had a smaller staff than any of these.[107]

Salaries were cut by 25 per cent in 1933. Teachers were often paid by warrants which some banks would not cash and others would convert to money only through substantial discounts. W. L. Stangel confided to a friend: "We all have taken a big slash in our salaries, and still we are all displaying NRA [the National Recovery Admin-

103. Chamber of Commerce, Levelland, August 22, 1934, to W. L. Stangel, TTSAP, WLS.

104. Quoted in Nall, "Agricultural History of the Texas Panhandle," 158-159.

105. *Ibid.*, 153, 159.

106. "The First Ten Years of Texas Technological College," in *Bulletin of Texas Technological College*, vol. 11, no. 5 (1935): pages not numbered.

107. *Ibid.*; Annual Report of the Division of Agriculture, 1934, TTSAP, DF.

istration of the New Deal] signs. If that is not optimism, I don't know what you call it."[108]

Cuts other than salaries were effected. Feed became scarce and expensive during the drouth and Stangel was forced to cut back the prize college herds in 1934. The college had 388 animals when the professor of animal husbandry announced that the herds were to be trimmed by 41 per cent. It was impossible to feed the remainder from the meager seventeen tons of feed produced on the college farm in 1934. In desperation, Stangel mowed green tumbleweeds from highway rights-of-way, to feed sheep and to grind into ensilage for cattle.[109]

The faculty teaching load worsened. In explaining to Max Bentley, editor of an Abilene newspaper, why it had been difficult for him to write an article requested by the editor, Stangel admitted: "I am teaching 28 hours per week, and that load with departmental, administration, and committee work, which every college man has a certain amount of, has kept me quite busy."[110]

In spite of obstacles the faculty made do with its limited resources. When Henry Clay, the staff agricultural engineer, was cramped into a doll-size office with agronomist Arthur W. Young, he decided to build a separate office. During the summer of 1936 he and some students built a fifteen by twenty-five foot adobe building. They made the bricks of clay from the college farm, insulated the ceiling with cotton "burrs", wired it for electricity, and constructed a heating system of junked water pipes.[111]

The determination of the faculty was matched only by that of the students who often remained in school in the face of great difficulty. To the consternation of the Lubbock city health department and of Stangel, a number of students brought cows from home, pastured them on vacant lots, and sold raw milk straight from the bucket to pay their expenses.[112]

Not all change was so bleak in the early part of the depression. The inauguration of a new president for Texas Tech brought the first agriculturally oriented chief executive to the institution. President Paul Horn died on April 13, 1932, perhaps because of the strain

108. *Ibid.*; A. H. Leidigh, September 18, 1934, to Tom Garrard, TTSAP, DF. W. L. Stangel, September 22, 1933, to Ike Dahlberg, TTSAP, WLS.

109. W. L. Stangel, August 24, 1934, to Bradford Knapp, TTSAP, DF. Personal interview with W. L. Stangel, March 7, 1973, at Lubbock by David Murrah, Southwest Collection.

110. W. L. Stangel, July 21, 1933, to Max Bentley. Stangel wrote to a banker friend at Bryan, Texas in 1931: "The banks of Lubbock are not honoring our warrants." W. L. Stangel, November 2, 1931, to Travis B. Bryan, TTSAP, WLS.

111. Thomas L. Miller, "Adobe—The House of Clay," *Texas Tech Magazine*, 1 (October 1937):10.

112. W. L. Stangel, August 8, 1939, to B. Wallin, TTSAP, WLS.

of steering the institution through the difficult early years of the depression. While the Board of Directors shopped for a successor, it created a kind of executive committee composed of a few of its own members to run the school. Operating under this executive committee was a council of the four academic deans, including Arthur Leidigh.[113]

Some Board members wanted "a man who leans quite strongly toward agriculture." On July 19, 1932, the Board announced that Bradford Knapp would be Horn's successor. W. L. Stangel observed that "everyone in the college as a whole, and certainly [everyone] in the School of Agriculture was pleased with his election."[114]

The heritage and career of Bradford Knapp revolved around agriculture. Born in Iowa, he was the son of the famous Seaman A. Knapp, President of Iowa State, author of the Hatch Act which created the system of federally subsidized state agricultural experiment stations, father of the concept of extension work embodied in home demonstration agents and county agents, and the first Director of the Extension Service. Bradford received a B.S. from Vanderbilt, and a degree in law from the University of Michigan before he became associated with his father in the Extension Service. When Seaman died, the younger Knapp was named head of Extension. Maryland Agricultural College later awarded him an honorary doctorate in agriculture. Before coming to Tech in the late summer of 1932, Knapp had served as Dean of the School of Agriculture at the University of Arkansas, President of Oklahoma A&M, and President of Auburn (Alabama Polytechnic Institute).[115]

Knapp had to deal with several problems affecting the School of Agriculture. The immediate issue was survival. Faced with declining revenues in state government resulting from the depression, a movement was underway in Texas in 1932 to do away with "duplication" in higher education programs. The State Board of Education recommended that the Schools of Agriculture, Engineering and Home Economics be wiped out and that Tech be reduced to a teacher training institution. A legislative committee began studying the proposal in January, 1933. Stangel wrote to a friend at the University of California: "We do not know what will come of all this propaganda, and yet we are looking for the worst."[116]

113. Andrews, *The First Thirty Years* pp. 36-40.

114. W. L. Stangel, May 17, 1932, to J. D. Blackwell; W. L. Stangel, July 19, 1932, to W. L. Blizzard, TTSAP, WLS.

115. Andrews, *The First Thirty Years*, 39.

116. *Ibid.*, 40. W. L. Stangel, January 24, 1933, to R. E. Miller, TTSAP, WLS. Floy Farrar Wilbanks, "The Life and Work of Dr. Bradford Knapp," M.A. thesis, Texas Technological College, 1940, pp. 80-81.

Led by Knapp and Clifford B. Jones, now Chairman of the Board of Directors, Tech defended itself. Knapp appeared before the Efficiency Committee of the legislature to oppose the change. Among other things, he trotted out past appropriation and enrollment figures to show that technical education at Tech cost less per student than at any other Texas institution. This, of course, was the result of legislative parsimony not of educational planning but the argument was effective. The legislature allowed Tech to keep its "schools," but in a parting swipe knocked 27.8 per cent from its appropriation.[117]

Knapp responded to the cut by reorganizing Tech to give the appearance of greater efficiency in 1933. The "schools" were scrapped and "divisions" substituted. Thus the School of Agriculture became the Division of Agriculture. Also, the Departments of Agronomy, Horticulture and Agricultural Engineering were brought together into the single Department of Plant Industry.[118]

Ties between the new President and the Division of Agriculture remained close throughout Knapp's tenure. At the invitation of Leidigh, Knapp taught a course in Rural Sociology, took an active interest in the Ropesville Resettlement Project (to be discussed in the next chapter), advised High Plainsmen to conserve their underground water and was continually defending West Texas agriculture. A good example was the controversy he stirred up with cotton buyers. In late 1937 he wrote a letter to the powerful cotton marketing concern, Anderson, Clayton and Company of Houston. He contended that "the best way to promote better staple of cotton was to pay farmers a premium according to the grade and staple of the cotton produced." Knapp insisted that cotton buyers were too preoccupied with wheeling and dealing in the market rather than in paying a higher price for good cotton. Within a few days after writing the letter, Knapp stayed up most of one night on a train while on his way to a conference arguing with a group of cotton buyers over the proposition after he heard one of them advise his fellows that " 'there was going to be good killing in cotton out here, if you knew the game,' " and urged all to stay out of the area until cotton had "piled up at the gins and compresses."[119]

In working for the improvement of cotton quality, Knapp told Dean Leidigh that the High Plains should develop its own cotton varieties for irrigated and dry land cultivation, that the region

117. *Ibid.*, 80-82. Andrews, *The First Thirty Years*, 40.

118. Wilbanks, "The Life and Work of Dr. Bradford Knapp," 82.

119. *Ibid.*, 92. Bradford Knapp, "Irrigation in the South High Plains," *The Progressive Farmer and Southern Ruralist*, 51 (May 1936):8. Bradford Knapp, November 6, 1937, to A. H. Leidigh, TTSAP, DF.

should cultivate its own seed farms, and that better cotton gins to protect the quality raw product should be built.[120]

Knapp, along with Leidigh, Stangel and other staff members, believed that diversification was a powerful weapon for farmers to use against the depression. In 1928, Leidigh had criticized West Texans for selling their cheap feed instead of feeding it to their equally cheap cattle, for failure to raise enough poultry to attract large buyers at higher prices, for not terracing their fields in order to hold more rainfall on the land, and for not developing a regional market for their wheat through cooperative efforts. Moreover, the Dean wanted to attract capital into the region for building packing plants, flour mills, and poultry-processing plants. The West Texas Chamber of Commerce preached the same message.[121]

The colonial, dependent status of West Texas was an old problem of the entire Great Plains region which, as almost exclusively a producer of raw products, was forced to purchase its manufactured goods from the industrialized areas of Chicago, Detroit, and the Northeast. One Great Plains historian has written that North Dakota, for example, "is, and always has been, dependent upon outside centers of finance, trade, and manufacturing and hence subject to a real degree to their control."[122] Like other Great Plains states, Texas was similarly disadvantaged at the time as evidenced by the following anonymous clipping gleaned from some state newspaper by Dean Leidigh in the 1920's.

WHAT IS WRONG WITH TEXAS?

Nothing's wrong with Texas, except entirely too many of us get up in the morning at the alarm of a Connecticut clock, button a pair of Ohio suspenders to a pair of Chicago pants. Put on a pair of Massachusetts shoes, wash in a Pittsburg tin basin, using Cincinnati soap, and a cotton towel made in New Hampshire, sit down to a Grand Rapids table, eat pancakes made from Minneapolis flour spread with Vermont maple syrup, and Kansas bacon fried on a St. Louis stove. Buy fruit put up in California, seasoned with Rhode Island spices, and sweetened with Colorado sugar. Put on a hat made in Philadelphia, hitch a Detroit mule fed on Oklahoma gasoline to a Ohio plow and work all day on a Texas farm covered with a New England mortgage, send our money to Ohio for tires, . . . and at night we crawl under a New Jersey blanket to be kept awake by a bull dog, the only home product on the place, wondering all the time, where in the hell all the money went in this wonderful State of ours.[123]

120. *Ibid.*

121. Mimeographed report of West Texas Chamber of Commerce field meetings October 16-17, 1928, in West Texas Chamber of Commerce folder, TTSAP, DF.

122. Elwyn B. Robinson, "Themes of North Dakota History," mimeographed (Grand Forks: University of North Dakota Department of History, *ca.* 1959), 3.

123. From various newspaper clippings in TTSAP, DF.

Knapp agreed completely. In a curious piece written for the golden anniversary edition of a San Angelo newspaper in 1934, the President envisioned West Texas fifty years in the future. He did not see the totalitarian 1984 of George Orwell's famous *Animal Farm* written in the 1940's. Knapp's 1984 was filled with rich diversified farms furnished with markets by local industries dispersed throughout the region ("great groups of small farms with factories in the center"). The region no longer supplied only raw products; it produced fabrics, clothing, meat products, dairy items, and many other manufactured goods.[124] Knapp's vision was not a prophecy; it was a hope held by those like Leidigh who preached diversification and the need for enlarging regional markets.

The dairy industry, an important prong of diversification which Stangel had worked hard to expand in the 1920's, became even more important to the region in the thirties as the drouth wiped out field crops and low market prices crushed profits for beef. By 1930, Lubbock produced one-fourth of all the butter manufactured in Texas and had forty-five wholesale and retail dairies producing milk and other products for the city. There were 291 "cream buying stations" in the South Plains area. And Hale County produced more cream than any other county in Texas.[125]

The production of cream by the small farmer, begun in the 1920's, was not caused by the desire for increased profits; simple survival furnished the motive. One dairy promoter asserted in late 1932, that "had it not been for the cream checks . . . this section would have been dependant upon Gov. releif for food." Stangel had heard more than one farmer say, "My cows have kept me going."[126] During the drouth, "cream" farmers even managed to make a living after purchasing alfalfa grown on irrigated farms of the region for their cows. In Hockley County, it was estimated in 1934 that the average "cream" farmer netted about $200 per year from his operations, enough to buy family groceries with the depression-deflated dollar. A Floyd County farmer said that in 1936 he made more money from his cream and eggs than from his cotton and wheat combined.[127]

124. "Dr. Bradford Knapp Wakes Up in 1984 and Finds West Texas Happy, Prosperous," *San Angelo Standard-Times*, Golden Anniversary Edition, May 3, 1934, section 4, pp.1,14.

125. A. H. Leidigh, "Agriculture on the South Plains," (unpublished manuscript, *ca.* 1935), TTSAP, DF. W. L. Stangel, December 15. 1930, to E. W. Provence; list of Lubbock dairies, *ca.* 1930, TTSAP, WLS.

126. Roy B. Davis, Plainview, December 18, 1932, to W. L. Stangel; W. L. Stangel, December 22, 1932, to Roy B. Davis, TTSAP, WLS.

127. Personal interview with Royal Crawford, December 29, 1965, by author at Tulia, Texas, Southwest Collection. *Lockney Beacon*, Special Irrigation Issue, April 30, 1937, section 2, p. 8. Clipping from Levelland newspaper entitled "Important Dairy Meeting Here on Night of August 28," *ca.* August, 1934, TTSAP, WLS.

The Division of Agriculture rendered a number of important services to the developing dairy industry of the region. Stangel, Leidigh, and Kenneth Renner, head of the new Department of Dairy Manufactures, spoke at a number of meetings throughout the region. Leidigh encouraged the formation of creamery cooperatives and Stangel spoke on economical feeding of dairy cattle. Renner was called upon by scores of creameries and dairy products manufacturers for advice. To inform farmers and their families on methods for keeping their cream pure so that they could get the highest market price, he wrote a one-act play performed by 4H and FFA groups entitled "Producing Quality Cream on the Farm." W. L. Stangel received numerous inquiries from farmers and county agents about dairy rations including some wanting a formula for feeding wheat. A typical inquiry, simple and to the point, was one from Quitaque: "Please send me formula for mixing home grown feed for milch cows. I am selling cream."[128] The Panhandle-Plains Dairy Show, with Stangel as manager continued to be held annually at Plainview. And in early 1934, the Texas Jersey Cattle Club, which Stangel served as a member of its Board of Directors, met in Lubbock.[129]

The Tech dairy served as a model for area dairymen. Kenneth Renner observed in 1937 that "practically all of the dairymen in Lubbock now holding permits to sell milk have secured the same since the college first entered the milk business in Lubbock." After brucellosis was discovered in the dairy herd, "Doc" Fred Harbaugh culled out the infected animals. When sediment tests showed that student milkers were careless in their work, Stangel sent a stern directive to the student milkers. The development of a model dairy, however, was not without some cost. Because of the growth of the college herd the decision was made to dissolve the Student Dairy in 1935. Ray Mowery sent word to the students that they would have to remove their cows from the Dairy Barn "before the night milking, Saturday, July 20, 1935." Thus ended what had almost become an institution on the campus.[130]

128. *Ibid.* A. H. Leidigh, May 31, 1930, to F. J. McClure, TTSAP, DF. R. B. Davis, Plainview, November 10, 1930, to W. L. Stangel; W. L. Stangel, November 21, 1930, to R. B. Davis; W. L. Stangel, December 16, 1931, to R. B. Persons; R. B. Persons, Quitaque, Texas, December 14, 1931, to W. L. Stangel; W. C. Calvert, Sweetwater, Texas, July 6, 1930, to W. L. Stangel, TTSAP, WLS. Kenneth M. Renner, "Producing Quality Cream on the Farm," *Bulletin of Texas Technological College*, vol. 10, no. 3 (1934).

129. R. C. Hopping and Charles Whitacre, Lubbock, April 16, 1938, to Dear Friend; W. L. Stangel, November 13, 1933, to A. B. Davis, TTSAP, WLS.

130. Kenneth M. Renner, February 4, 1937, to Bradford Knapp, February 4, 1937, TTSAP, DF. Personal interview with Fred G. Harbaugh, May 29, 1973, by David Murrah at Lubbock, Southwest Collection. W. L. Stangel, August 26, 1933, to Fred G. Harbaugh; W. L. Stangel, November 18, 1931, to R. C. Middleton *et al.*; R. C. Mowery, July 12, 1935, to Ray Dunlap, TTSAP, WLS.

Under the leadership of Renner, the Department of Dairy Manufactures furnished important leadership not only for the developing dairy manufactures of West Texas, but for the state as well. Renner's objective was "to train competent men who can take their place in the Dairy Industry of Texas and make their training and influence felt for the betterment of the Industry."[131]

Demands upon the Department grew in the 1930's. At the beginning of the fall term in 1935, the increase of freshmen and sophomores in the introductory dairy manufactures courses required the creation of two new lecture sections and setting up two additional laboratory sections. By 1935, seventeen courses were offered in areas of manufacturing, management and marketing of dairy products. Renner added to his staff an assistant professor, Mart G. Pederson, who had graduated from Tech in 1932 and obtained his M.S. in dairy manufactures from Kansas State in 1936.[132]

Growth of the dairy industry in Texas was a reflection of two things: first, growing urbanization as more people flocked to the towns and cities from the farm, an accelerating movement already more than three-quarters of a century old in the United States, and second, the new consumer demand for what had once been a luxury—ice cream. Almost every town had at least one ice cream parlor by the 1920's, and as townsmen purchased the new electric refrigerators they began to stock pints and quarts of "store-bought" ice cream in their homes. Renner reported in 1934 that three-fourths of the requests for his graduates were for "ice cream makers."[133]

Renner remained abreast of the latest research in ice cream production, applying those techniques to his own plant and to the frequent services rendered to private manufacturers. Typical was his service to the Bell Ice Cream Company of Lubbock in locating the cause for "reactions to sweet cream" after the company's own cream experts were unable to isolate the trouble. In 1933, Renner assisted by William L. Ray of the Chemistry Department developed a low cost solids tester for ice cream mix suitable for the small manufacturer. The first test conducted with the device was on egg yolk solids by student J. Bryan Stine, later chief chemist for the Kraft Company. In 1937-38, Renner was called upon by fifteen manufacturers for advice on various problems and served as Secretary of the West

131. Kenneth M. Renner, February 4, 1937, to Bradford Knapp, TTSAP, DF.

132. Kenneth M. Renner, September 18, 1935, to A. H. Leidigh, TTSAP, DF. *Bulletin of Texas Technological College*, vol. 11, no. 4 (1935):73-74.

133. Annual Report of the Division of Agriculture, 1934; R. C. Smith, March 4, 1935, to Bradford Knapp; Kenneth M. Renner, "Research Contributions for 1934, Milk and Ice Cream Investigations" (unpublished paper presented to Texas Ice Cream and Milk Dealers Annual Convention, Mineral Wells, Texas, 1935), TTSAP, DF.

Texas Cream Improvement Association, and on the Educational Committee of the Texas Cream Improvement Association, the Advisory Board on Milk Sanitation of the State Health Department, and the Milk and Cream Weight and Test Regulation Committee of the Texas Weights and Measures Association. As small West Texas towns passed ordinances requiring milk inspection, he provided still another important service by running cheap laboratory analyses of milk samples.[134] He also worked with home demonstration and county agents in cream improvement demonstrations for farmers and their wives, and organized a number of one-day short courses for dairy manufacturers.[135]

Renner's most significant contribution to the industry, however, was his assistance in creating a uniform cream grading standard for Texas. At a meeting of dairy producers and manufacturers at Texas A&M on January 3, 1934, he and a professor from "A&M" were instructed to draft a preliminary bill on grading for the Texas legislature. The result was the Texas Cream Grading Law of 1934 which established three grades of cream based on freshness and purity. Price differentials were established and penalties were attached for using adulterated cream in dairy products. By late 1934, Renner was working with Oklahoma authorities for the purpose of bringing that state's standards in line with those of the Texas law. Standardization was desirable because most of the cream produced north of Amarillo and Childress was marketed through Oklahoma creameries.[136]

Animal Husbandry headed by W. L. Stangel not only made its contribution toward the cause of diversification but also remained the most popular department in the Division. M. E. Heard, head of Textile Engineering, was disturbed because more students were not majoring in agronomy and specializing in cotton production. He found that throughout the South and Southwest, animal husbandry was generally more popular than other departments of agriculture. Why? Heard believed that "one of the reasons is that all of us admire a beautiful animal, and the fact that we have the Ft. Worth Fat Stock Show, the Royal Livestock Show at Kansas City, and the International at Chicago, and that these boys prepare themselves to make many nice trips, and the opportunity to win beautiful prizes, adds a powerful incentive to their program. Why somebody has not

134. Lawrence G. Harmon, "The Limit of Error of the Simplified Vacuum Solids Test as Applied to Ice Cream Mix, Evaporated and Sweetened Condensed Milk," M.S. thesis, Texas Technological College, 1940, p. 2. Kenneth M. Renner, September 22, 1934, to A. H. Leidigh, TTSAP, DF.

135. Annual Reports of Division of Agriculture, 1935, 1936, and 1938, TTSAP, DF.

136. Kenneth M. Renner, January 5, 1934, to A. H. Leidigh, including draft of the Cream Grading Bill; K. M. Renner, November 13, 1934, to A. H. Leidigh, TTSAP, DF.

attempted to do the same thing for cotton is more than I can understand."[137] The engineer perhaps put too much emphasis upon prize-motivation, but there is no doubt that the sons of cotton farmers, for the most part, found cattle more attractive than cotton. Moreover, the out-of-state judging trips were obviously attractive to young men from the farm eager to see the sights of the big city.

Livestock judging was the core of animal husbandry. In addition to offering one course in Advanced Livestock Judging, many of the other courses such as Breeds of Livestock and Beef Production were related to judging. The department retained registered "teaching" herds of Hereford, Aberdeen-Angus, Holstein, Guernsey, and Jersey cattle in addition to its swine, sheep, and horses. All senior animal husbandry majors had the opportunity to compete for places on the teams. A team was composed of five members and one alternate. Funds for traveling expenses to judging events were not provided out of state appropriations. Students themselves raised the needed money through ventures such as the annual "Pig Roast" first sponsored by the Agricultural Club in 1929, an agricultural fair, and the Tech rodeo.[138]

No man was better known in the Southwest for judging show cattle than W. L. Stangel. While still at Texas A&M, he had coached the First Place team at the International in 1919. After moving to Tech, he had been instrumental in organizing a number of regional and local livestock shows such as those at Lubbock, Abilene, Big Spring, Odessa, and Amarillo. When Texas held its Centennial Exposition in 1935-36, Stangel took his only leave of absence from Tech in order to accept the position of superintendent of livestock exhibits.[139]

It was under Stangel and Ray Mowery, the livestock judging coach, that the Tech teams emerged as winners in national competition, placing consistently among the top 20 per cent. A Tech team first entered the International Livestock Exposition in Chicago, the most prestigious show of them all, in 1928. In 1933, Tech placed third at the event. The next year, the team won Second Prize at the American Royal Livestock Show in Kansas City in November, and the following month placed first at the International. Another Tech team won First Prize at the American Royal in 1937.[140]

137. M. E. Heard, September 3, 1938, to John C. Thompson, Secretary of the Texas Cotton Ginners Association, TTSAP, DF.

138. W. L. Stangel, October 31, 1934, to Executors of the W. L. Ellwood Estate, TTSAP, WLS. *Bulletin of Texas Technological College*, vol. 11, no. 4 (1935):71-72.

139. W. L. Stangel, July 17, 1952, to R. E. Post, TTSAP, WLS. See chapter 2. *Lubbock Avalanche-Journal*, August 18, 1940, p. 6.

140. Annual Reports of Division of Agriculture, 1934, 1935, and 1938, TTSAP, DF.

The department also showed its animals regularly at the Fort Worth Fat Stock Show and the State Fair, winning awards with them, selling the prize animals (a number of them to Board member and Tech booster Amon G. Carter), and plowing the earnings back into the program.[141]

Livestock judging was only the topping on the cake for Animal Husbandry. The department served the region in a myriad of ways. It was estimated that in 1938 about 1,500 farmers per year contacted the department about animal health problems, primarily through "Doc" Fred Harbaugh. Harbaugh later recalled that area farmers usually did not seek a "vet" until the animals were in pretty bad shape.

As advisor, veterinarian, and teacher of the meat processing courses, Harbaugh was constantly hampered by lack of equipment, another casualty of inadequate state appropriations. He complained to Leidigh in 1935: "In the eight years the veterinary service has been given the college herds and flocks, there has been furnished a few pairs of forceps, a laboratory table, and $12.00 with which to build stocks to confine animals. An old calf stall in the dairy barn was walled off in which to place the stocks. A mouth speculum, and 3 dental instruments complete the equipment." The department owned an autoclave and bacteriological incubator only because it used money made from its blood-testing laboratory. The lack of equipment only added to "Doc's" burden in often working up to two or three o'clock in the morning. Harbaugh also complained about the lack of equipment for teaching his course in meats. In the absence of a meats laboratory building, he butchered his animals under any available tree. J. H. Baumgardner, an early student who later joined Tech's Animal Husbandry Department, recalled in later years: "Doc scalded the hogs in a barrel over a bonfire. That was all the meats lab we had." Finally, he summed up his complaint by inquiring: "I would appreciate knowing just what is expected of the instructor of these courses. Is he to teach as a college professor, or is he to teach as he has for the past eight years?"[142]

Stangel did all he could to increase those appropriations. Of all the members of the staff, W. L. Stangel probably knew more men of influence than anyone else through his long association with wealthy cattle breeders and agri-businessmen. Such men occasionally put pressure on the legislature to increase appropriations. For

141. Annual Report of Division of Agriculture, 1934, TTSAP, DF.

142. Annual Report of Division of Agriculture, 1938; Fred G. Harbaugh, September 24, 1935, to A. H. Leidigh, TTSAP, DF. Personal interview with F. G. Harbaugh. Texas Tech news release on Harbaugh testimonial, April 10, 1969.

example, Stangel wrote letters asking for more money for the Division of Agriculture to Texas legislators in 1934. One legislator, Clint C. Small, responded that "if the stockmen throughout West Texas would only get enthused over this situation, we might be able to get an appropriation at the next regular session."[143]

One of Stangel's most important contributions was his early promotion of feeding out West Texas cattle on West Texas feed. He taught his students and advised farmers to utilize local feedstuffs. In the fall of 1925, H. W. Stanton of Lubbock asked Stangel's advice in working out a feed ration of grain sorghum heads and cottonseed meal. With a single hammer mill and the formula, Stanton started the Standard Milling Company with feedstuffs grown on his farm. In 1931, he built the first feed lots near Lubbock on the rim of Yellow House Canyon. By December he had ten large lots capable of holding 300 steers each.[144] A few feedlots, primarily small operations, were on the Plains by the early 1930's. There were few operations as large as Stanton's and another at Levelland where B. B. Roberts was feeding out 2,000 steers a year.[145]

Stangel noted in the fall of 1932: "There is more interest in livestock feeding this fall than has ever been displayed before, and we are having more cattle and lambs on feed than we have ever fed before." The publisher of *Western Live Stock* of Albuquerque asked him for an article on "the possibility and practicability of an expansion of feeding operations in the West Texas section." Stangel, however, was too burdened with other commitments to oblige. He replied that "more experiments in livestock feeding were needed in order to determine fully the potential of locally grown feedstuffs."[146]

In 1929 the Department of Animal Husbandry began lamb feeding experiments in cooperation with the Texas Agricultural Experiment Station. Some cattle feeding experiments were begun in 1931. The Department had an experiment in progress with forty Hereford steers divided into two lots by 1933. Feed rations consisted of milo maize, cottonseed meal, and grain sorghum "bundles" for both lots. One lot was fed cottonseed cake while the other was fed cotton-

143. C. R. Garner, Amarillo, January 29, 1934, to W. S. [sic] Stangel; C. C. Small, Amarillo, January 27, 1934, to C. R. Garner, TTSAP, WLS.

144. W. L. Stangel, October 19, 1931, to John C. Burns; W. L. Stangel, December 16, 1931, to J. W. Boog-Scott, TTSAP, WLS. Personal interview with J. H. Baumgardner, October 4, 1972, by R. Sylvan Dunn and David Murrah at Lubbock, Southwest Collection.

145. W. L. Stangel, January 23, 1931, to C. W. McCampbell, TTSAP, WLS.

146. D. J. Biggs, Albuquerque, New Mexico, October 22, 1931, to W. L. Stangel; W. L. Stangel, October 29, 1931, to D. J. Biggs, TTSAP, WLS.

seed.[147] This type of feeding experiment became a common sight at Tech within the decade.

Feeding experiments received virtually no financial support until the Texas Cottonseed Crushers' Association (TCCA) became interested in the possibilities of using the experiments to demonstrate the superiority of crushed cottonseed products to whole cottonseed in feeding. Cottonseed oil mills had long been involved directly and indirectly in cattle feeding. They had built the first large commercial feedlots in the nation about the turn of the century in order to fatten cattle on what was then a high protein waste by-product—cottonseed meal and hulls. In April, 1937, the TCCA extended an invitation to Stangel and his wife to attend its annual convention at San Antonio in May with expenses paid by the organization. Later that year, the TCCA established a fellowship of $500 for graduate students to be used in experimental feeding. The first one was awarded to Merrill Polson in 1937 for an experiment in lamb feeding. In 1938 the fellowship was awarded to A. T. Fowler and in 1939, Stangel announced that John Henry Baumgardner would be the recipient. Students used their experiments as projects for master's theses.[148] The projects used varying mixtures of cottonseed meal, hulls, and "cake" combined with milo and grain sorghum ensilage. The objective of the TCCA program was to demonstrate the increased profits to be made by lacing locally grown feedstuffs with cottonseed products. Typical results were those experiments conducted in 1938-39, in which the animals receiving a higher protein ration of additional cottonseed meal made the highest net profit.[149]

The feeding experiments were publicized in a number of ways including local newspapers, county agents, and by word of mouth. But the most effective was undoubtedly the exhibition of Texas Tech in Dallas the week that Tech's Red Raiders met the Gaels of St. Mary's of California in the Cotton Bowl on New Year's Day, 1939. In cooperation with the Educational Service of the National Cottonseed Products Association, Stangel and M. E. Heard, head of the Department of Textile Engineering, set up an exhibit of cotton and cotton-

147. Annual Report of Division of Agriculture, 1934, TTSAP, DF. W. L. Stangel, March 11, 1933, to T. G. Gill; "7th Annual Feeding Project, Department of Animal Husbandry in Cooperation with Texas Cottonseed Crushers' Association," mimeographed (Texas Tech, 1939), pages not numbered, TTSAP, WLS.

148. B. Wallin, Dallas, April 8, 1937, to W. L. Stangel; W. L Stangel, April 12, 1937, to B. Wallin; W. L. Stangel, January 10, 1938, to G. A. Simmons; Report of Conference of College Relations Committee, Texas Cottonseed Crushers' Association, [October 12, 1938]; "7th Annual Feeding Project;" W. L. Stangel, August 10, 1939, to B. Wallin; A. H. Leidigh and W. L. Stangel, June 13, 1939, to members of Texas Cottonseed Crushers' Association, TTSAP, WLS. Personal interview with J. H. Baumgardner.

149. "7th Annual Feeding Project," TTSAP, WLS.

seed products and by-products in the lobby of the Adolphus Hotel. A flying shuttle made red and black (Tech's colors) cloth from West Texas cotton. The Postex Cotton Mills of Post displayed their Garza sheets. Also included were sacks of a flour named Co Flo made from cottonseed, and various plastic products such as radio cabinets and photographic film made from cotton. Central to the exhibit were sheep wrapped in Texas Tech blankets in small pens, and a number of photographs showing feeding practices at Tech and in the Lubbock area on the paneling in the background. A large overhead sign declared: "Texas Tech Feeds Cotton By-Products To All Kinds & Classes of Livestock."[150]

As a result of the feeding experiments, Stangel received numerous requests from farmers for information on feed rations for cattle, hogs and sheep. Requests ranged from questions on self-feeders for calves and trench silos to results on feeding experiments. But the most usual query was usually as ambiguous as, "Please send me a ration for steers."[151]

Although occasionally overshadowed by an aggressive Animal Husbandry Department, the Department of Plant Industry played a number of important roles during the depression. C. E. Russell, the horticulturist who had served for several years as head of the department, resigned in 1937. Agronomist Arthur W. Young (Ph.D., Iowa State), who came to Tech in 1935, succeeded Russell. Other new personnel in the department by 1938 included Henry P. Clay, the agricultural engineer; W. W. Yocum, another horticulturist; and Earl T. Duke, instructor of agronomy. Last, but far from least, was O. B. Howell, a professor of horticulture who held a B.S. in landscape and floriculture and an M.S. in plant pathology from Michigan State. Howell's experience before coming to Tech in 1935 included working on Michigan grain and fruit farms, serving as a landscapist and florist, and working with the federal Civil Works Administration.[152]

One of Howell's jobs was to beautify the Tech campus, a rather formidable task at that time. Working with President Bradford

150. "Thousands See Cotton's Many Uses Stressed at Cotton Bowl Jubilee," *Cotton and Cotton Oil Press* (January 7, 1939):6-7, clipping in TTSAP, WLS.

151. P. W. Horn, January 17, 1931, to A. H. Leidigh; W. L. Stangel, January 23, 1931, to T. J. Allen; L. J. Halbert, Plainview, September 30, 1932, to W. L. Stangel; W. L. Stangel, October 11, 1932, to L. J. Halbert; T. G. Gill, Strawn, Texas, January 21, 1933, to W. L. Stangel; W. L. Stangel, October 11, 1932, to O. T. Williams; D. O Williams, Abernathy, Texas, February 6, 1932, to Agricultural Department of Texas Tech; W. L. Stangel, February 17, 1932, to D. O. Williams; E. T. Abbott, Menard, Texas, October 13, 1931, to W. L. Stangel, TTSAP, WLS.

152. Annual Report of Department of Plant Industry, 1938; vita of O. B. Howell in Howell file, TTSAP, DF.

Knapp, the horticulturist laid plans for a massive tree planting to be held on February 22, 1938. When the day arrived students and faculty planted some 5,000 trees and shrubs. Howell, Knapp, W. T. Gaston (the Business Manager of Tech), state Senator G. H. Nelson, Ray Chapelle (head of the Department of Agricultural Education), and J. H. Grimsley (Superintendent of Buildings and Grounds) supervised the operations by horseback. Horticultural students acted as instructors for each of nine large planting groups. And W. W. Yocum directed the transference of trees from the campus nursery by way of trucks.[153]

Howell also served the public in a number of other ways. He spoke to garden clubs, home builders associations, and Rural Electrification Association (REA) meetings. In at least one case he was in too much demand to escape criticism. One summer while not teaching, the Cabot Company employed him to landscape the grounds of its plant in Kermit. The Texas Association of Nurserymen criticized Howell for competing with private businessmen and protested to Dean Leidigh. The Dean patiently pointed out that the horticulturist had performed the service on his own time.[154]

The establishment of a branch seed testing laboratory at Tech was not the least of the services of the Plant Industry Department. Need for such a service was evident. About 80 per cent of the grain sorghum in Texas was being raised in the High Plains area by the early 1930's. Growers had to send samples of their seed all the way to Austin for tests of purity and germination. At the same time demand for good seed was growing and more farmers were buying "certified" varieties. The Department had been testing some seed on a limited basis since the 1920's, but the demand now exceeded the Department's resources. Leidigh asked the Texas Commissioner of Agriculture in 1931 to establish a branch seed laboratory in Lubbock. The Dean wanted the laboratory on campus but thought that it should be located elsewhere in Lubbock because "the School of Agriculture is absolutely crowded to death, [and] is poorly financed."[155]

Disregarding the plea about lack of space, the Texas Department of Agriculture opened a branch seed lab on the campus in the spring of 1933. G. L. Beene, a Tech senior agronomy major, was placed in charge of the facility. It was open for two years before be-

153. Norma Lee Mills, "Tree Planting Time at Texas Tech," *Texas Tech Magazine*, vol. 1, no. 5 (1938):5, 18.

154. Annual Report of Department of Plant Industry, 1938; Harvey Mosty, Secretary of Texas Association of Nurserymen, Kerrville, Texas, February 9, 1939, to A. H. Leidigh; A. H. Leidigh, March 6, 1939, to Harvey Mosty, TTSAP, DF.

155. A. H. Leidigh, October 23, 1931, to J. E. McDonald, TTSAP, DF.

ing closed due to inadequate funds. But in 1937, an act of the legislature reopened the laboratory with an annual budget of $2,000. The new facility helped to implement a law passed by the same legislature requiring all salable seeds of field crops to be labeled with an analysis of contents, purity, and rate of germination.[156]

Tech consequently became the center for the production of certified seed on the High Plains. Most active in this new service was Arthur W. Young, head of the Department, who directed short courses on growing certified grain sorghum seed from time to time. He also served in an advisory capacity to the State Certified Grain Sorghum Seed Association, and was made a permanent member of the Texas Seed and Plant Board.[157]

As in other departments, research projects were modest, funded little if at all, and usually conducted in cooperation with students as course or thesis projects. Research was conducted along such lines as soil moisture retention, long-term effects of manure on dryland crops, native grasses, rammed-earth housing construction, a new arid land legume called Fenugreek, the growing of sugar beets, and, in cooperation with the Department of Textile Engineering, observations on High Plains cotton maturation. An exception was a grant of $4,300 funded in part by the Texas Brewers Association for research on the feasibility of growing malt barley on the High Plains. Some of the money was used to create a fellowship for a graduate student to work on the project.[158]

Because of the rapid conversion from horse-power to tractor-power, as well as the growth of pump irrigation on the High Plains in the 1930's, agricultural engineering work in the Plant Industry Department took on a new importance. From 1934 to 1940, irrigated acreage on the High Plains increased from 35,000 to 250,000 as more and more farmers began to tap the "underground rain" beneath the surface with turbine pumps, gear heads, and automobile engines. When an irrigation conference was conducted at Plainview in 1934, E. C. Buie, the Department's only agricultural engineer, spoke on

156. J. E. McDonald, Austin, Texas, October 3, 1933, to A. H. Leidigh; Annual Reports of Division of Agriculture, 1934 and 1935, TTSAP, DF. Pauline Phillips, "Seed Testing—A Service to West Texas," *Texas Tech Magazine*, vol. 1, no. 3 (1937):7.

157. "Program of One-Day School of Instruction in Breeding Grain Sorghums, Texas Tech, March 2, 1935" (printed program); Annual Reports of Division of Agriculture, 1936 and 1938, TTSAP, DF.

158. Annual Report of the Department of Plant Industry, 1938; Annual Report of the Division of Agriculture, 1934; memorandum on possible future research at Texas Tech, *ca.* 1939, in agronomy and range management folder, TTSAP, DF.

the topic of "Power Requirements and Costs of Irrigation" to a group of 250 farmers and businessmen.[159]

Some farmers began turning to the Division of Agriculture in the hot dry summer of 1934 for advice on sinking irrigation wells and irrigation practices. But experimentation in semi-arid land irrigation was needed before much advice could be given. A dual purpose irrigation well was needed by the college for experiments as well as for growing feed for college herds. On August 10, 1934, Leidigh asked Knapp to push the matter of financing a well before the Board. Knapp showed an interest in the matter and brought it before the body. The Board voted the money. Buie, Hershel M. Bell, another agronomist, and Leidigh prepared plans and estimates for the well, and it was installed in 1935. But no funds were forthcoming for research purposes. Plant Industry attempted unsuccessfully to establish cooperative projects with the Texas Agricultural Experiment Station and with the Soil Conservation Service's Division of Irrigation. By 1940, the two wells had been drilled on the farm but they were primarily used to raise feedstuffs for the herds.[160]

Although the Texas Agricultural Experiment Substation near Lubbock began research on High Plains irrigation in 1938, experimentation lagged behind development. In 1941, the results of experiments dealing with "preplanting" irrigation and the timing of watering cotton by Don L. Jones (Director of the Substation) and Frank Gaines were publicized, but the next Texas Agricultural Experiment Station (TAES) bulletins on High Plains irrigation did not appear until the 1950's. The first cost studies were not published by the TAES until 1952.[161]

By the 1930's the Panhandle-Plains was also rapidly becoming one of the most mechanized farming regions in the nation. In the Panhandle counties, the number of horses and mules dwindled from

159. Green, *Land of the Underground Rain*, 119-143. Annual Report of Division of Agriculture, 1934, TTSAP, DF.

160. A. H. Leidigh, June 30, 1934, to Fred D. Weyl; A. H. Leidigh, August 10, 1934, to Bradford Knapp; Bradford Knapp, August 18, 1934, to A. H. Leidigh; Bradford Knapp, December 22, 1934, to A. H. Leidigh; A. H. Leidigh, January 25, 1935, to Bradford Knapp; Bradford Knapp, December 6, 1935, to A. H. Leidigh; A. H. Leidigh, December 4, 1939, to George Mahon; Dean W. Bloodgood, Austin, Texas, December 8, 1939, to A. H. Leidigh, TTSAP, DF.

161. Leota Lightfoot Matthews, "The History of the Lubbock Experiment Station, Substation No. 8," M.S. thesis, Texas Tech, 1959, pp. 85-87. D. L. Jones and Frank Gaines, *Pump Irrigation on the South Plains*, ed. A. D. Jackson, Texas Agricultural Experiment Station (TAES) Progress Report no. 728 (College Station, 1941); William F. Hughes and Joe R. Motheral, *Irrigated Agriculture in Texas*, TAES Miscellaneous Publication no. 59 (College Station, 1950); A. C. Magee, C. W. McArthur, C. A. Bonnen, and William F. Hughes, *Cost of Water for Irrigation on the Texas High Plains*, TAES Bulletin No. 745 (College Station, 1952).

52,243 to 18,548 between 1930 and 1940. During the same period, farmers added 3,942 tractors to their holdings, an increase of about 32 per cent. During the first six months of 1935, South Plains farmers bought a half million dollars worth of tractors. A number of factors stimulated this growth. First, tractors increased productivity, thus lowering the cost of producing crops per acre. Second, the New Deal agricultural program put money into farmers' hands with which to make down payments to implement companies. The growing use of tractors, in turn, enabled farmers to cultivate larger farms. In the process, the movement toward smaller farms during the 1920's was reversed. Agricultural units grew larger (a process which is still continuing) and the small farm tenant began to disappear from the scene.[162]

The Division of Agriculture had been given Fordson tractors in the 1920's, but offered no courses in farm machinery until the middle 1930's. In February, 1930, a farm machinery dealer in Plainview offered Tech a Caterpillar tractor for instructional purposes. Leidigh was forced to decline the offer "because up to date we have not been able to recognize the importance of farm machinery in our student instruction." The Division did not even employ an agricultural engineer at the time. The Dean wrote President Horn of the "embarrassing incident."[163]

Just as all farmers did not move rapidly toward tractors, not all members of the faculty were eager to move away from horses. When one views photographs of Tech's beautiful Percherons or sees the team of Clydesdales used for current advertising purposes by a brewery, an emotional attachment to such magnificent animals is easy to understand. Perhaps because of such an attachment, W. L. Stangel continued into the late 1930's to believe in horse and mule power. He wrote to a friend in 1926 that "I cannot help but feel that our cheapest farm power is the horse and mule and we at the South Plains Fair should encourage his propagation." During the depression he professed to the Percheron Society of America: "The depression is having a healthy reaction in favor of horse power on the farm. While money was plentiful the farmers did not stop to think that by purchasing tractors, they were destroying a market for their feeds. I feel confident that the horse and mule will come back on the farm to stay." By 1934, he still believed that "horses and mules are our cheapest form of power," but six years later he was forced to admit,

162. Nall, "Agricultural History of the Texas Panhandle," 186-189. Green, *Land of the Underground Rain*, 123.

163. A. H. Leidigh, February 17, 1930, to Paul Horn, TTSAP, DF.

"We can see the horse and mule slipping every day." Even then he thought that the farmer should keep some horses and mules for certain types of work "that can not easily be done with the tractor or truck."

His mind, however, was not closed on the subject. When a couple of agricultural economists, C. A. Bonnen and A. C. Magee, published an article in the *Journal of Farm Economics* in 1938 calling attention to the rapid change toward tractors on the High Plains for purposes of economy, they sent a copy of it to Stangel. The Department head responded by asking them to appear before a session on horses and mules, over which Stangel was presiding, at the forthcoming American Society of Animal Production meeting in Chicago. In November 1939, E. K. Hufstedler, a farm implement dealer of Lubbock and Plainview, with the support of the Department of Plant Industry, helped put on a "tractor show" on the Tech campus. At about this time, perhaps during the tractor show, Hufstedler challenged Stangel to a good natured debate on the subject of tractor versus horse. "Runt" declined but some of his students accepted. The debate was held at the Wilson school south of Lubbock. Stangel attended the exchange. The implement dealer asserted that the tractor could do anything that a horse could do, but better. At that point, a student challenged him to produce a single tractor which had ever given birth to a "baby" tractor.[164]

Because of the increased demands from students, Plant Industry hired Eugene C. Buie (B.S. from Texas A&M) as "ag" engineer, and began offering courses in agricultural engineering, farm shop, and farm machinery in 1934. A temporary wooden shop building was constructed. Dean Harmon (A. H., '38), who became a Swisher County farmer, remarked in later years that the agricultural engineering courses in welding and building construction proved to be among the most useful for him. During 1937-38, several tractors were loaned to the Division for instructional purposes. Two of the monthly programs of the new Plant Industry Club in 1936 involved speeches and discussions on tractors and power machinery. Students in 1939 attempted to form a Farm Machinery Club. Henry P. Clay, who succeeded Buie, offered to be the sponsor. But Dean Leidigh turned down the petition because he thought that the Division of Agriculture already had enough clubs. Nevertheless, the attempt to

164. W. L. Stangel, June 29, 1926, to I. E. Barr; W. L. Stangel, June 24, 1932, to Percheron Society of America; W. L. Stangel, January 2, 1934, to John W. Carpenter; W. L. Stangel, November 4, 1938, to C. A. Bonnen; C. A. Bonnen, College Station, October 19, 1938, to W. L. Stangel; Clifford B. Jones, November 7, 1939, to A. H. Leidigh, TTSAP, WLS. Personal interview with W. L. Stangel.

form such an organization shows the emerging new interest among the students.[165]

There is some evidence that the growth in the number of students in agronomy in the thirties and the demands for offerings in power farm machinery were related to the growing number of agricultural students from the High Plains counties north of Lubbock, the center of the movement toward pump irrigation and mechanized power implements. In the Report of the Division of Agriculture for 1934, the head of the Department of Plant Industry stated: "It seems that considerably *more emphasis will have to be placed upon the teaching of crop farming* due to the fact that as time goes on *more of our students are coming from the area north of us* [italics mine]." By 1934, it was indeed apparent that more were coming from that area. Floyd County with its 14 agricultural majors was second only to Lubbock County in the number of students in the Division. And by 1939, the five top counties next to Lubbock in number of agricultural majors were all High Plains counties. Floyd was still second with 20 majors, Crosby was third, followed by Lamb, Hale, and Parmer.[166]

The Department of Agricultural Economics, Farm Management, and Rural Sociology was one of the more innovative departments at Tech. J. O. Ellsworth, the head, taught courses in agri-economics and farm management as well as economics for the Division of Liberal Arts. He was aided by Elmer L. McBride (M.S. from Oklahoma A&M) who joined the staff in 1935, and by President Knapp and Dean Leidigh who taught courses in Rural Sociology.[167]

A number of long-distance field trips were launched from Tech in the mid-thirties. Composed of professors and students, they were exercises in exploration and research. As early as 1928, C. H. Mahoney conducted his Horticulture upperclassmen on a one-week tour of Rio Grande Valley citrus groves. The Biology Department began its field trips in 1935 and took one of them to the Pacific Northwest. The most important for research purposes was undoubtedly the expedition headed by W. C. Holden of the Department of History and Anthropology to the Yaqui Indians of Sonora, Mexico, in 1934. But one of the earlier extended Tech field trips was led by Ellsworth in 1933 through the Mississippi Valley where his few stu-

165. Annual Reports of Division of Agriculture, 1935 and 1938; Henry P. Clay, April 22, 1939, to A. H. Leidigh; A. H. Leidigh, May 19, 1939, to Henry P. Clay. Minutes of Plant Industry Club, May 18, 1936 and November 20, 1936, in Plant Industry Scrapbook, TTSAP, DF. Personal interview with Dean Harmon by author, November 28, 1975, Tulia, Texas.

166. Annual Report of the Division of Agriculture, 1934; memorandum on hometowns of Agricultural students at Texas Tech, 1938-39, February 18, 1939, by Dean A. H. Leidigh, TTSAP, DF.

167. For Ellsworth's background, see chapter 2.

dents viewed various farming operations, agri-business concerns, experiment station projects, and talked with farmers and agricultural economists. The course, "Field Problems in Agricultural Economics," was repeated in the summer of 1935.[168]

The "travel course" of 1935 was typical of Ellsworth's broad approach for his students, as well as his killing pace. The group left Lubbock in his not-so-new Packard on July 19 and returned on August 30. The 6,500 mile venture extended through El Paso and Tucson to the West Coast, up to Washington, east to Montana, Utah, and Wyoming, and back home through Colorado and New Mexico. Students studied irrigation enterprises, cooperatives, importing and exporting businesses, experiment stations, vineyards, fruit farms, ranches, and virtually every type of agricultural enterprise in the west.[169]

As was his teaching, Ellsworth's approach to the farm-constituency was innovative. In late 1932, he proposed to organize a corporation to be called American Farm Service. His plan was to utilize the specialties of the agricultural staff at Tech in offering management services to farmers, expecially to the 62 per cent of Lubbock County who were tenants. His objective was to increase profits for both renter and owner. He also envisioned the corporation operating outright larger farms, ranches, and foreclosure lands held by banks, handling land investments and appraising the value of agricultural holdings. Costs were to be met by charging owners 10 per cent of their rents, and owner-operators 50 per cent of all income over and above profits averaged over the previous five years. The Service would also act as a clearing house in bringing competent tenants (college graduates where possible) and absentee owners together.[170]

Ellsworth's American Farm Service was too ambitious for his limited resources. It never materialized. But he and his students acted as consultants without pay for a number of tenants. They began by showing them how to keep detailed farm records in as simple a form as possible. Ellsworth noted in 1935: "Existing agencies seem to be doing very little in actually assisting tenants in the adoption of better methods [of farming]. To illustrate, not one of the few

168. Andrews, *The First Thirty Years*, 44-47. "What Agriculture at Texas Technological College Offers You," *Bulletin of Texas Technological College*, vol. 4, no. 3 (July 1928): 26-27. J. O. Ellsworth, December 31, 1936, to A. H. Leidigh, TTSAP, DF.

169. Detailed itinerary for travel course in 1935, copy in J. O. Ellsworth folder, TTSAP, DF.

170. J. O. Ellsworth, November 21, 1932, to A. H. Leidigh, with outline of his "Farm Management" and "American Farm Service: An Organization for Group Farm Management," TTSAP, DF.

farmers we are assisting ever used contour planting before we began working with them and now every one of them has adopted the practice."[171] In 1934-35, he spent most of his holidays and spare time "after five o'clock" visiting farmers. His students used questionnaires in conducting surveys of farms in order to pinpoint problems.[172]

Ellsworth took a one-year leave of absence to work for the federal Resettlement Administration at Amarillo in 1936-37 and given a $50,000 budget for research in regional farm management. He returned to Tech in 1937 but the Division lost him that same year when he resigned to become head of the new Department of Economics and Business Administration.[173]

The addition of a vocational agriculture teacher training program was still another important development. Leidigh had been trying since 1925 to establish such a program. It had to be approved by the State Board of Education and the State Board of Control. In 1930, only Texas A&M and Sam Houston State at Huntsville had programs under the Smith-Hughes Act leading to teaching certificates in vocational agriculture. Leidigh believed that "politics" was the only stumbling block in the way of Tech getting its own department. So far as need was concerned, Leidigh observed: "There are actually more schools teaching vocational agriculture within 50 miles of Lubbock than there are within 50 miles of Texas A&M, and about twice as many as there are within 50 miles of Huntsville." In 1933, the program was finally approved. Courses in the teaching of vocational agriculture were introduced, and Cyril Luker who held a B.S. from "A&M," was hired to teach the courses. The Department of Vocational Agricultural Education was established in 1936. Luker resigned the same year and Ray L. Chappelle (B.S. from Texas A&M and recent M.S. from Tech) succeeded him as head. In 1938 the name of the Department was changed to Agricultural Education.[174]

In spite of the hard times, students enjoyed the fellowship and fun of the Agriculture Club, oldest students' organization on campus. The club was enlightened by speakers on such subjects as "Agriculture of China" and "Fruit Regions of the United States." On January 9, 1934, Dean Leidigh showed a "4-reel picture" to the club entitled "The Four Sons," produced by the John Deere Company to

171. J. O. Ellsworth, June 4, 1935, to Bradford Knapp, TTSAP, DF.

172. *Ibid.*; J. O. Ellsworth, February 23, 1935, to Bradford Knapp, TTSAP, DF.

173. J. O. Ellsworth, April 17, 1936, to A. H. Leidigh; J. O. Ellsworth, May 27, 1936, to Bradford Knapp; E. L. McBride, October 18, 1939, to A. H. Leidigh, TTSAP, DF.

174. J. H. Hinds, Nacogdoches, Texas, December 6, 1930, to A. H. Leidigh; A. H. Leidigh, December 11, 1930, to J. H. Hinds; Annual Report of Division of Agriculture, 1934, TTSAP, DF. Andrews, *The First Thirty Years*, 120-121.

demonstrate the advantages of mechanized power farming. At other times, the group was entertained by fellow Aggie Casey Fine on his violin, or a Miss Allie Eason singing "Spanish songs." But even more fun were such occasions as "a Kangaroo Court . . . featuring the trial of R. C. Mowery for 'ungentlemanly conduct' in a Chicago theatre and advances toward chorus girls. Mowery was convicted and sentenced to take the next [livestock judging] team to same theater." The most popular entertainment of all appeared to be assigning extemporaneous speeches to Aggies on such humorous, and sometimes off-color, topics as "The Art of Castrating a Hydraulic Ram," "How to Neck a Giraffe," and "How to Grow Steel Wool."[175]

As has been noted, much of the staff was research oriented. In addition to his many staff duties, Dean Leidigh was still carrying on his research on wheat rust in the late 1920's. Ellsworth, Young, and others had projects in mind worthy of support, but lack of a respectable research budget and facilities handicapped the Division throughout the 1930's. A few isolated instances of research, funded for the most part by private interests such as the barley malt project and the cottonseed products feeding experiments were conducted. But no comprehensive program of research existed.[176]

Three obstacles hindered research: (1) the heavy class load of each staff member, (2) the lack of state appropriations, and (3) perhaps most important, the absence of a direct link with a research station. As noted in chapter 1, research in all land-grant institutions was stimulated in the late 1880's when the Hatch Act provided federal funds for the establishment and support of agricultural research experiment stations. The great majority of those stations were subsequently put under the authority of the land-grant institutions. Thus the Texas Agricultural Experiment Station was located at A&M with a number of substations, such as those at Lubbock and Spur. But no satisfactory sustained cooperative work between Tech and the Lubbock station had been achieved by the early 1930's.[177]

Despite the lack of official cooperative research, a good relationship between the Division of Agriculture and the Texas Agricul-

175. Agricultural Club Minutes, History File, Dean's Files, Texas Tech College of Agricultural Sciences.

176. A. H. Leidigh, November 9, 1928, to C. O. Johnson of Kansas State Experiment Station, TTSAP, DF.

177. Leidigh wrote in 1931 after Stangel conducted some cooperative feeding experiments with sheep: "We have had a very unprofitable experience in our relations with Mr. Conner [Director] of the Texas Agricultural Experiment Station, with regard to Mr. Stangel's feeding work. I am so definitely convinced that no just treatment is possible from that source that I am dropping my wheat breeding for the Experiment Station and I am going to go it alone from now on." A. H. Leidigh, October 15, 1931, to J. O. Ellsworth, October 15, 1931, TTSAP, DF.

tural Experiment Substations at Lubbock and Spur did exist, based largely on old and lasting friendships. Leidigh, formerly associated with the TAES, had installed R. E. "Dick" Dickson at the Spur station in May, 1914. R. E. Karper, a former student of Leidigh at Kansas State, served at the Lubbock station as superintendent from 1915 to 1925 before he went to College Station to succeed Leidigh. From 1928 to 1940 Karper served as vice-director and agronomist in charge of grain sorghum investigations. In that capacity he was instrumental in developing many of the common varieties of "combine maize" grown on the High Plains. Dickson's work was primarily in the area of cattle feeding and soil erosion, and he maintained a close relationship with W. L. Stangel, as well as Dean Leidigh, through the years. The staff also retained a similar relationship with Don L. Jones who succeeded Karper as superintendent of the Lubbock research facility.[178]

Dickson kept Stangel abreast of his work in cattle feeding. For example, he notified him in 1931 of the greater gains to be made in feeding "chopped" milo over "bundles". Stangel regularly attended Dickson's annual "All West Texas Feeder's Day" at Spur. And Dickson, Don L. Jones, and Stangel occasionally toured West Texas together in one-day excursions looking at farms, crops, and feedlots. In the summer of 1938, "Dick" Dickson and some friends while driving through Lubbock's Mackenzie Park observed a large group of picnickers enjoying the shade of Chinese elms which R. E. Karper had first introduced to West Texas in 1919. Someone in Dickson's party suggested that the trees be named for Karper. Dickson took the initiative in getting permission from the park authorities and soliciting funds from Karper's friends to pay for the bronze plaque which now commemorates Karper Grove. Of course, Stangel and Leidigh also did their part in this effort. Leidigh nominated "Dick" Dickson for Lone Star Farmer in 1938, calling him "the single and leading investigator in practical things having to do with the saving of soil moisture in the United States and the prevention of soil erosion."[179]

178. See chapter 2 for more on Leidigh's background. A. H. Leidigh, June 17, 1938, to J. B. Rutland, TTSAP, DF. Everett Aldren Gillis, "R. E. Karper," pp. 611-113 in *Builders of the Southwest*, edited by Seymour V. Connor (Lubbock: Southwest Collection of Texas Tech, 1959).

179. W. L. Stangel, December 23, 1934, to R. E. Dickson; W. L. Stangel, April 11, 1932, to R. E. Dickson; R. E. Dickson, Spur, Texas, May 15, 1937, to D. L. Jones and W. L. Stangel; W. L. Stangel, May 17, 1937, to R. E. Dickson, TTSAP, WLS. R. E. Dickson, Spur, Texas, June 6, 1939, to W. L. Stangel; W. L. Stangel, August 9, 1939, to R. E. Dickson, TTSAP, WLS. A. H. Leidigh, June 17, 1938, to J. B. Rutland, TTSAP, DF.

Dean Leidigh probably believed that the best hope of Tech to get a research facility was with federal rather than state money. He wrote to Congressman Marvin Jones of the Panhandle congressional district in 1930 asking him to push for the establishment of a United States Department of Agriculture experiment station on the Tech campus such as the one at Big Spring. Jones replied that he had been trying to get one for the South Plains since 1925. As late as 1932, Leidigh was still attempting to interest the federal government in establishing the station, but to no avail. Because Lubbock already had a state experiment substation, it was difficult to justify building another research facility only a few miles away. When the federal government finally established the Southwestern Great Plains Research Center, it was located near Amarillo in Congressman Jones's district.[180]

Bradford Knapp raised hopes that some research money might be forthcoming from federal or state sources in 1935 when he asked his divisional deans for ideas on research projects "if we had the means to undertake a limited amount and character of work of this kind." Leidigh then passed the question to his departmental heads. Members of the staff suggested projects, ranging from farm surveys to feeding experiments, to research in the terracing of permanent pastures, to "an investigation of the various types of wind machines and their efficiency in the producing of power." It was obvious that a small amount of money would only satisfy a fraction of the proposals. Hopes were raised but research funds amounted at best only to a trickle.[181]

The college farm and its organization underwent some significant changes in this period. In 1926, the college had operated 862 acres under its farm superintendent, seven hundred of which were in pasture, and leased the remaining 832 acres to six neighboring farmers. The farm was operated by a separate farm department under the farm superintendent. The superintendent was directly under the dean's office. But gradually the farm enlarged its operational acreage, dropping the leases one by one.[182]

President Knapp, dissatisfied with the organization of the farm, abolished the farm department in the fall of 1934. He placed responsibility for the draft horses, implements, and tractors, as well as most

180. A. H. Leidigh, March 10, 1930, to Marvin Jones; Marvin Jones, Washington, D.C., March 22, 1930, to A. H. Leidigh; A. H. Leidigh, April 28, 1932, to J. O. Ellsworth, TTSAP, DF. Nall, "Agricultural History of the Texas Panhandle," 226-227.

181. Bradford Knapp, April 20, 1935, to Dean Leidigh *et al.*; sheaf of interdepartmental correspondence accompanying the letter above, TTSAP, DF.

182. A. H. Leidigh, January 18, 1926, to P. W. Horn, TTSAP, DF.

of the farm, in Stangel's Animal Husbandry Department which already used most of the land for pasture and feedstuffs. Plant Industry was given four fields. Animal Husbandry, of course, had to coordinate the use of the implements. Knapp summed up the key to making the new organization work when he wrote the staff members: "We shall have to rely upon good cooperation to make this plan succeed. We must think more of the College and of the larger institutional interest and welfare than we think of departmental development."[183] Under Stangel's administration, the farm became the showcase for the Division of Agriculture. In late afternoons, Saturdays and Sundays, cars loaded with farmers and townsmen drove through to observe its well-kept buildings, weed-free fields, and fat show animals.[184]

Division of responsibility frequently produces conflict. Knapp's reorganization consequently resulted in some interdepartmental friction. Plant Industry had to go through Animal Husbandry to plant, irrigate, cultivate, plow, or harvest its plots. A few administrative blunders are normal in any complex organization. Thus, Arthur Young perhaps had some cause for irritation when he sent memoranda to W. L. Stangel complaining that the farm superintendent had shifted the irrigation water from the experimental malt barley before completion of the watering, that the parched alfalfa field needed watering rather badly, and that a borrowed combine had been returned before all grain had been harvested. In turn, Stangel informed Young that the farm superintendent needed sufficient lead time to plan his work.[185]

Far more important than the minor conflicts within the division of agriculture over operation of the farm were the harmonious efforts made by the staff to satisfy the increasing demands by farmers for personal services. A few requests were rather unique. A farmer in Isolation, Kentucky wrote to Stangel: "Could you advise me where I could get some of those western burros cheap. . . . I want some to work on my farm and for my children to ride." A school boy from Sweetwater, Oklahoma wanted to know not only if planting crops by the dark of the moon would produce heavier yields; he also wanted to know the effect of the moon's phases upon the breeding of

183. Memorandum on farm department by Bradford Knapp, August 29, 1934, to A. H. Leidigh *et al.*, TTSAP, DF.

184. Newspaper clipping from *Lubbock Avalanche-Journal* about the college farm, *ca.* late 1930's, TTSAP, WLS. Personal interview with F. G. Harbaugh. Personal interview with W. L. Stangel.

185. W. L. Stangel, March 13, 1937, to Arthur W. Young; Arthur W. Young, March 11, 1937, to W. L. Stangel; Arthur W. Young, July 7, 1938, to W. L. Stangel; W. L. Stangel, March 8, 1939, to Arthur W. Young, TTSAP, WLS.

livestock! And then there was the letter from a man in Roswell, New Mexico, addressed to the "Fur Department" of Tech which asked, "Do you have a short course on fur farming?" M. E. Heard of textile engineering first received the query. He sent it to Stangel with the notation that "fox farming is somewhat out of our bailiwick."[186]

The Thirties expanded and deepened the ralationship between the Division of Agriculture and West Texas. In addition to the new demands created by the Dust Bowl experience (to be discussed in the following chapter), more farmers than ever sought advice about plant diseases, weed control, animal health, feeding, and other such matters. The relationship between staff and farmer-constituency was based not only upon the actual needs of West Texas agriculture, but also upon the staff's insights in dealing with the farmer himself. Since the days of W. A. Henry at the University of Wisconsin and Eugene Hilgard at the University of California, agricultural scientists who related to farmers had taken off their professional frock coats, rolled up their sleeves, donned work clothes and talked to their constituents on an equal plane in non-technical terms. It involved a triple role in which staff members had to be scientists, teachers, and farmers. Occasionally, even those with the best of intentions committed blunders. For example, young Henry P. Clay of agricultural engineering set up a short course on farm machinery for January, 1938. One part was to be a noon luncheon to cost sixty-five cents at the Hotel Hilton. But because of lack of interest, Clay had to cancel the luncheon. Bradford Knapp understood the problem. He took Clay aside and told him that a farmer was not in the habit of paying sixty-five cents for a meal "even though he had made $4,000 or $5,000 on a cotton crop." On the other hand, Knapp suggested, if Clay had pit-barbequed a sheep or a pig, brewed up a little coffee over the fire, and charged ten cents each, he would have gotten a crowd.[187]

In spite of hard times, the thirties was an era of progress for the fledgling Division of Agriculture. The Division profited from having a President who was an agricultural leader of national stature. It was Bradford Knapp who put Tech on the national map. When the agricultural and technical divisions of Tech were threatened, it was Knapp who played a leading role in preserving those functions. Student enrollment continued to expand at a steady pace, the var-

186. Bedford Bowman, Isolation, Kentucky, May 16, 1935, to W. L. Stangel, TTSAP, WLS. Y. Hendricks, Roswell, New Mexico, February 3, 1937, to "Fur Department of Texas Tech"; Opie Henson, Sweetwater, Oklahoma, January 28, 1935, to Division of Agriculture, TTSAP, DF.

187. Bradford Knapp, January 18, 1938, to Henry P. Clay, TTSAP, DF.

ious departments interacted with the region to satisfy, so far as possible, the constituency's needs in different ways. The advent of Franklin D. Roosevelt's New Deal in the midst of hard times would produce still other opportunities for the Division of Agriculture.

THE DIVISION OF AGRICULTURE AND THE NEW DEAL

The New Deal was the nation's response to the economic and social dislocations caused by the Great Depression. Immediately after his inauguration as President in 1933, Franklin D. Roosevelt and his Democratic Congress began to create the host of alphabetic agencies from the Agricultural Adjustment Administration (AAA) to the National Youth Administration (NYA) which affected virtually every aspect of American life including farm and campus.

The Public Works Administration (PWA) sponsored the first program to affect Texas Tech directly. As noted in the preceding chapter, the Texas legislature sharply decreased appropriations for the institution in 1933. That same year the PWA furnished $650,000 in grants and loans to Tech for the construction of two new dormitories. And through the Civil Works Administration (CWA), federal money was used to pave the primary streets of the campus for the first time. The only money appropriated by the state of Texas for major buildings on the campus during the thirties was $275,000 for a library in 1937.[188]

One program which had an impact upon the Division of Agriculture was the National Youth Administration (NYA) created in 1935 to subsidize college students by paying them for working on campus projects. At its height in 1936, the NYA had 290 students on campus drawing $3,885 per month, an average of about $13 each. A number of the students were involved in agricultural projects, particularly in the Department of Plant Industry. Under the supervision of C. E. Russell, head of the Department, students assisted in several early research projects mentioned in the preceding chapter such as measuring the rate of moisture penetration in various types of soils, crop experimentation, and rammed-earth housing construction for farms. The Department of Agricultural Economics also used several NYA students in conducting rural surveys. And still another group of students was reported preparing a history of the Division of Agriculture.[189]

188. Floy Farrar Wilbanks, "The Life and Works of Dr. Bradford Knapp," M.A. thesis, Texas Technological College, 1940, pp. 40-43.

189. Deborah Lynn Self, "The National Youth Administration in Texas," M.A. thesis, Texas Tech University, 1974, pp. 63-64. *Texas Tech Magazine*, vol. 1, no. 1 (1937): 11, 20.

A less popular undertaking begun in March, 1938, was the Non-Collegiate NYA. Administered by Dean Leidigh and Ray L. Chappelle of the Department of Agricultural Education, the Non-Collegiate NYA consisted of young men lacking the background for college work who spent about three hours per day in general campus work and took special short courses offered by the Division of Agriculture. Known officially as the NYA Resident Training Project, its members tended shrubs, watered trees, constructed farm buildings, and performed a number of similar tasks. Unlike the regular NYA, the Non-Collegiate program received much criticism. The "residents" themselves complained that too much of the teaching in their special courses was done by visiting vocational agriculture high school teachers in night classes. In response, President Bradford Knapp told the state NYA director that the classroom space and staff was already overtaxed and that the Division of Agriculture was doing the best job possible under the circumstances. There were also complaints about the Non-Collegiate men. Echoing the sentiments of Tech personnel and Lubbock citizens, Knapp stated that "some of them are evidently very much below par, morally, intellectually, and otherwise." He referred specifically to a few of the men "making 'raw cracks' " to coeds, "loafing on the streets," and leaning "on their shovels, spit[ting] tobacco juice." Ray Chappelle, while admitting that both students and the college had received some benefit from the program, recommended in March of 1939 that it be discontinued. The program, however, was prolonged into 1940.[190]

Most of the farmers of the region and the staff of the Division of Agriculture approved of the New Deal agricultural program. The Agricultural Adjustment Administration (AAA) created by Congress in 1933 attempted to reduce agricultural overproduction and raise commodity prices of such staples as wheat and cotton. Farmers voluntarily agreed to reduce their acreage in exchange for federal subsidies. More than 90 per cent of the farmers in some Panhandle counties approved of the wheat program by 1935. The government subsidies became even more important during the severe Dust Bowl drouth. In 1934, a study made in Dallam County showed that the average wheat farmer received 57.5 per cent of his income from the AAA. When the Supreme Court declared the Agricultural Adjust-

190. A. H. Leidigh, memorandum [*ca.* 1937], to Ray L. Chappelle; Bradford Knapp, April 1, 1938, to A. H. Leidigh; J. C. Kellam, State Director of National Youth Administration, Austin, March 30, 1938, to Bradford Knapp; Bradford Knapp, April 1, 1938, to J. C. Kellam; A. H. Leidigh, March 2, 1939, to Ray L. Chappelle; Ray L. Chappelle, March 22, to A. H. Leidigh; A. H. Leidigh, September 15, 1939, to Ray L. Chappelle; Ray L. Chappelle, July 19, 1938, to J. M. Gordon, TTSAP, DF.

ment Act to be unconstitutional in 1936, the reaction of the Clarendon Chamber of Commerce that the court's decision was "deplorable to all West Texas" voiced the sentiments of most in the region.[191] Upon the heels of the AAA's cotton plow-up and pig-kill in 1933, W. L. Stangel approved the plan of J. W. Ridgway, his former dairy instructor at "A&M" and then manager of the Borden Company's dairy plant in Fort Worth, to "plow up some dairy cows" in order to reduce the industry's surplus butter. When the cattle-kill was inaugurated in 1934, however, Stangel concurred with Roy B. Davis of the Panhandle-Plains Dairy Association in counseling dairymen to use the opportunity to cull their herds rather than sell off their good stock.[192]

Another important New Deal effort which involved the agricultural faculty was a program of the Federal Emergency Relief Administration (FERA) later absorbed by the Resettlement Administration in 1935. The National Rural Rehabilitation Program of the FERA was charged with buying large blocks of land, subdividing those into small units for rent (for sale later) to landless farmers who had not yet joined the Okie Migration to California, and financing their farming operations. The national director of the project and assistant of FERA Administrator Harry Hopkins was Lawrence Westbrook, who had been a member of the Texas legislature, had helped to organize the Texas Cotton Cooperative Association, and had served as Director of the Texas Relief Commission in 1933-34.[193]

Westbrook was instrumental in founding Texas Rural Communities, Inc., to work with the FERA in establishing the projects. John W. Carpenter, a Dallas utilities company executive, was elected president of the organization. Others named to its board of directors included Westbrook, H. Y. Benedict, President of the University of Texas, T. O. Walton, President of Texas A&M, and Bradford Knapp. When A. B. Davis, Secretary-Manager of the Lubbock Chamber of Commerce, read an article in February, 1934, about Westbrook's work, he suggested that the Lubbock Chamber of Commerce take the lead in establishing such a project for West Texas. A few months

191. Nall, "Agricultural History of the Texas Panhandle," 161-163, 171-172.

192. J. W. Ridgway, Fort Worth, September 4, 1933, to O. E. Reed, Chief of Bureau of Dairy Industry, U.S.D.A.; J. W. Ridgway, Fort Worth, September 13, 1933, to W. L. Stangel; W. L. Stangel, September 20, 1933, to Clyde L. King, Chief of Dairy Section of AAA; W. L. Stangel, July 24, 1934, to Roy B. Davis; Roy B. Davis, Plainview, July 23, 1934, to W. L. Stangel, TTSAP, WLS.

193. *Who's Who in the South and Southwest*, vol. 6 (Chicago: Marquis, 1959) *s.v.* "Westbrook, Lawrence." Arthur M. Schlesinger, Jr., *The Politics of Upheaval* (Boston: Houghton Mifflin, 1960), 352. Bernard Sternsher, *Rexford Tugwell and the New Deal* (New Brunswick: Rutgers University Press, 1964), 263-265.

later, Davis recalled: "This story intrigued our interest and, after careful consideration and study, we were convinced that the idea was . . . one of the few worthwhile proposed experiments in the New Deal. In our judgment, it was one of the few ways that had been thought of that would actually rehabilitate humans instead of doping them with the dole."[194]

The Lubbock Chamber of Commerce appointed a committee to "investigate and study 'New Deal Colonies' " and to work out a plan for establishing at least one in the Lubbock area. Members of the committee included Dean Leidigh, W. L. Stangel, President Knapp, Don L. Jones (Superintendent of the State Experiment Substation at Lubbock), A. B. Davis, and Judge R. C. Hopping, who was sales manager of the extensive Ellwood Lands on the South Plains. The Chamber committee put together a proposal within a few weeks. Texas Rural Communities approved the plan in February, 1934, and a site on Ellwood property was selected southwest of Lubbock near Ropesville.[195]

In addition to a humanitarian purpose, the Lubbock Chamber wanted the project for two other reasons by 1935: (1) to prove that small farmers could make a living on the High Plains, and consequently (2) to show that the area was really not a part of the Dust Bowl. This motivation was apparent in the conflict which arose between the committee on one side and Texas Rural Communities and Resettlement Administration officials on the other. The Lubbock Chamber resented its area being classified as part of the Dust Bowl in 1935 when the South Plains was placed in the newly created Region XII of the Resettlement Administration with its headquarters in Amarillo.[196] The Region encompassing parts of Texas, Oklahoma, Kansas, New Mexico, and Colorado was viewed by the government and those outside the region as the Dust Bowl. A. B. Davis complained after meeting with Resettlement Administration officials in Dallas: "all too many of those in authority who have to do

194. Vèrnon C. Stafford, "The Ropesville Resettlement Project," *West Texas Historical Year Book*, 25 (October, 1949):88-90. A. B. Davis, Lubbock, October 25, 1935, to Victor Schoffelmayer, TTSAP, DF. The article which influenced Davis was Gene Cooper, "Rural Colonization Plan in Texas Hits at Unemployment," *Dallas Morning News*, February 4, 1935, section 1, p. 10.

195. Spencer W. Wells, Chairman of Ropesville Project Local Advisory Committee, Lubbock, December 10, 1935, to D. P. Trent, Regional Director of the Resettlement Administration, TTSAP, DF.

196. The dates of Vernon Stafford (1932 and 1933) for the genesis of the project by the Lubbock Chamber of Commerce in Stafford, "The Ropesville Resettlement Project," 89, are apparently wrong. See A. B. Davis' account of the genesis of the idea in A. B. Davis, Lubbock, October 25, 1935, to Victor Schoffelmayer, and Spencer A. Wells, Lubbock, December 10, 1935, to D. P. Trent, TTSAP, DF. These and numerous other letters pertaining to the Ropesville Project may be found in the Ropesville Project folder of TTSAP,DF.

with this project just don't believe in this country. They speak of it as being a country of 'low rainfall.' They just can't get it out of their heads that this is not a desert." Knapp also objected to the area being placed in the Dust Bowl. Although the President of Tech did not deny that the South Plains had its dust storms, he did deny that the extreme drouth conditions of the Oklahoma Panhandle, the northern part of the Texas Panhandle, southeastern Colorado, and southwestern Kansas prevailed on the South Plains. "*I insist that this area is not now and never has been in anybody's 'Dust Bowl.'* [italics by Knapp]"[197] When Leidigh protested to Congressman Mahon about the Dust Bowl designation, Mahon in turn complained to Resettlement Administration officials about including the South Plains in Region XII, but to no avail.[198]

The Lubbock Chamber of Commerce wanted to demonstrate through the Ropesville Project that a farmer could make a living by cultivating forty to sixty acres with possibly up to three acres of vegetables and orchards under irrigation from windmills. Some leaders and land developers had for some time been interested in determining the minimum amount of land required for a family farm on the South Plains. As early as 1931, Clifford B. Jones, manager of Spur Lands and then Chairman of the Tech Board of Directors, had raised the question before President Paul Horn. He suggested that the School of Agriculture conduct an experiment with tracts of 80, 160, and 320 acres to determine the minimum unit. The Board agreed and the suggestion made to Leidigh, but the college had no funds for the experiment.[199]

Originally, the Chamber of Commerce committee proposed to settle at least one hundred families on farms containing forty acres in cultivation. When the project was shifted from the FERA to the Resettlement Administration, the latter agency along with Texas Rural Communities decided to increase the minimum to 120 acres and settle only thirty-three families. Irritated by the change, A. B. Davis wrote confidentially to the agricultural editor of the *Dallas Morning News*:

> Hell—any and everybody that knows anything about this country knows that any intelligent farmer, properly starting out and capitalized, can make a good living on 120 acres on the South Plains. . . . Therefore, we

197. Nall, "Agricultural History of the Texas Panhandle," 185. A. B. Davis, Lubbock, December 27, 1935, to members of the Ropesville Local Advisory Committee; Bradford Knapp, January 27, 1936, to A. B. Davis, TTSAP, DF.

198. A. H. Leidigh, January 16, 1936, to Congressman George Mahon; George Mahon, Washington, February 4, 1936, to A. H. Leidigh, TTSAP, DF.

199. P. W. Horn, October 14, 1931, to A. H. Leidigh, TTSAP, DF.

> know that if this thing is to be worth anything as an experiment and a demonstration that it should be held down to 60 acres with a minimum of 100 units.

Davis asserted that if the small unit experiment proved successful, "it would induce the large landowners of this section to follow suit on similar plans, and in the final analysis, that is *the big objective* [italics mine]." In other words, it was hoped that the Project would set off a population and land development boom on the South Plains which, in turn, would demonstrate that the region was not part of the Great American Desert. Spencer Wells, chairman of the Ropesville Local Advisory Committee, wrote to the regional director of the Resettlement Administration that if the project were to "achieve the results originally intended . . . the farms must be 60 acres instead of 120 acres."[200]

In private committee meetings, Leidigh was skeptical of the forty acre plan. When the committee first proposed Ropesville, there was talk of including small manufacturing concerns within the project so that its settlers could supplement their incomes with factory work. Bradford Knapp was especially interested in this (remember his vision of West Texas in 1984?), and at that point he supported the forty-acre unit. But by December 1935, with the manufacturing idea discarded somewhere in the planning stage, Knapp told Davis that he favored a variety of units ranging from 60 to 120 acres depending upon the ability of the individual farmer. "I believe in a two-horse man holding a two-horse farm, and a four-horse farmer holding a four-horse farm." The final size of the unit, incidentally, was sixty acres on alternate one-eighth sections, leaving an additional sixty acres for future use between each farm.[201]

Leidigh, Stangel and Knapp remained on the advisory committee throughout the creation of the project. Leidigh made important contributions about crops to be grown and helped lay out terraces. Stangel offered valuable advice on farm animals to be purchased, and Knapp screened the applicants through interviews. In 1936, the first family moved into Ropesville, and the settlers signed contracts with the government to purchase the land in 1941.[202]

200. A. B. Davis, Lubbock, October 25, 1935, to Victor Schoffelmayer, and Spencer A. Wells, Lubbock, December 10, 1935, to D. P. Trent, TTSAP, DF. This evidence clearly contradicts the assertion of Vernon Stafford that the governmental officials wanted to saddle the project with smaller units while the Lubbock Chamber wanted larger units. Actually, the opposite was true. Compare the letters above with Stafford, "The Ropesville Resettlement Project," 93-94.

201. Bradford Knapp, December 30, 1935, to A. B. Davis, TTSAP, DF. Stafford, "The Ropesville Resettlement Project," 90-91, 94-95.

202. *Ibid.*, 90-100. A. H. Leidigh, November 20, 1940, to James A. Bush, TTSAP, DF.

Tech maintained an active interest in the work through the late thirties. Knapp visited the farms frequently, meetings involving the Ropesville Project and the Farm Security Administration (successor to the Resettlement Administration) were held on campus, and by 1938 a Tech dairy manufactures major, James P. Williams (class of '31), was serving as manager of the project.[203]

The New Deal effort which produced the greatest impact upon the Division of Agriculture was undoubtedly the soil conservation program, a response to the drouth and erosive dust storms which began raking the southern Great Plains in the middle thirties. The worst dust storm hit the region on April 14, 1935. It rolled out of southwestern Kansas and southeastern Colorado, across the Oklahoma Panhandle and into eastern New Mexico and the Panhandle-Plains of Texas, resembling, as one old timer put it, "a big headrise comin' down the Canadian River after a heavy rain." Visibility dropped to below fifty feet. Dust sifted through windows into houses creating a haze indoors. Sand drifted around fence rows until wire and post were almost covered. And people held wet cloths over their noses to filter out the powdery dust.[204] The storms were hard on livestock as well as people. An observer in New Mexico noted: "Cattle worse after one of these than . . . after a blizzard." A sense of hopelessness sank over the region as dusters scraped out precious soil to the hardpan. The same New Mexican wrote to Stangel: "We are having one of those dust storms this morning. It seems that there is no end to them."[205]

A ray of hope emerged in the government's creation of the Soil Erosion Service in 1933. Originally a part of the Department of the Interior, the name was changed to the Soil Conservation Service in 1935 and put into the Department of Agriculture. The Service began its first project in West Texas in 1934 under the leadership of H. H. Finnell, formerly director of the Oklahoma State Experiment Substation at Goodwell, who was named supervisor of the Dalhart Wind Erosion Control Project Number 27, in eastern Dallam County. Farmers in this 27,000-acre area agreed to a five-year program of soil conservation practices including terracing, contour plowing

203. Wilbanks, "The Life and Work of Dr. Bradford Knapp," 92-96. Program of Farm Security Administration Meeting at Lubbock, Texas, June 8, 9, 10, [1938], TTSAP, DF. *Texas Tech Magazine*, vol. 1, no. 8 (1938):9.

204. Nall, "Agricultural History of the Texas Panhandle," 156-158. Vance Johnson, *Heaven's Tableland: The Dust Bowl Story* (New York: Farrar, Straus & Co., 1947), 155-156. Fred Floyd, "A History of the Dust Bowl," Ph.D. dissertation, University of Oklahoma, 1950, p. 100.

205. B. Carmichael, Kenna, New Mexico, April 28, 1935, to W. L. Stangel, TTSAP, WLS.

and the planting of cover crops. Dallam County became a model for similar projects throughout the southern Great Plains.[206]

The new Soil Conservation Service (SCS) needed trained personnel and offered salaries to attract such men. The subsequent recruiting affected the Division of Agriculture in two ways. First, the Service raided the faculty. A recruiter arrived on campus on March 14, 1935, and asked Dean Leidigh for permission to talk to some of his staff members. Leidigh granted the request but confided to a friend at Kansas State: "On account of our present very low salary scale, this has me considerably worried. . . ."[207]

Tech, as well as a number of other agricultural schools, lost men to the higher salaries of the SCS in 1935 and 1936. Hershel M. Bell, who had joined the Department of Agronomy in 1927, resigned in 1935 to work for the Soil Conservation Service. Cyril Luker, head of the Department of Agricultural Education, resigned to work for the SCS at an increase in salary of $100 per month. And J. O. Ellsworth took a leave of absence from the Department of Agricultural Economics in 1936 to work with the Resettlement Administration at Amarillo. Leidigh complained to Knapp that the resignations and changes in personnel indicated that salaries were about 50 per cent "too low" and that staff members were being overworked by 30 per cent.[208]

In at least one instance, however, the soil conservation movement provided an opportunity for adding a valuable new faculty member. When Leidigh began looking for an addition to the Plant Industry Department in 1935, Bradford Knapp suggested that he contact a youthful professor at Panhandle A&M College in Goodwell, Oklahoma, whom the President had met a few months before at a soil conservation meeting in Dalhart. Because of Knapp's family ties to Iowa State where his father once served as president and his brother was employed in the business office, mutual interests emerged in the conversation with agronomist Arthur W. Young (Ph.D., Iowa State). The Soil Conservation Service also offered Young a job, but he chose Tech at a lower salary because he preferred to teach.[209]

Even more important was the Soil Conservation Service as a market for graduates of the Division of Agriculture. H. H. Finnell wired Stangel on April 26, 1935: "Can you recommend available

206. Nall, "Agricultural History of the Texas Panhandle," 177-180.

207. A. H. Leidigh, March 15, 1935, to R. I. Throckmorton, TTSAP, DF.

208. A. H. Leidigh, January 3, 1936, to Bradford Knapp; Annual Reports of Division of Agriculture, 1935 and 1936, TTSAP, DF.

209. Personal interview with Arthur W. Young, March 6, 1973, by Beth Schneider, Lubbock, Southwest Collection.

agricultural graduates with training and practice but not necessarily professional experience in soil survey to take special training in erosion survey preparatory to permanent appointment soil erosion service [?]" Leidigh responded, "When do you want them [?]"[210] By the fall of 1935, seventeen Tech graduates were in the SCS. Because the work was primarily with soils and plants, the greatest demand was for agronomy majors. Thus, twelve of the men were agronomists, but two were agricultural economists, two were from dairy manufactures, one was in animal husbandry and one had a degree in general agriculture. By 1938, twenty-eight ex-students were employed by the Soil Conservation Service.[211]

Dean Leidigh kept abreast of the work of the SCS. He queried former students about their training and made notes on the contents of their in-service courses. In the summer of 1936, he wrote to Cyril Luker, a former staff member then with SCS, that Tech would offer a course in soil conservation for the first time in the summer of 1937 designed for vocational agriculture teachers and "younger" staff members of the SCS. The Dean stated further that he would like to use some SCS personnel in teaching the course.[212]

Farmers in the region moved rapidly toward adopting the new soil conservation techniques. The Soil Conservation and Domestic Allotment Act of 1936 offered incentive by providing payments for conservation practices. For example, farmers received 25 cents per acre for contour plowing and 50 cents an acre for planting cover crops on contour rows. At least one county agent who also acted as supervisor of the conservation program in his area worked round the clock for months to meet local demands. By the end of 1937, more than 6,000 High Plains farmers had contoured acreage.[213]

Tech personnel also aided farmers, especially in surveying terraces. Some staff members in agricultural engineering and their students engaged in such work without pay.[214] When plans were announced for a soil conservation meeting sponsored by the County Judges Association to be held at Amarillo in January, 1936 and involving everyone from county judges to SCS people, Leidigh noted

210. Telegrams, H. H. Finnell, Dalhart, April 26, 1935, to A. H. Leidigh, and A. H. Leidigh, April 26, 1935, to H. H. Finnell, TTSAP, DF.

211. List of "Agricultural Men Employed in the Soil Conservation Service," October 22, 1935, TTSAP, DF. *Texas Tech Magazine*, vol. 1, no. 8 (1938).

212. A. H. Leidigh, August 22, 1936, to Cyril Luker; "Soil Erosion Project at Dalhart, Texas," notes made by Dean Leidigh in a talk with Ralph Cogdell on May 11, 1935; "Wind Erosion Science, Outline of the Course," by O. T. Williams, mimeographed (May 31, 1935), in Soil Erosion folder; Annual Report of Division of Agriculture, 1938, TTSAP, DF.

213. Nall, "Agricultural History of the Texas Panhandle," 179-180.

214. Personal interview with Arthur W. Young, May 27, 1975, by author at Lubbock, Southwest Collection.

that Tech was not invited to send a representative. Angered at the snub, he wrote the South Plains' Congressman, George Mahon, asking that he "use your influence and good offices to secure us, particularly our Dr. A. W. Young, a permanent place in these councils." Because it was a state rather than a federal meeting, Mahon could do nothing. Leidigh felt it was simply one more case of representatives of the South Plains being ignored by officialdom.[215]

The state did not ignore Tech, however, when it established the Soil Conservation Committee of the Land Use Committee of the Texas Planning Board in 1938. Leidigh was named chairman of that committee. When E. A. Wood, Director of the State Planning Board, sent the Dean a list of names suggested for his committee with the notation that the chairman could add any others he wished, Leidigh penned in the names of R. E. Dickson, an old friend who was director of the State Experiment Substation at Spur; James A. Bush, an influential Amarilloan; and Robert A. Manire, Director of State Agricultural Education.[216]

By 1939, the Division of Agriculture had awarded degrees to 301. Of that number, 88.7 per cent were engaged either in agriculturally related fields of employment or directly in agriculture. The largest number, 106, was employed by government, exclusive of teaching, in such areas as extension work, the Soil Conservation Service, other areas of the U.S. Department of Agriculture, and state departments of agriculture. The next largest group (61) taught high school vocational agriculture. Forty-one were in agri-business concerns, sixteen taught and/or conducted research in colleges of agriculture, eleven were graduate students working toward advanced degrees, and thirty-two, about 10 per cent of the total, were farmers and ranchers.[217]

Not all students, of course, who returned to the farm from Tech chose majors in agriculture. Perhaps typical of these was a football player from Littlefield who decided on another major field because (1) he thought he "knew enough about agriculture to make a living at farming," (2) his father "owned considerable farm land, enough to support several generations," and (3) perhaps most important, if he

215. A. H. Leidigh, January 16, 1936, to Congressman George Mahon; George Mahon, Washington, January 22, 1936, to A. H. Leidigh; A. H. Leidigh, January 28, 1936, to George Mahon, TTSAP, DF. The meeting itself was probably conducted in accordance with a law enacted by the Texas legislature to establish wind erosion conservation districts in each county under the auspices of the county commissioners court. The county judge, by law, served as presiding officer of the commissioners court. (Nall, "Agricultural History of the Texas Panhandle," 179.)

216. E. A. Wood, Austin, February 22, 1938, to A. H. Leidigh, TTSAP, DF.

217. Report of the Employment of Agricultural Graduates, February 25, 1939, TTSAP, DF.

"took agriculture, the laboratories would prevent him from having enough time for [football] practice."[218]

There are a number of conclusions which may be drawn from these statistics. (1) Only 10 per cent of those with agricultural majors went "back" to the farm. But this is no surprise since national economic and technological forces were increasing the size of farms and decreasing the number of farmers. (2) Tech graduates were now vocational agriculture teachers in a large number of regional high schools. This was extremely significant in terms of future sources of Tech agricultural students because those teachers were responsible for orienting their students toward Tech. (3) Agri-business was now furnishing a new market for graduates, an important trend for the future. (4) And perhaps most significant of all, agricultural programs set in motion by the New Deal or expanded by both federal and state governments furnished the largest market for graduates. If one lumps teachers and professors with this number, 60 per cent of the graduates were employed by government.

Depression, Dust Bowl, and New Deal formed a trinity which influenced the development of and which offered service to the region for the Tech Division of Agriculture. It is impossible to estimate how many students and farmers in West Texas shared the belief of the football player who said he already knew enough about farming to make a living and therefore needed no college training in agriculture, but by the end of the decade, it was less in evidence. Experience with the depression and Dust Bowl exposed a sense of desperation among farmers and their sons. New Deal programs brought scientific agricultural practices within the grasp of more farmers than ever before. Dean Leidigh noted in December 1931 that "the last ten years have enabled the teacher to secure a more sympathetic understanding of the application of science to Agriculture."[219] And in the process of readjustment, the Division of Agriculture became an important focal point of scientific agriculture in West Texas, thanks in part to the readiness on the part of the faculty to serve their farmer constituency in spite of low pay and heavy loads.

218. J. O. Ellsworth, December 6, 1932, to A. H. Leidigh, TTSAP, DF.

219. "Article written for Miss Weeks to use at the meeting of the Agricultural Workers Association" [by Dean Leidigh], December 16, 1939, TTSAP, DF.

THE WAR YEARS

The eruption of World War II produced unforeseen changes at Texas Tech and within the Division of Agriculture, as well as on the national and international scenes. A new president furnished the leadership for most of the period. Bradford Knapp died of heart disease on June 11, 1938. For the next few months, the College was headed by a three-member executive committee made up of J. M. Gordon, Dean of the Division of Arts and Sciences; W. T. Gaston, the Business Manager; and Harry L. Kent, the Director of Administration whom Knapp had brought to Tech.

In a controversial meeting on November 26, the Board of Directors, by a vote of four to three, chose Clifford B. Jones, one of its own members, to be the new president. The deciding vote for Jones was cast by the presiding officer, Spencer Wells of Lubbock. The dissenters asserted that the move was illegal. Technically, because Jones had sent his resignation on the Board to the governor just prior to the meeting, he was not a member at the time of the voting. But this point was clouded because the governor was on a hunting trip and had not yet officially accepted the resignation.

Clifford B. Jones became the third president of Texas Tech on February 1, 1939, but not without controversy. The next month the Texas attorney-general reversed his office's earlier approval of the action made in October 1938, and declared that the appointment was illegal. A few days later, a district judge at Groesbeck issued an injunction to prevent the Board from choosing Jones a second time. Risking contempt of court charges, the Board reelected him. The incident was not finally closed until the Texas Court of Civil Appeals axed the injunction on May 1.[220]

As one of the most active civic leaders in West Texas, the new president had long been a friend to Tech. Born in Colorado, Jones grew up in Kansas City where he completed a university preparatory course in high school. He decided to go into business rather than attend Yale, and in 1907 was made vice-president and treasurer of Jacques Steel Company in Kansas City. His father became manager of the vast S. M. Swenson and Son's Spur Ranch properties in West Texas and employed Clifford as his assistant in 1911. When the Swenson family moved the elder Jones to the Gulf Coast to man-

220. Andrews, *The First Thirty Years:* 50-53. For the most complete account of the controversy surrounding Clifford B. Jones' appointment, see Rushing and Nall, *Evolution of a University*, 71-90.

age their sulphur-extraction enterprises in 1913, Clifford succeeded his father at the age of 28.

Jones' interest in Tech preceded its founding. He was among those who established the West Texas Chamber of Commerce and worked toward the reality of a "West Texas A&M." Governor Pat Neff appointed him to Tech's first Board of Directors which he served as chairman from 1925 to 1938. At the time of his inauguration, he was one of the best known citizens of West Texas.[221]

Jones's relationship to the Division of Agriculture began when Arthur Leidigh and "Runt" Stangel arrived on the scene in 1925. Jones solicited implement dealers and livestock breeders for much of Tech's earliest machinery and livestock. The connection continued as he sent books, bulletins, and bits of information to staff members for their use and asked the advice of Leidigh and Stangel on various agricultural problems.[222]

Like his predecessor, Jones was oriented toward agriculture. Although he had never been a farmer, he fully understood its important economic relationship to West Texas. He differed from Bradford Knapp in one respect. Whereas Knapp was an agricultural sociologist interested in farming as a way of life rather than as a business, Jones was essentially an agricultural businessman. This does not necessarily imply that Clifford Jones had no deep feelings for the problems of average farmers, nor does it mean that Knapp did not appreciate agriculture as business. Each man came from a different background with different training, and each viewed agriculture primarily from his particular frame of reference. The significant point is that from 1932 until 1944 when Clifford Jones resigned, Tech had presidents whose foremost interests were in agriculture.

The Board of Directors renewed the contract of Clifford Jones for a five-year period in March, 1941, and the war broke out in December. The international conflict affected Tech in a number of ways. Faculty and students joined or were drafted into the armed forces. Even Spencer Wells, chairman of the Board, entered the army. Tech offered correspondence courses to enlisted men at reduced tuition rates. New courses in Chinese and Portuguese were

221. Seymour V. Connor, "Clifford B. Jones," pp. 102-105 in *Builders of the Southwest.* Jones had no college degree, but neither did T. O. Walton, President of Texas A&M from 1925 to 1943. George Sessions Perry, *The Story of Texas A&M* (New York: McGraw-Hill, 1951), 95-96, 100.

222. See Clifford B. Jones correspondence folders in TTSAP, DF and TTSAP, WLS for numerous examples of information ranging from pink boll worm infestation to federal agricultural programs.

offered by the Department of Foreign Languages. The Board of Directors in one of its least memorable acts, but in tune with the national racist anti-Japanese-American mood, prohibited persons of Japanese ancestry from entering Tech. (Nothing was said, of course, of German descendants.)

Enrollment dropped sharply during the war. In 1938-39, Tech had reached a high of 3,896 students. By 1943-44, the number had plummeted to 1,928.[223] In the Division of Agriculture, enrollment from the later thirties through 1941 had been above 600 per year, and in 1941, eighty-five students received degrees in agriculture. By the fall term of 1942, enrollment was down to 120. Seventy-two students dropped out of the Division that term. Of these, thirty-two entered the armed services and twenty-three went into draft-deferred farm and ranch work.[224] Several staff members resigned to go into the services or war industries. Neil Casey Fine, a brilliant graduate of Tech who had returned in the late thirties to teach in Animal Husbandry, left to become a naval officer. George O. Elle of Plant Industry and James Huffman, creamery superintendent, entered the army. O. B. Howell, also of Plant Industry, got a job in a defense-related industry. To add to an already critical faculty shortage, Earl T. Duke, a young instructor in Plant Industry, died on May 11, 1942. And Mart G. Pederson left the Department of Dairy Manufactures to enter commercial creamery work, as did also Forrest Baumgardner, the new Tech creamery superintendent. Vacancies were usually not filled due to the difficulty of finding qualified personnel. For example, when Casey Fine resigned, the Division hired Tech graduate Jamie Caviness to take his place. Caviness resigned within the year to go into the army and the position remained vacant.[225]

The most pressing immediate problem faced by the Division was the need for a new agricultural building. The original stucco and wood structure had been completed in 1927. It was sufficient for the first few years. But cramped conditions soon forced the college to partition much of the Livestock Judging Pavilion into offices and classrooms, to build some "shacks" and even to hold classes in the barns. More than forty students were often cramped into 19½ by 19½-foot classrooms. As the old Agricultural Building became more crowded, professors moved their equipment into "shacks" some dis-

223. Andrews, *The First Thirty Years*, 54, 57-59, 63.

224. A. H. Leidigh, "The Agricultural Division at Texas Tech," *Sheep and Goat Raiser* (October 1941):8. Annual Report of Division of Agriculture, 1943, TTSAP, DF.

225. Annual Reports of Division of Agriculture, 1942, 1943, and 1944, TTSAP, DF.

tance away and even into the hall. In 1939, a campus journalist observed that soon "a student will have to have a map to find his way down the hall." Instructors as well as students were affected. Some classes ran until 10 p.m. and others were conducted on Saturday mornings. Even Saturday afternoon laboratory sections were commonplace. Dean Leidigh was convinced that the crowded, unsatisfactory conditions turned numbers of agricultural students away from Tech altogether.[226] Moreover, Leidigh wrote to Horn that the situation "is affecting the viewpoint of the agricultural students [who] . . . consider our part of the College is not well provided for and does not have the conveniences, furniture, and similar equipment available for the other parts of the institution."[227]

The old building was not only overcrowded. During the winter it was frequently cold due to "the inexpensive nature of the construction." And in the summer months, the steam radiators which had proved to be insufficient during the winter could not be completely turned off. By 1938 the building's roof had some bad leaks. During one heavy rain, water flowed under the north doors, through the vestibule, and into Leidigh's office. To make matters worse, the electrical circuits were inadequate for the overtaxed facility. As the Dean put it: "It is usual for us to have a partial lack of electric lights and power service . . . due to a blown fuse. This practically always happens whenever the classrooms are full, the laboratories are full, and it is dark or cloudy."[228]

The Dean seldom missed an opportunity to inform his constituency of the problem. When Tech held its tenth anniversary celebration in 1935, arrangements were made for visitors to be guided through the College's facilities. The handout sheet for visitors to the Division of Agriculture, probably written by Leidigh, contains this laconic observation: "The State has never furnished the Division of Agriculture with an adequate building."[229]

Leidigh encouraged students to prod their state legislators into appropriating funds for better quarters. J. H. Baumgardner, President of the Agricultural Club, sent out a memo to Aggies in the summer of 1938 urging them to contact their legislators "and any other influential man in your community" about the pressing need for a building. Members of the staff put together a map showing the

226. "Campus Highlights," *Texas Tech Magazine*, vol. 2, no. 8 (1939):4. Report on Questions Pertaining to Appropriations by A. H. Leidigh, December 14, 1938, TTSAP, DF.

227. A. H. Leidigh, September 10, 1930, to P. W. Horn, TTSAP, DF.

228. A. H. Leidigh, April 22, 1938; January 11, 1932; and June 17, 1938, to W. T. Gaston, TTSAP, DF.

229. Decennial Celebration Notice for Visitors, Division of Agriculture, Texas Technological College, November 9, 1935, TTSAP, DF.

hometown and legislative district of every agricultural major. In March, 1939, the staff supplied each student with the names and addresses of his respective state representative and senator. A broadside was circulated containing the bold headline, "WRITE YOUR CHOSEN REPRESENTATIVES IN AUSTIN—THEY WANT TO KNOW YOUR VIEWS. WRITE THEM TODAY—NOW!" An announcement stating, "Strike while the iron is hot. Write your Representative!! Write your Senator!!!" was posted on a bulletin board.[230]

The appropriation was defeated, but the Tech Aggies did not give up. J. R. Bertrand, President of the Agricultural Club for 1939-40, wrote his fellow students to continue the battle.[231] Alumni also added their support. One ex-student, then superintendent of a High Plains creamery, wrote his senator and representative of the problem. He noted that during a recent conference of creamery men on the campus, the group of one hundred had to move three different times in order to find a large enough room. Irritated and still angry, he complained, "Nowhere on the campus will you find a permanent [agricultural] building, due to the fact that the Department of Agriculture has in plain words up to date 'SUCKED A DRY TIT' "[232]

Student and alumni pressure finally bore fruit in 1941 when the legislature appropriated $250,000 for a permanent building. Leidigh was ready to begin construction almost as soon as the money was provided. As early as 1938, he had been collecting plans and ideas for the building from officials of a number of agricultural colleges. For example, Dean Ernest T. Anthony of Michigan State strongly recommended that he use the University of Illinois Agricultural Building for a model. Plans for a 48,000 square-foot structure with the Tech traditional red tile roof were decided upon and bids were let on October 4. On Friday, October 31, 1941, at 2 p.m., Dean Leidigh, President Clifford Jones, and officers of the Agricultural Club conducted the groundbreaking ceremonies while faculty and board members, along with local and state dignitaries, looked on.[233]

230. Bulletin board announcement in red pencil, March 2, 1939, broadside telling students to write their state legislators [*ca.* 1939], and map in folder labeled "Agricultural Building"; J. H. Baumgardner to members of Agricultural Club (mimeographed), August 19, 1938; Ray L. Chappelle, October 30, 1936, to Walter Jones, TTSAP, DF.

231. J. R. Bertrand, September 5, 1939, to members of the Agricultural Club, TTSAP, DF.

232. Plant Superintendent [Guy C. Blanton], February 24, 1941, to Grady Hazlewood and G. H. Little, TTSAP, DF.

233. A. H. Leidigh, "The Agricultural Division at Texas Tech," 8; Ernest T. Anthony, Lansing, Michigan, May 11, 1938, to A. H. Leidigh, and other letters in the "Agricultural Building" folder; Staff memorandum by A. H. Leidigh, October 31, 1941, TTSAP, DF.

The building was to be completed in time for occupancy during the early part of the fall semester, 1942. But the war intervened. The building was not finished until early 1943. And its first occupants were GI's instead of Aggies. Early in the war, the Board of Directors offered Tech's facilities to the war effort. Consequently, the 309th College Training Detachment of the Army Air Corps moved in right after its completion and occupied the structure for over a year. When the soldiers moved out, Leidigh inspected the facility and estimated that, "The dirt marks, uncleanness, and wear damage to the building while the Army was in it sixteen months was about equal to sixteen years damage to somewhat similar equipment in the old Agricultural Building." After some reconditioning and replacing missing furniture, the Division of Agriculture moved in during the fall of 1944.[234]

Courses in "farm shop" conducted by the Department of Plant Industry in cooperation with the Department of Agricultural Education became very popular during the war for three reasons: (1) the rapidly growing power-mechanization of agriculture, (2) the farm implement shortage created by the industrial demands for the production of war goods, and (3) the farm worker labor shortage apparent during the war. Within a decade the majority of farmers in the region had progressed from horse-drawn machinery to farm tractors, combines, and detachable implements of every kind from cultivators to mechanical cotton harvesters. Moreover, the continued expansion of pump irrigation with its own complex technology of pump, gearhead, and engine made it even more necessary for farmers and their sons to advance their mechanical skills. Intercession of the war created shortages in steel products. As farmers entered a period of unprecedented prosperity during the war due to climbing commodity prices, they found it next to impossible to replace worn or broken machinery. The farmer was forced either to build his own repair shop or waste precious time taking his ailing equipment to the local machine shop.

Farmers turned to the local vocational agriculture teacher for assistance in developing skills such as arc welding and using an acetylene torch. Teachers, in turn, looked to the Division of Agriculture for help. Henry P. Clay, agricultural engineer of the Plant Industry Department, aided agricultural education in meeting the new demand. In the summers of 1942 and 1943, advanced shop courses were conducted, and more than forty teachers attended each year.

234. Andrews, *The First Thirty Years*, 59-63. A. H. Leidigh, December 17, 1942, to Clifford B. Jones; A. H. Leidigh, July 17, 1944, to W. T. Gaston, TTSAP, DF.

Even after the war was over, the Division's expanded offerings in shop work remained popular as farmers maintained their shops to cut repair costs, modify implements, and even manufacture some of their equipment from scrap iron.[235]

President Jones directed Cecil Horne of the Journalism Department, in late 1942, to do an article on Tech's contribution to the war effort. Horne asked Dean Leidigh for "a statement of not over 100 words" on the subject. If the Agricultural Building had been completed, Leidigh could have cited the army's occupancy of that structure as one of the Division's primary contributions. The Dean replied that Agriculture's most important gesture was "the loss of a large number of fine students to the different branches of the armed services together with the loss of four of our regular staff members."[236]

Not only did Agriculture give manpower and building to the cause, but also it contributed in a number of other ways. Maximum food production was crucial to the war effort and the federal government encouraged farmers to produce more food and fiber. President Roosevelt proclaimed January 12, 1943, as Farm Mobilization Day. After stating that, "Food is no less a weapon than tanks, guns, and planes," the President asked that U.S. Department of Agriculture officials, farm organization officers, vocational teachers, representatives of state government, and all those connected with agriculture meet on that day to discuss methods for growing the largest harvests ever in 1943.[237] In response, the Division began supplying staff members for short courses sponsored by the Texas Division of Vocational Education of the State Department of Education and offered by local school vocational agriculture departments. In one such course, J. D. Strickland of Animal Husbandry compiled material for a course entitled "Increasing Milk Production." When the West Texas Chamber of Commerce inaugurated a series of broadcasts over local radio stations encouraging farmers to plant more cotton, Leidigh and Clifford Jones delivered two of the addresses. Jones spoke on "New Uses of Cotton", and the Dean addressed listeners on the subject "Can We Raise Peanuts and Soybeans?" advising farm-

235. Nall, "Agricultural History of the Texas Panhandle" Ph.D. dissertation, University of Oklahoma, 1973, pp. 199-203. Green, *Land of the Underground Rain*, 148-153, 125-130. Annual Reports of the Division of Agriculture, 1942 and 1943, TTSAP, DF.

236. Cecil Horne, December 9, 1942, to A. H. Leidigh; Report of A. H. Leidigh to Cecil Horn, [December 1942], TTSAP, DF.

237. Mimeographed copy of President Roosevelt's proclamation, December 16, 1942, in TTSAP, DF.

ers to produce some peanuts and soybeans for the war, but to stay basically with cotton.[238]

Another contribution was in the attempt to produce ersatz or substitutes. In the early part of the war, the Japanese cut off the flow of rubber to the United States and this set off a nationwide search for some other type of latex. The Cabot Company wrote to Leidigh asking for samples of rabbitbrush (*Chrysothamnus nauseosus*) plant, located on the western edges of the High Plains, for experimental purposes. The West Texas Chamber of Commerce became interested in possibilities for producing rubber from small grains. But the single effort by Tech was an experiment carried on for the government by Arthur W. Young, head of Plant Industry, in growing guayule, a shrubby plant indigenous to northern Mexico, southwest Texas and southern New Mexico. The plant, long known to produce a gum from which rubber could be made, was said to have been used by the Aztecs in making balls for their games. The Agricultural Act of 1942 gave the Secretary of Agriculture the authority to fund research for rubber substitutes. About 36,000 acres of guayule were subsequently planted in the southwest, including three or four acres on the Tech farm. But the plants required several years to mature, and by then chemists had developed a chemical synthetic rubber.[239]

In addition to Young's work with guayule, the Plant Industry Department aided the war effort in other ways. W. W. Yocum spoke to various groups on the subject of growing "victory gardens." And several members taught courses in "preflight physics" to the air corps students occupying the Agriculture Building.[240]

Of immediate benefit to the military was the work of the Department of Dairy Manufactures. The military conscription law enacted by Congress in 1940 created not only an army within a matter of months but also an increased demand for milk products for the new soldiers. By the spring of 1941, Kenneth M. Renner reported that "the call for men capable of operating Market Milk Plants having Army contracts has completely exhausted the supply of graduates from this Department." Renner even had to give James Huffman, the

238. Mimeographed outline of course for Rural War Production Training Program entitled "Increasing Milk Production," by J. D. Strickland [1943]; Notes of A. H. Leidigh for radio speech, March 6, 1943, on topic, "Can We Raise Peanuts and Soy Beans?"; D. A. Bandeen, Abilene, Texas, February 19, 1943, TTSAP, DF.

239. R. G. Allen, Pampa, May 7, 1942, to Director of School of Agriculture, Texas Tech; A. H. Leidigh, May 11, 1942, to R. G. Allen; Max Bentley, Abilene, Texas, June 19, 1942, to Clifford B. Jones, TTSAP, DF. Personal interview with Arthur W. Young, May 27, 1975, by author, Lubbock, Southwest Collection. *Encyclopedia Americana*, 1958 edition, *s.v.* "Guayule."

240. Annual Reports of Division of Agriculture, 1943 and 1944, TTSAP, DF.

creamery superintendent, a four-month leave of absence to manage the Banner Creamery at Brownwood which was supplying the Texas national guard training camp with milk.[241]

The war strained the resources of the Department. Renner moved into a temporary Dairy Manufactures Building made of wood and stucco in 1939, but it was not until December, 1943 that Dairy Manufactures moved its equipment into the new Agricultural Creamery Annex. Renner and his associates, Mart Pederson and L. G. Harmon, worked as licensed graders for butter and cheese set aside by commercial creameries for military use. During the period June 1, 1943 to May 1, 1944, they graded forty carloads of cheese and eleven carloads of butter at points all over Texas and New Mexico. Renner reported that the three of them traveled 7200 miles from June 1 to October 31, 1943. In addition, compliance with many new government regulations associated with military purchases put an even greater demand upon Renner's time. By 1942, he had received technical assistance requests from more than two hundred dairy plants in 13 different states and 3 foreign nations. Over seventy-five calls alone were from Texas plants. He was able to assist only twenty. Most of the calls were for assistance in meeting the new demand for dry milk created almost overnight by government contracts. Noting the trend, Renner asked for money to purchase dry milk processing equipment to strengthen his program.[242]

The manpower shortage created by the war also placed great demands upon the Department of Agricultural Education. In a fifty-nine county area of West Texas, the number of schools offering vocational agriculture increased from forty-nine in 1936 to eight-three by 1941. Some 69 per cent of the vocational agriculture teachers in those schools were Tech graduates. The Department, composed of Ray L. Chappelle, its head; the "itinerant teacher trainer," T. L. Leach; and the state area supervisor, O. T. Ryan, found it impossible to supply enough graduates for openings. By 1943, the junior and senior male students in Agriculture at Tech had all but vanished from campus into the armed forces or back to the farms. Temporary vocational agriculture certificates were issued to teachers of other disciplines and the Department worked primarily in the area of in-service training for those.[243]

241. Annual Report of Division of Agriculture, 1941, TTSAP, DF.

242. Kenneth M. Renner, January 6, 1943, to A. H. Leidigh; Annual Reports of Division of Agriculture, 1940, 1942, 1943, and 1944, TTSAP, DF.

243. Annual Reports of Division of Agriculture, 1943 and 1944, TTSAP, DF.

The war also offered opportunities for other services. It was ironic that the bloody conflict set the stage for the beginnings of research at Texas Tech. Only a few months prior to the attack on Pearl Harbor in 1941, the Texas legislature appropriated the first significant research funds for Tech, $50,000 to be spread over a two-year period. President Jones pushed the cause of research before the legislature and was clearly pleased when the *San Antonio Express* carried an article in October, 1942, about Tech's involvement in the guayule experiment. The new injection of research funds would have accomplished little had it not been for the accompanying sharp drop in student enrollment while legislative appropriations remained comparatively high. Thus an opportunity arose to decrease the teaching load of those involved in research. Jones told his deans and department heads in a memorandum of May 27, 1943, that because of the small number of students "the time is auspicious to endeavor to inaugurate this [research] policy, recognizing therein a vehicle for great good to the institution and to the state." He suggested that interested faculty members should apply for released time through their department channels to a new Special Committee on Research.[244]

With this encouragement, a number of projects were conducted. Since 1938, Arthur Young had been conducting experiments in cooperation with the American Crystal Sugar Company and the Santa Fe Railway Company to determine the best variety of sugar beet for production under High Plains irrigation. By 1944, he had found a suitable variety. That summer the agronomist went to Rocky Ford, Colorado to study the new mechanization for thinning, topping, digging, and loading beets in order to share the information with potential growers in West Texas. Three years later beet culture began on the High Plains when American Crystal Sugar made contracts with area farmers to grow 1440 acres of the crop.[245]

The Department of Plant Industry also concluded its experiments with malt barley and the application of manure to dry-land farms in 1943. Because castor oil was much in demand during the war as a lubricant for precision tools, an experiment in growing castor beans was begun by Earl T. Duke in 1941. Henry P. Clay de-

244. "Texas Tech Shows Remarkable Growth in Varied Fields," *Sheep and Goat Raiser* (October 1941):7. Clifford B. Jones, November 3, 1942, to M. M. Harris; Clifford B. Jones, May 26, 1943, to Deans and Heads of Departments, TTSAP, DF.

245. *Texas Tech Magazine*, vol. 7, no. 8 (1943):4. Arthur W. Young, June 22, 1944, to A. H. Leidigh, TTSAP, DF. Nall, "Agricultural History of the Texas Panhandle," 218-219. For information on earlier experiments with sugar beets in the region, see Nall, 60-62; Garry L. Nall, "Panhandle Farming in the 'Golden Era' of American Agriculture," *Panhandle-Plains Historical Review*, 46 (1973):90-91; Green, *Land of the Underground Rain*, 132-133.

signed and built a threshing machine to harvest the beans. As a result of the experiments, a number of farmers in counties north of Lubbock began raising the crop under irrigation and an extraction plant was built at Plainview.[246]

Dairy Manufactures proposed nine research projects for the period 1941-1943. Two were started and completed by 1943: "The Effects of Acidity on the Mold Mycelia Content of Butter" and "The Use of Various Sweetening Agents in Ice Cream." Results of the former were published in the *Journal of Dairy Science* in 1943 and copies of the latter experiment were distributed to more than three hundred ice cream manufacturers.[247]

The Department of Animal Husbandry continued its cottonseed-products livestock feeding experiments. The Texas Cottonseed Crushers Association continued to support the program with an annual graduate student fellowship. J. H. Baumgardner, who would join the Department after the war, was awarded the fellowship in 1939-40. At the conclusion of that experiment, the Division held its first Livestock Feeder's Day in 1940. Some 250 people attended. The Block and Bridle Club, national honorary organization for animal husbandry majors, furnished much of the required manpower for the event. Pit barbeque cooked on campus was served the guests. Baumgardner climbed up on a wooden corral fence and spoke to the visitors surrounding the feeder pens of the experiment's results. Thereafter, Feeder's Day became an annual event. The next year the Texas Feed Manufacturers Association held its annual meeting in Lubbock and W. L. Stangel spoke on "Range and Group Feeding of Beef Cattle."[248]

The Department of Agricultural Economics, Farm Management and Rural Sociology failed to become actively involved in staff research. Composed of Elmer L. McBride (M.S., Oklahoma A&M), who took J. O. Ellsworth's place as head in 1937, and Marshall B. Harrison (M.S., Kansas State), who had come to Tech in 1935, the earlier dynamic thrust of Ellsworth's work in county surveys in the thirties was no longer apparent. McBride stated in his part of the annual reports to the president: "Because of absolutely no funds and also because of heavy teaching duties very little research is at-

246. *Texas Tech Magazine*, vol. 5, no. 3 (1941):4; vol. 7, no. 9 (1943):4. Interview with Arthur W. Young by author. Annual Report of Division of Agriculture, 1942, TTSAP, DF.

247. Annual Report of Division of Agriculture, 1942 and 1943; Proposed Research Projects, Dairy Manufactures Department, 1941-43 legislative biennium, attached to Kenneth M. Renner, September 10, 1941, to Clifford B. Jones, TTSAP, DF.

248. Annual Reports of Division of Agriculture, 1940, TTSAP, DF. W. W. Bridges, Fort Worth, March 31, 1941, to W. L. Stangel, TTSAP, WLS.

tempted." This is not to say that the department rendered no service. McBride gave freely of his time to area farmers who called on him. For example, he worked with Scurry County farmers to establish a poultry marketing cooperative. And he maintained on the departmental bulletin board a record of daily price fluctuations of commodities marketed on the South Plains. Moreover, M.S. theses done by graduate students in the Department made some fine contributions to the knowledge of agriculture in the region. For example, John R. Bertrand did a study of more than three thousand former vocational agriculture students from twenty-eight high schools on the South Plains and found that the sons of farmers who owned their own land were more likely to become farmers than the children of tenant farmers and that "the odds are 8 to 1 against vocational agricultural sons of skilled workers entering farming."[249]

The first opportunities to acquire additional research facilities appeared during the war and postwar period. In late 1943, J. H. Burkett of Clyde, Texas, offered to give his 6½-acre pecan tree experiment farm and library to Tech. Burkett, who had developed the famous Burkett and several other varieties of pecans, was eighty years old at the time, working on a type of pecan suitable for a semi-arid climate, and wanted his experiments to continue. The elderly, largely self-trained horticulturist had enjoyed a distinguished career. In 1916 he had been appointed Chief of the Division of Edible Nuts of the Texas Department of Agriculture. He served in that capacity for about fifteen years before retiring to continue his cross-breeding experiments. Through Max Bentley of the West Texas Chamber of Commerce, Burkett approached Leidigh in November, 1943. As conditions of the proposed gift, Burkett wanted his farm to remain intact for research purposes. In a letter to Dean Leidigh signed by "the pecan crank," Burkett wrote: "The Pecan is destined to become the most valuable horticultural species in Texas or the entire United States."[250]

Leidigh sent Arthur Young to look into the proposition. Young visited with Burkett at his home on January 23, 1944, and reported to the Dean that some expenditures would be necessary for repairs and improvements to machinery and buildings. It would also be

249. Annual Reports of Division of Agriculture, 1941 and 1942; Ray E. Dickson, Secretary of Scurry County Chamber of Commerce, Snyder, Texas, April 5, 1940, TTSAP, DF.

250. J. H. Burkett, Clyde, Texas, November 28, 1943, to A. H. Leidigh; Max Bentley, Abilene, Texas, November 24, 1943, to A. H. Leidigh; Arthur W. Young, January 24, 1944, to A. H. Leidigh, TTSAP, DF. H. L. Crane, C. A. Reed, and M. N. Wood, "Nut Breeding," *United States Department of Agriculture Yearbook, 1937* (Washington, D.C.: Government Printing Office, 1937), 847.

necessary to employ a caretaker to live on the property. To defray part of the expenses, the hundred or so mature trees were yielding about 1500 pounds of pecans annually. Valuation of the property was placed at $5,000. Unfortunately, there was no legal way to spend state money on the property. The Board of Directors reluctantly declined the offer.[251]

On at least one and possibly other occasions, the Board of Directors declined offers of land for the same reason. The creation of the Texas Tech Foundation by Clifford B. Jones, Spencer Wells, and W. T. Gaston through the Board of Directors on May 29, 1939, had provided the framework through which non-state money donated to the institution could be funneled into maintaining such gifts, but the Foundation did not begin functioning until November, 1945, more than a year after the Burkett offer.[252]

The Foundation was in operation when an even more significant proposal surfaced after the War. The federal government loaned the 16,076-acre site of its Pantex Ordnance Plant north of Amarillo to Tech in cooperation with the Texas Agricultural Experiment Station and the United States Department of Agriculture in 1947. The government deeded the land to Tech in 1949 with a "recapture clause." During the Korean War, the government exercised that option and took back more than 10,000 acres. Thus the 5,822-acre PanTech Farm was established. Its first research project was a study of wheat pasture poisoning in cattle.[253]

Like the war period, the postwar years were full of change. Clifford Jones resigned as president in 1944. He was succeeded by William M. Whyburn, a forty-two year old academician with a Ph.D. in mathematics who had been a member of Tech's first faculty. At the time of his appointment he was serving as chairman of the Mathematics Department at UCLA. Enrollment at Tech rocketed upward as ex-servicemen funded by their GI Bill of Rights flocked to the campus. The number of students from 1943 to 1947 went from 1,928 to 6,698, one-half of whom were veterans. Arthur H. Leidigh retired from the Deanship in 1945 at the age of 65 to return to the classroom as a member of the Plant Industry Department. W. L. Stangel was elevated to Dean, and Ray Mowrey became head of

251. Arthur W. Young, January 24, 1944, to A. H. Leidigh; Clifford B. Jones, May 20, 1944, to A. H. Leidigh, TTSAP, DF. Personal interview with Arthur W. Young by author.

252. Andrews, *The First Thirty Years*, 55. Personal interview with Arthur W. Young by author. Rushing and Nall, *Evolution of a University*, 89.

253. W. L. Stangel, August 21, 1947, to J. R. Emmons, TTSAP, DF. *Twenty Years of Progress in Agricultural Research, Education, and Public Service*, ICASALS Special Report no. 27 (Texas Tech, 1969), 5. *Texas Techsan*, vol. 10, no. 8 (1961):14.

Animal Husbandry. The auditorium of the new Agriculture Building, the largest meeting room on campus at the time, was named Aggie Memorial Auditorium in honor of those graduates killed in the war.[254]

During World War II there had been few festive events on campus. An indication of a more carefree mood was the inauguration of the first All-Western Days on April 12-13, 1946. A sunrise chuckwagon breakfast, a street dance and a parade kicked off the festivities. "Western" dress for all was required. A "sheriff" and his "posse" were appointed to dunk offenders in a water trough. Climax of the celebration was the rodeo sponsored by the Block and Bridle Club.

Origins of the annual Aggie Rodeo went back to May 3, 1929, when students of the old School of Agriculture held the First (and last) Annual Aggie Fair in the Livestock Judging Pavilion. Events included bucking horse and calf roping contests among students, a carnival and a vaudeville show featuring Aggie talent. Highlight of the Fair was probably the polo game between Aggies and Liberal Arts students.

Next year, the first Aggie Rodeo was held October 9-10 in a makeshift arena built south of the Dairy Barn. Virginia Wester, a New Mexico coed, was crowned queen and a downtown parade led off the activities. Contests included steer riding, "bronc" riding, "musical chairs on horses," women's riding, and "mounted wrestling." Lubbock merchants, including Hemphill-Wells, Carter-Houston, Sherrod Brothers, and Caprock Embroidery Company contributed such prizes as a Stetson hat, sweater, lariat rope, and gloves. "Doc" Harbaugh and W. L. Stangel gave a loving cup.

The Rodeo of 1932 added wild cow milking, relay riding, and a beef and mutton barbeque to its program. A "special cigar race" for faculty members was a highlight of the 1933 Rodeo, sponsored for the first time by the Block and Bridle Club organized that year.

La Remuda succeeded the Annual Rodeo in 1935. The first Remuda held at Matador Field, the football stadium, featured a play, "Ag School Farce," a mock combat of "knights" on donkeys, a polo game on donkeys, a pillow fight, and exhibits of Tech livestock and Lubbock saddle horses. The Remuda, however, was not as popular as the old Rodeo, and in 1940, the Aggie Rodeo was reintroduced but not held again until 1946 when All-Western Days began.

254. Andrews, *The First Thirty Years*, 103, 65-68. W. M. Whyburn, "Preliminary Report to the Board of Directors, Texas Technological College," April 24, 1948, in W. L. Stangel Papers.

The primary objective of the Rodeo, Remuda, and All-Western Days, as well as the annual Pig Roast, was to raise funds for the senior livestock judging team's expenses to the International and the American Royal. Although intended only as a fund-raising activity, a byproduct was the establishment in 1947 of the Texas Tech Rodeo Association which joined the Western Intercollegiate Rodeo Association. That same year, the Tech team won first prize in the national Intercollegiate Association Rodeo.[255]

High Plains farmers continued to prosper after the war. The devastated condition of Europe coupled with the massive new American foreign aid program called The Marshall Plan expanded markets for agricultural products pushing both prices for commodities and land upward. Irrigated land by 1947 was selling for $100 to $150 per acre, and dryland farms were bringing $40 to $100 per acre. Lubbock County in 1947 produced more cotton than any other county in the state—180,935 bales. In fact, the sixteen-county area of which Lubbock was the "hub" produced 24 per cent of the cotton in Texas and led the state in regional farm income.[256]

The growth in farm prosperity was reflected in the Division of Agriculture. By 1949, there were 825 agricultural majors. One hundred sixty-three graduates of the Division received their degrees in June. The staff consisted of thirty members, not including four who were on leaves of absence. A number of Tech graduates such as J. H. Baumgardner in Animal Husbandry and T. L. Leach in Agricultural Education, had been added to the faculty, while Casey Fine and George Elle returned after the war.

New buildings consisted of a $65,000 Beef Cattle Barn, the Agricultural Engineering Building, an addition to the Meats Laboratory, and some more farm buildings. Dairy Manufactures had a new three-quarter-ton panel truck and Animal Husbandry sported an equally new "7-passenger Dodge" for its judging teams. The farm had six irrigation wells and the Plant Industry Department was cultivating an additional 160 acres resulting from a brush eradication program. The Aggie Club and attendance at the traditional annual Pig Roast was larger than ever. The Block and Bridle Club and the Rodeo Association cooperatively sponsored the All College

255. Andrews, *The First Thirty Years*, 124-127. Information on early rodeo in loose-leaf notebook entitled "History" [*ca.* 1933 and 1934], in W. L. Stangel Papers.

256. *Dallas Morning News*, January 13, 1946, section 1, p. 4. George Bond, Jr., Director of Agricultural Activities of Lubbock Chamber of Commerce, Lubbock, November 30, 1948, to Conference Members of Beltwide Cotton Mechanization Conference; W. L. Stangel, February 3, 1947, to Claude F. Cannon, Jr., TTSAP, DF.

Rodeo in 1949 for the first time on Tech's new football field—in the Clifford B. Jones and Audrey Jones Stadium.[257]

The Division suffered a tragic loss when forty-seven year-old Kenneth M. Renner, who had built the Department of Dairy Manufactures, died suddenly on September 2, 1947. J. J. Willingham replaced Renner in 1948, and became head of the Department in 1949. He had a B.S. degree from Texas A&M (1931) and the M.S. and Ph.D. (1941) from Iowa State. From 1931 to 1935, Willingham had worked for commercial dairy plants in Texas. He was on the faculty of Iowa State from 1935 to 1943, and during 1944-1948, served as associate technical director for the Mrs. Tucker's Foods Company of Sherman, Texas.[258]

One indication of the success of the Division of Agriculture was the career accomplishments of its graduates. In addition to the Tech graduates who constituted a majority of the area vocational agriculture teachers, as mentioned earlier, and the growing number of Tech county agents in West Texas, about 10 per cent of the graduates went into farming or ranching. That minority, such as Raleigh Middleton (D.M., '29), formerly the college farm superintendent; Elton Mims (A.H., '28); J. E. Couch (Agron., '30); Harold Osborne (A.H., '35); and Dean Harmon (A.H., '38) undoubtedly exerted some influence upon neighbors' agricultural practices and served as community leaders.

Still others occupied positions in higher education, the U.S. Department of Agriculture and agri-business concerns. Among these were: Ogden King (Ag. Econ., '29), who received his Ph.D. from Cornell in 1937, taught at the University of Nanking, and was working in the Bureau of Agricultural Economics by 1941; R. C. Tom (A.H., '29), head of the Department of Animal Husbandry at Colorado State; J. Bryan Stine (D.M., '33), chief chemist for the Kraft Cheese Company; Curtis B. Williams (D.M., '33), chief milk sanitarian for the New Mexico Department of Public Health; Morris Hill (D.M., '38) and Clayborn Harrell (D.M., '39), plant superintendents for the Borden Company in Oklahoma City and San Antonio; Leon Havis (Hort., '31), who took his Ph.D. from Ohio State and obtained a position with the U.S. Plant Industry Experiment Station at Beltsville, Maryland; John Havis, a brother, (Hort., '42) took the Ph.D. from Cornell and later became superintendent of the Waltham Field Experiment Station in Massachusetts; and W. D. Holley (Hort., '38), professor at Colorado State. Holley, along with Charles Weddle

257. W. L. Stangel, [spring 1949], to Division of Agriculture Alumni, TTSAP, DF.
258. Andrews, *The First Thirty Years*, 117. *Texas Techsan*, vol. 13, no. 7 (1962):12.

(Hort., '36) and Claude Hope (Hort., '29), organized Pan American Seeds, Incorporated, in 1948, which specialized in growing and marketing hybrid flower seeds.

Among other influential graduates were John H. Burroughs, Governor of New Mexico; John C. White, Texas Commissioner of Agriculture; L. N. Hazel, professor of Animal Husbandry at Iowa State; Rex Johnston, Regional Director of Soil Conservation Research for the USDA; John R. Bertrand, Dean of Agriculture at the University of Nevada; Casey Fine and J. H. Baumgardner, members of Tech's own Animal Husbandry Department; Cecil I. Ayers of Tech's Plant Industry Department; and both Ray Chappelle and T. L. Leach of the Agricultural Education Department of Tech.[259]

The theme of the U.S. Department of Agriculture Yearbook for 1940 was "Farmers in a Changing World." Change was also the dominant trait of the Division of Agriculture during the decade of the forties. The Division entered the decade inadequate in quarters and equipment, although much progress had been made since 1925. During this period, Agriculture moved into its new permanent building and received its first stimulus toward becoming a research institution. Its graduates were involved in pursuits from farming to agricultural research. And although enrollment was off during the war, in the postwar years it turned up sharply with the large influx of veterans on campus.

259. Annual Report of Division of Agriculture, 1944; list of graduates of Department of Dairy Manufactures, Texas Tech, November 1, 1941, TTSAP, DF. Andrews, *The First Thirty Years*, 108-122.

EXPANDED PROGRAMS AND THE MOVEMENT TOWARD A RESEARCH-ORIENTED INSTITUTION

Texas Tech celebrated its Silver Anniversary in 1950 only a few months after the Korean War broke out. Optimistic of its future, a host of speakers including the noted Western American historian Carl Coke Rister and the junior U.S. Senator from Texas Lyndon B. Johnson launched the institution on its next twenty-five years. Another drouth began to expand in the region the same year and lasted until 1957. Although of longer duration than the Dust Bowl era, less soil erosion and hardship resulted because of improved soil conservation practices fostered by the Soil Conservation Service and various federal drouth relief programs. Moreover, the dry weather stimulated pump irrigation development. Between 1950 and 1954, irrigated acreage ascended from 1.86 million to 3.5 million, making the Texas High Plains one of the most extensively irrigated and prosperous agricultural regions in the world.[260] A group of eastern Arkansas farmers from the rich Mississippi delta toured the region in the spring of 1955 to view the dynamic, complex agricultural economy with its churning irrigation pumps, large farms, four-plow tractors, supportive local manufacturers, and Texas Tech. Upon returning home, a spokesman exclaimed, "I've never seen anything like it."[261]

The expansion of Texas Tech proceeded in step with the agricultural economic development of the High Plains. The Korean War hindered enrollment at first, but the number of students climbed from 6,511 in 1949 to more than 10,000 by 1957. As the anniversary celebration got underway in the fall of 1950, Dean Stangel, Arthur W. Young, and President Dossie Wiggins, who succeeded Whyburn in 1948, broke ground for the new Agricultural Engineering Building. In 1951, the Ag Engineering Building, the Ag Engineering Annex, a new battery of greenhouses, the Veterinary Science Building, and the Beef Cattle Pavilion were all completed. The College

260. Ruth Horn Andrews, *The First Thirty Years*, 80-82. Green, *Land of the Underground Rain*, 148.

261. H. W. Newell, "Farming in the Great Plains As Seen By Arkansas Farmers," mimeographed (Earle, Arkansas: Peoples Mercantile and Implement Company, June 1955), W. L. Stangel Papers.

herds were enlarged by the addition of Milking Shorthorns in the late forties, Brahmans in 1951, and Beefmasters in 1954.[262]

Agriculture at Tech went through a period of rapid reorganization and change during the fifties. The divisional structure created by Bradford Knapp in the early thirties was scrapped, and the old divisions were changed back to schools in 1956. The Division of Agriculture became the School of Agriculture once again. The Department of Dairy Manufactures was changed to Dairy Industry in 1955. The Department of Plant Industry was split into three separate departments in 1951—Agronomy, Agricultural Engineering, and Horticulture and Park Management.[263]

Ira L. Williams (M.S., University of Iowa) was hired to head the new Department of Ag Engineering in 1952. To meet the growing demand of students for more specialized approaches to agricultural technology, Williams, in cooperation with Tech's Division of Engineering, organized the course offerings into four branches—land improvement (including irrigation), rural electrification, farm power and machinery, and farm structures (including crop drying and processing).[264]

The National Cotton Council, aware of the responsibility of ginners for processing quality cotton, urged in early 1956 that Clemson in South Carolina and Texas Tech develop cotton gin engineering curricula. Dean Stangel and Dean J. R. Bradford of Tech's School of Engineering appointed a committee composed of Ira Williams, Ray Flege of Textile Engineering, and Arthur Young as chairman to draw up the program. The committee visited gin research centers at Chickasha, Oklahoma, and Mesilla Park, New Mexico, before putting together the program which was approved by the Tech Board of Directors on June 3, 1957.[265]

One of the more innovative programs at Tech in the fifties was undoubtedly the new Department of Horticulture and Park Management headed by a native Texan named Elo Joe Urbanovsky. The new program was related to the campus beautification work started in 1949 by Urbanovsky. Campus landscaping had been practically nonexistent at Tech in the earlier years. As mentioned in a previous

262. Andrews, *The First Thirty Years*, 81, 107. *Texas Techsan*, vol. 5, no. 4 (1954):2; vol. 1, no. 6 (1950):7. Ira L. Williams, March 28, 1958, to President E. N. Jones, W. L. Stangel Papers.

263. Andrews, *The First Thirty Years*, 107, 119.

264. *Texas Techsan*, vol. 5, no. 3 (1954):3. Personal interview with Arthur W. Young, March 6, 1973, by Beth Schneider, Lubbock, Southwest Collection. Andrews, *The First Thirty Years*, p. 115.

265. Ira L. Williams, "Training Future Cotton Gin Engineers," clipping, and memorandum on "Cotton Gin Engineering" by Williams, [*ca.* 1957], W. L. Stangel Papers.

chapter, Bradford Knapp and O. B. Howell had started the annual Arbor Day tree plantings in 1938, but the budget for grounds maintenance was inadequate and no overall plan had been developed. Horticulturist W. W. Yocum resigned his position on the Campus Beautification Committee in 1946 when the administration allowed an unsightly water tower to be constructed near the Broadway Street entrance to the campus. Arthur Young had approached President Clifford Jones and President W. M. Whyburn about providing funds for the horticultural staff to landscape the campus, but both had denied the request. When Dossie Wiggins became president in 1948, Young made the same proposition. Wiggins responded: "Can you find a man to do it?" Delighted with the new President's attitude, Young replied that he and Dean Stangel believed they could hire the right person.[266]

Young and Stangel agreed to find a man who would not only landscape the campus, but head up a future separate horticulture department. In November, 1948, Stangel asked Fritz Hensel of the Department of Landscape Art at Texas A&M to suggest someone for the job. Without hesitation Hensel wrote, "The man for you is E. J. Urbanovsky." Urbanovsky had a B.S. from Texas A&M in architecture and landscape design (1929) and had done graduate work at Massachusetts State, Amherst. His experience was even more important than his academic background. He had worked with Hensel on the A&M campus, and also as landscape architect with the New Deal's Resettlement Administration for northwest Texas and Oklahoma. In connection with the latter position, Hensel noted that "he made an outstanding record with the Administration, and his plans were generally adopted all over the United States." Urbanovsky also worked with the U.S. Park Service, taught awhile at A&M after World War II, and then joined the Veterans Administration as landscape architect for that agency's facilities in Texas, Louisiana, and Mississippi. Hensel characterized him as "energetic, enthusiastic, full of initiative . . . and . . . extremely talented. . . . With your cooperation he will make your campus what you want it to be."[267]

Dean Stangel made Urbanovsky an offer and asked him to prepare a landscaping budget for the campus. The landscapist responded favorably, a budget was agreed upon and plans were laid to establish a "department of landscape art" in the future. Urbanovsky

266. Personal interview with Arthur W. Young, May 27, 1975, by author, Lubbock, Southwest Collection.

267. *Ibid.* F. W. Hensel, College Station, November 29, 1948, to W. L. Stangel, TTSAP, DF.

arrived in the spring of 1949 to teach half-time in the old Department of Plant Industry and to begin the campus beautification program. Under his leadership a master plan for campus expansion emerged which emphasized areas of landscaped spaciousness immune from building construction projects. The resulting appearance of the Tech campus sprang from Urbanovsky's belief that the physical campus environment is important in developing "attitudes and character of the individual and in the development of future behavior systems in our society."[268]

When the new Department of Horticulture and Park Management was organized Urbanovsky lost little time in establishing one of the top park management training programs in the nation. In February, 1956, he initiated the first annual Southwest Park & Recreation Training Institute at Lake Murray Lodge in southern Oklahoma. Sponsored by the American Institute of Park Executives and the Oklahoma Planning and Resources Board, as well as the Institute, the week long event drew about 250 participants from nine states and more than fifty speakers. Workshop topics varied from "State Park Planning" to "Flowers for Color in the Municipal Park."[269]

Expansion is usually not incurred without cost. As the Tech campus and the city of Lubbock spread out in the 1950's, both began to nibble away at the college farm. During most years, the farm had made some money for the School of Agriculture from livestock and crop sales. Between 1952 and 1957, Agronomy alone grossed over $48,000 growing certified wheat, cotton, barley, and grain sorghum seed. In 1958-59, Agronomy and Animal Husbandry brought in over $90,000, not enough to meet the operating expenses of both departments but sufficient to help defray the high cost of maintaining the farm. Even more important were the teaching functions of the farm conveniently located next to the campus. The first significant blow to the integrity of the farm occurred in the mid-fifties when a freeway cut diagonally across the farm to connect northern Lubbock to the Brownfield highway. Stangel opposed the move, but the city and Tech joined hands to build the road. During construction, the problem of moving cattle across the highway came up for discussion.

268. Texas Tech Public Information Office News Release, April 30, 1969. E. J. Urbanovsky, Dallas, Texas, February 4, 1949, and March 5, 1949, to W. L. Stangel; W. L. Stangel, March 17, 1949, to President D. M. Wiggins; W. L. Stangel, March 26, 1949, to E. J. Urbanovsky, TTSAP, DF.

269. *Lubbock Avalanche-Journal*, February 2, 1956 and *Fort Worth Star-Telegram*, April 1, 1956, clippings file; Program of Second Annual Southwest Park and Recreation Training Institute, February 4-8, 1957, Urbanovsky folder, TTSAP, DF.

Dean Stangel suggested building an overpass for the cattle. That idea was quashed as being too costly. Instead, the highway engineers built a narrow underpass which frightened rather than attracted cattle.[270]

When the possibility of building a new Tech football stadium on farm land arose in the summer of 1956, Stangel strongly opposed the move. In a letter to President E. N. Jones, he recounted his stand on the highway issue:

> As you know, I was not in favor of the freeway, but I gave in. I opposed to the last the underpass which we now use but which definitely has handicapped our operations. I contended for an overpass for the college and an underpass for the traffic on the highway. They said that it would not be safe. All of the arteries now leading into and out of Lubbock are [now] underpassed. . . . Of course, it cost less to underpass the college than it would have to underpass the highway.[271]

Stangel was not opposed to "expansions which are just and fair," such as the proposed new dormitories, and he probably did not oppose the construction of the National Guard Armory, the Army Reserve facility, or the Municipal Coliseum-Auditorium on the northeastern edge of the farm. But he did oppose highways and roads across the farm such as the extension of Indiana Avenue from Nineteenth Street to Fourth Street which the city already had "her sights on" in 1956 in order to save automobile drivers a little time.[272]

Judging events continued to play a large part in the Animal Husbandry program. Since the late 1920's the annual "Pig Roast" had been held just prior to the senior livestock judging team's exodus for the International in Chicago. This remained a tradition. Teams at various shows in the Southwest and at the national expositions judged dairy cattle, dairy products, hogs, quarter horses, meats, crops, and, of course, the popular breeds of beef cattle.

Times had changed since the thirties when M. E. Heard of Textile Engineering had complained that there were no contests for judging cotton. The Agronomy Department's crops judging teams brought back their full share of the honors. Coached by Cecil Ayers, who had taken his B.S. in agronomy from Tech in 1936 and returned to teach in 1942, the teams placed either first or second in both the International and the American Royal from 1947 to 1953, scoring high on seed judging, crop grading, and identification. The team

270. *Texas Techsan*, vol. 10, no. 8 (1959):6-7. Arthur W. Young, March 18, 1958, to E. N. Jones, W. L. Stangel Papers. Personal interview with W. L. Stangel, March 7, 1973, by David Murrah, Southwest Collection.

271. W. L. Stangel, July 17, 1956, to E. N. Jones, W. L. Stangel Papers.

272. *Ibid.*

won the International again in 1956. And by 1959, Ayers' teams had won the International five times and the American Royal six times, to give the Agronomy Department the most first places in national competition of any of Tech's agricultural teams.

The year 1953 was the most memorable of all for Tech's teams. The crops judging team, composed of Rollie Taylor, Max Von Roeder, Duane Mounts, and Clarence Mertins, repeated the Tech team's performance of 1952 by winning both the International and American Royal. The day after the crops team won top honors at the International, the livestock judging team won first place at the same event under the coaching of Stanley E. Anderson (M.S., Texas Tech, 1951), a native of Iowa who had come to Tech as graduate student and instructor in 1948. At the Southwestern Exposition in Fort Worth, other Tech teams won first place in judging Jersey cattle for three consecutive years, and continued to score high in dairy cattle, hog, and quarter horse judging contests.[273]

The Animal Husbandry Department faculty also remained active in judging contests. Dean Stangel who had served as Livestock Director of the Texas Centennial Exposition in 1935-36, held a similar position with the Texas State Fair from 1946 until the middle fifties. And Ray Mowery acted as master of ceremonies at the awards ceremonies of the Chicago International in December 1954, delighting the audience with "tall" West Texas tales such as the one about the early pioneer who drove his team of oxen across the plains during a hot day. One dropped dead of a heat stroke, and while the fellow was skinning the animal, a "norther" blew up and froze the other to death. Mowery, whose spontaneous demonstrations of animal behavior delighted his students, remained one of the more popular teachers in the School of Agriculture. He resigned as head of the department in 1954, taught for six more years, and retired in 1960.[274]

Since its beginnings, the School of Agriculture had worked closely with its farmer-constituency as noted in previous chapters. Its role was expanded in the fifties as West Texas agriculture became more highly mechanized, more intensively capitalized and more reliant

273. *Texas Techsan*, vol. 4, no. 8 (1953):7; vol. 4, no. 1 (1953):18. *Austin Statesman-American*, November 26, 1956 and *Fort Worth Star-Telegram*, November 22, 1956, clipping file, TTSAP, WLS. *What's Happening in Lubbock*, 2 (January 1960):18-19; *Texas Tech Block and Bridle Club Yearbook* (1962), 1, Dean's Files, Texas Tech University College of Agricultural Science, hereafter cited as DF, TTCAS.

274. "Farm News," *Lubbock Avalanche-Journal*, August 30, 1953, p. 2; Cotton John Smith, "Folks from Texas Talk a Tall Legend on Visit to Chicago," *Amarillo Daily News*, December 2, 1954, clipping file, W. L. Stangel Papers. Author's conversation with J. H. Baumgardner, July 22, 1975.

upon chemicals for crop production. Few did more than Arthur W. Young for the development of the grain sorghum industry, the most extensively irrigated crop on the Texas High Plains. Beginning in 1948, he served for a number of years as chairman of the statutory Texas State Seed and Plant Board. He was state representative of Texas to the board of directors of the International Crop Improvement Association (ICIA) from 1948 through the middle 1950's. In addition, he served as chairman of the ICIA's Committee on Pathological Standards and the Millet Committee, and was elected President of that organization in 1959. Under his leadership, the Agronomy Department continued to sponsor an annual Certified Seed Growers meeting, various high school and 4H crop judging contests on campus, and to send speakers to farmers' meetings when requested. Speaking engagements, if not paid for by the local organization, were often done at the faculty member's own expense because Tech had no budget for agricultural extension work. When Young on one occasion traveled 180 miles to speak at a meeting of 125 farmers, he had to take his own car because his leave request was kicked back due to an error made in someone's initials on the form. Piqued at the bureaucratic red tape, Young remarked to Stangel: "It is discouraging to rush around and arrange to be away to make such talks as a representative of the College and have items such as this one cause difficulty. Would it be better to turn down all such requests?"[275]

Dean Stangel understood the need to disguise extension work under some other name. He observed, "The administration takes the position that such an activity does not have any educational value to the college and therefore is not of direct benefit." The solution? Staff members had to justify such trips with the rationale that the experience would provide them with information which could be used in their classes.[276]

Short courses became commonplace on the campus. The American Cotton Congress held its annual meeting at Lubbock on June 25-27, 1953, and the controversial Secretary of Agriculture, Ezra Taft Benson, delivered the main address at Clifford B. Jones Stadium. A southwestern Cotton Gin Operators' School was held March 21-22, 1957, sponsored by the Texas Agricultural Extension Service, the Texas Ginners' Association, and the Cotton Gin Machinery Manufacturers. Annual Grain Drying and Storage Con-

275. Arthur W. Young, April 27, 1955, to W. L. Stangel, W. L. Stangel Papers. Arthur W. Young, vita; Gerald W. Thomas, May 8, 1961, to R. C. Goodwin, DF, TTCAS.

276. W. L. Stangel, April 27, 1955, to Arthur W. Young, W. L. Stangel Papers.

ferences were begun in 1954. The Department of Agricultural Engineering played a major role in conducting those programs, and Welding Short Courses continued to be held in cooperation with the Agricultural Education Department.[277]

In addition, events such as the First Agricultural Chemical Conference held January 13-14, 1954, and the First Annual Southwest Soil Management Demonstration and Plowing Contest conducted at the PanTech Farm on October 1, 1952, demonstrated the variety of new short courses and programs for farmers and agribusinessmen.[278]

Emergence of a new irrigated vegetable industry on the High Plains offered more opportunities for expanded services. As early as 1932, a farmer in Hale County named M. B. Jewell planted and harvested twenty acres of irrigated potatoes. In Lubbock County, J. B. McCauley planted six acres of the root crop in 1936. But it was not until a group of twenty-five farmers from Idaho arrived in the Hereford area in the late thirties that vegetable production got a sustained boost. "Tater Joe" Ballinger became well known for his potato crops, and in 1939, the group formed a marketing cooperative called Hereford Potato Growers, Inc. By the fifties, crops of onion, carrots, lettuce, cantaloupes, cucumbers and other vegetables were being grown on the Plains north of Lubbock. These vegetable crops combined with the emerging sugar beet culture made Hereford the center of the new industry.[279]

Arthur Young and horticulturist George O. Elle visited a number of farmers in the area in the spring of 1953 and found that they were in need of both research and advice on plant varieties, weed control, and "cultural practices," as well as insect and disease control measures. The Texas Agricultural Experiment Station (TAES) had proposed the establishment of a substation at Hereford, but the research proposed by the TAES over a ten to fifteen year period was too long range for the farmers. They had immediate problems and they looked to Tech for immediate solutions.

The West Texas Vegetable Growers Council was formed at Plainview in February, 1956, and on April 12, the group representing

277. Memorandum, Ira L. Williams, May 21, 1953, to staff of School of Agriculture, TTSAP, DF. Program of Southwestern Cotton Gin Operators' School, March 21-22, 1957; Program of Fourth Annual Grain Drying and Storage Conference, February 20-21, 1958; Programs of Welding Short Courses, June 1-3, 1955 and June 2-5, 1958, W. L. Stangel Papers.

278. Announcement of First Annual Chemical Conference, January 13-14, 1954; Program of First Annual Southwest Soil Management Demonstration and Plowing Contest, October 1, 1952, TTSAP, DF.

279. Nall, "Agricultural History of the Texas Panhandle," 217-221. Green, *Land of the Underground Rain*, 132-134.

thirty High Plains towns held a meeting. The next year, Elle and entomologist Donald Ashdown asked President E. N. Jones for permission to act as consultants for the vegetable producers. In forwarding their requests to the president, Urbanovsky, head of the department, noted that Ashdown and Elle were "the only individuals in the West Texas area who have received the technical training necessary to provide such information [to the growers]."[280]

President E. N. Jones, who succeeded Dossie M. Wiggins in 1952, led Texas Tech and its College of Agriculture toward a more active participation in research. Jones was a native of Kansas with a Ph.D. in biology from the University of Iowa. He had served as Academic Dean of Baylor University and President of Texas A&I at Kingsville before coming to Tech in 1948 as the institution's first vice-president. Jones completed the building program begun under Wiggins and then launched a research expansion policy as his first priority. His emphasis was apparent in a speech before a group of Lubbock citizens in 1956 when he noted: "It has been said that a faculty which both teaches and researches is both interested and interesting."[281]

The most important breakthrough in research was the new spirit of cooperation between the Texas Agricultural Experiment Station and the Tech School of Agriculture. Cooperation between the two institutions was not new, but it had been limited primarily to occasional cattle feeding experiments of the early 1940's. Acquisition of the PanTech Farm in the late forties brought the two closer together because the government, while ceding the facility to Tech, required involvement of the TAES and the United States Department of Agriculture. The relationship moved toward a more permanent and comprehensive arrangement when a rider providing the School of Agriculture with $50,000 for use in cooperation with the TAES Lubbock Substation was attached to the 1953 appropriations bill for the TAES. In the spring of 1953, a joint committee of the Tech and A&M Boards met for the first time to work out a policy of joint research. In the spring of 1955, both Boards signed a "Joint Statement on Coordinated Policies in Agriculture." The most significant part of that policy concerned "joint appointments." Those professors at Texas Tech selected for joint appointments were given reduced

280. W. L. Stangel, April 27, 1953, to E. N. Jones; Arthur W. Young, April 11, 1953, to W. L. Stangel, W. L. Stangel Papers. *Lubbock Avalanche-Journal*, April 12, 1956, clipping file, TTSAP, WLS. W. L. Stangel, July 26, 1957, to E. N. Jones; E. J. Urbanovsky, July 16, 1957, to W. L. Stangel; Donald Ashdown and George O. Elle, July 12, 1957, to E. J. Urbanovsky, W. L. Stangel Papers.

281. Andrews, *The First Thirty Years*, 87-88. E. N. Jones, "The Role and Value of Research on the High Plains" (public address, August 14, 1956, Lubbock), TTSAP, DF.

teaching loads and enjoyed TAES staff membership in the Lubbock Substation.[282]

Typical of the new research made possible by Tech's acquisition of the PanTech farm was the greenbug control program. The Southern Great Plains wheat crop was severely damaged by hordes of the tiny aphids in the late 1940's and early 1950's. Two characteristics made the pest extremely difficult to control: (1) reproduction was by parthenogenesis and (2) occurred at temperatures as low as 40 degrees farenheit. Because biological feeders or enemies of the greenbug, such as the lady bird beetle, do not reproduce rapidly at temperatures below 55 degrees and because there were a number of cool, late, dry spring seasons favorable to the pests' rapid growth in numbers, wheat farmers endured several consecutive crop failures. The wheat crop of 1950 was the worst disaster of all.

The greenbug problem prompted Dean W. L. Stangel to obtain the names and addresses of area Texas Farm Bureau county presidents from Swisher County Farm Bureau President Dean Harmon, an alumnus of Tech and former student of Stangel. Harmon enthusiastically supplied the list and his support for a research program at PanTech. Stangel and J. P. Smith, manager of the farm, solicited support for the proposal from regional farmers through the Farm Bureau leadership. Stangel appealed to the U.S. Department of Agriculture and Harmon wrote the Director of the Texas Agricultural Experiment Station about possible federal and state funding. But no government money was available for the project in 1950.[283]

Representatives of agricultural colleges, experiment stations, the U.S. Department of Agriculture, wheat producers, and grain industries from all over the Southern Great Plains attended a Wheat Insect Conference at Amarillo on April 20, 1951, to underscore the greenbug threat. Both Texas and Oklahoma State Experiment Station personnel reported that each had begun pesticide experiments into the problem, but that a much more "year-round history of the insects' activities" was needed. Even more attention was focused on

282. *Ibid.*; Annual Report of Division of Agriculture, 1943, TTSAP, DF. James W. Witherspoon, Hereford, March 13, 1953, to E. N. Jones; W. L. Stangel, August 9, 1953, to R. D. Lewis, W. L. Stangel Papers. Personal interview with Dean Anson R. Bertrand, June 2, 1975, by author, Lubbock, Southwest Collection.

283. A. Dean Harmon, Tulia, Texas, April 18, 1950 and May 22, 1950, to W. L. Stangel; G. E. Wesley, Happy, Texas, May 27, 1950, to W. L. Stangel; G. T. Hackney, Lubbock, Texas, May 23, 1950, to J. P. Smith; J. Don Parel, Associate Director, American Farm Bureau Federation, Washington, D.C., June 12, 1950, to J. Walter Hammond, President of Texas Farm Bureau Federation; J. Walter Hammond, Waco, Texas, June 16, 1950, to W. L. Stangel; A. Dean Harmon, Tulia, Texas, December 1, 1950, to R. D. Lewis, Director of Texas Agricultural Experiment Station; *Lubbock Avalanche-Journal*, February 8, 1952, clipping on Donald Ashdown; all in Greenbug Research folder, DF, TTCAC.

a variety of wheat pest and disease problems at a regional meeting at Dodge City, Kansas, September 26-28, 1951. Experiment station representatives from Kansas, Colorado, Nebraska, Oklahoma and Texas attended the meeting. At the invitation of the chairman, H. H. Laude of the Kansas State Experiment Station, Arthur W. Young and J. P. Smith participated in the meeting in order to offer the Pan-Tech facilities for the research.

The greenbug control project became a reality in 1952 when Texas Tech, the Texas Agricultural Experiment Station, and the U.S. Department of Agriculture entered into a joint research effort at PanTech supported by private sources including the Santa Fe and Rock Island Railway Companies, Harvest Queen Mill and Elevator Company of Fort Worth, Burrus Mills of Dallas, some thirty-five other grain elevator concerns of West Texas, and other interested parties. To head the endeavor, Tech hired its first agricultural entomologist, Donald Ashdown (Ph.D., Cornell), who at the time was working with R. G. Dahms at the Oklahoma State Agricultural Experiment Station on greenbug research for the U.S.D.A.'s Bureau of Entomology and Plant Quarantine. Ashdown assumed his new post on March 1, 1952, and over the next eighteen years he and his staff made a number of important discoveries about the hardy little pest and other wheat insects, and also tested the effectiveness and residue persistence of new pesticide controls. An important by-product of this effort was Ashdown's addition to the Tech teaching faculty in 1953 and his leadership in the new entomology program which resulted in a B.S. degree in entomology being offered in 1958 and an M.S. degree in the subject being approved in 1964.[284]

Other early fruits of cooperation were obvious when bulletins of the TAES authored by Tech faculty began to appear. Eldred A. Jordan and Ira L. Williams of Agricultural Engineering published the successful results of their experiment in drying freshly harvested grain sorghum by cheap, unheated air in 1954, and H. R. Crookshank of Animal Husbandry was joint author of a publication on a remedy for wheat pasture poisoning of cattle in 1957.[285]

284. "Report of the Wheat Insect Conference at Amarillo, Texas, April 20, 1951," mimeographed; "Report of Conference Held at Dodge City, Kansas, September 26, 27, 28," mimeographed; Donald Ashdown and Eldon A. Cleveland, "Progress Report on Texas Technological College Greenbug Research Project," January 15, 1953, mimeographed; *Lubbock Avalanche-Journal*, February 8, 1952, clipping on Donald Ashdown, DF, TTCAC. *Twenty Years of Progress in Agricultural Research, Education, and Public Service*, ICASALS Special Report No. 27 (1969), 22-23. "The Entomology Program," typewritten copy (1973), Dr. Donald Ashdown's files.

285. Eldred A. Jordan and Ira L. Williams, "Drying and Conditioning Sorghum Grain in Storage on the High Plains of Texas by the Use of Unheated Air," Texas Agricultural Ex-

The new faculty research aided by graduate and undergraduate students involved virtually every aspect of High Plains agriculture, including irrigation projects. Irrigation produced maximum yields but also severely exhausted soil nutrients. In 1943, Dean Leidigh had noted that High Plains farmers fertilized their land little, if any. About the only fertilizer in use at that time was super-phosphate for vegetable gardens. By 1950, Arthur Young was experimenting with a new type of concentrated nitrogen compound manufactured from natural gas called anhydrous ammonia. Using "anhydrous" supplied by a Phillips Petroleum Company plant at Etter, Texas, Young at first applied the highly toxic gas to his experimental wheat pasture plot by simply dropping the hose from the fertilizer tank into the irrigation ditch. Water absorbed the gas and spread it over the land. The danger of using this type of application became apparent when a near fatal accident almost occurred to an overly curious observer driving through the college farm who spotted the hose and stopped to inspect it. Young, at the other end of the field, saw the unknown investigator pull the hose from the water to inspect the nozzle end. He stuck the spewing gas into his face and collapsed. Before the agronomist could reach the unconscious form, the fellow regained consciousness, climbed into his automobile, and sped away. The Phillips Company continued to sponsor Young's experiments with anhydrous ammonia through the early 1950's. Other more successful methods of application, such as injecting the gas into the ground with chisel-plows, were used. By 1958, about 67 per cent of all grain sorghums and 31 per cent of all cotton on the High Plains were being fertilized, primarily with anhydrous ammonia, and a new multi-million dollar fertilizer manufacturing industry had emerged in the region.[286]

Charles T. Bourns of Agricultural Engineering did a study sponsored by concrete pipe manufacturers of "Seepage Losses from Irrigation Ditches on the South Plains of Texas" and disseminated the results in a bulletin printed by the Texas Tech Press. Regional newspapers such as the *Plainview Herald* readily picked up the research item for its readers. The impact of such publicized research upon Tech's farmer constituency is difficult to measure. A few closed irrigation conduit systems had been on the High Plains since the

periment Station Progress Report No. 1714, mimeographed (College Station, 1954); *Dalhart Texan*, January 4, 1957, clipping file, TTSAP, WLS.

286. A. H. Leidigh, October 8, 1943, to J. M. Arnold; W. L. Stangel, July 3, 1950, to Ralph H. Wooten, TTSAP, DF. W. L. Stangel, April 13, 1953, to E. N. Jones, W. L. Stangel Papers. Author's conversation with A. W. Young, May 27, 1975, Lubbock. Green, *Land of the Underground Rain*, 155-156.

1940's, and underground concrete pipe was placed on part of the Tech farm in 1952, but few had been installed before the middle fifties. By 1958, about 50 per cent of the irrigated acreage on the Plains was served by closed-conduits, the overwhelming majority of which were made of concrete pipe. Eighty per cent of this pipe was put in from 1954 to 1958, upon the heels of Bourns's study.[287]

Ira Williams requested money to build an irrigation laboratory on the east end of the Agricultural Engineering Annex in May, 1954. Dean Stangel forwarded the request and notified Williams that "from our conference with Dr. [E. N.] Jones, it is doubtful that the laboratory will be allowed, but I want you to know that one will never get such a facility unless he requests it and having requested it you cannot be blamed for certain things that should have been done in irrigation that are not now being done."[288]

There were a number of other irrigation and water conservation research projects. The Agronomy Department began an experiment in 1953, funded by the Toro Company, to determine the minimum moisture needed for "satisfactory Bermuda grass turf." The same year, Horticulture and Park Management attempted to broaden this to include all turf and hoped to obtain research money from a number of sources including the city of Lubbock and the High Plains Underground Water Conservation District. In 1953, the Agricultural Engineering Department began to evaluate irrigation pumps on the college farm for efficiency and to compile a report on the decline of the water table at the farm. Animal Husbandry began experimenting with gains of beef animals on various kinds of irrigated pastures in 1952.[289]

Research projects proliferated during the period. In Agricultural Economics, the new head of the department, Wayland Bennett, worked on "A Survey of Potential Markets for Sweet Potatoes Produced in West Texas." Elo Urbanovsky began tests on decomposed cotton burs as a cheap mulch for flower beds and shrubs and a year-round green grass mixture for West Texas lawns. George O. Elle conducted a number of experiments on various vegetables to determine planting dates, yield, and quality in the High Plains en-

287. Ira L. Williams, June 28, 1955, to Herbert S. Hilburn; W. L. Stangel, July 8, 1955, to Ira L. Williams, TTSAP, DF. *Texas Techsan*, vol. 3, no. 5 (1952):19. Green, *Land of the Underground Rain*, 153-155.

288. Ira L. Williams, May 17, 1954, to W. L. Stangel; W. L. Stangel, June 2, 1954, to Ira L. Williams, TTSAP, DF.

289. Memo cards on research projects in the School of Agriculture, *ca.* 1952 to 1956; "A Program of Water Conservation at Texas Technological College," research proposal submitted by Department of Horticulture and Park Management, *ca.* 1953; W. L. Stangel, June 5, 1953, to H. B. Pingrey, TTSAP, WLS.

vironment. In Animal Husbandry, "Doc" Harbaugh and Koy L. Neeley conducted some tests on fluoride (common to High Plains ground water) ingestion by dairy cattle, Stanley Anderson studied the effects of antibiotic additives on swine, and graduate students continued the cottonseed products feeding experiments on beef cattle started in the late 1930's.[290]

In spite of the new thrust toward a research oriented School of Agriculture, and the new cooperation with the TAES, research funds were primarily from corporate grants and private gifts rather than state funds. For the fiscal year 1955-56, Tech spent $196,271.98 on research. Of this amount, the School of Agriculture's share was $35,309 or about 18 per cent. Some $12,601 of that amount was from corporate and private sources and $10,000 came from profits of the PanTech Farm. Only $12,907 of state-appropriated money went into Tech's agricultural research.[291]

High Plainsmen themselves began to support collective private research efforts through several projects. The West Texas Chamber of Commerce proposed that Tech establish a Bureau of Business Research. The Board of Directors acted favorably on the proposal on April 18, 1956, and the WTCC responded by underwriting the program for three years at $20,000 per annum. The same year, the Board established an Engineering Research Institute and the Office of Coordinator of Research on campus. Sylvan J. Kaplan was appointed to the latter position.

Area farmers and businessmen also launched a successful project in 1956 to establish their own private agricultural research facility, The High Plains Research Foundation, at Halfway in Hale County. Under President E. N. Jones's leadership, Dean Stangel and other Texas Tech leaders joined hands with the Lubbock Chamber of Commerce in raising funds for the research farm. When the drive to solicit money for the Foundation ended successfully, the solicitation machinery was then directed toward raising funds for agricultural research at Tech.[292] Before the end of the year, the College of Agriculture launched its drive with the announcement that it would need $136,500 over a five-year period from private sources, in addition to state appropriations, for its research thrust. To coordinate

290. Memo cards on research projects, *ca.* 1952 to 1956; *San Angelo Standard-Times*, November 6, 1955, clipping file, TTSAP, WLS. E. J. Urbanovsky, November 13, 1951, to W. L. Stangel; Report on Research, School of Agriculture, *ca.* 1957, TTSAP, DF.

291. E. N. Jones, "The Role and Value of Research on the High Plains" (public address, August 14, 1956, Lubbock), TTSAP, DF.

292. *Ibid.*; E. N. Jones, February 5, 1957, to W. C. Omara, TTSAP, DF. Nall, "Agricultural History of the Texas Panhandle," 227-228.

research within the School, Donald Ashdown was appointed chairman of the Agricultural Research Committee in 1957.[293]

By the end of the fifties, increased emphasis upon research and the inauguration of new programs were pushing the School of Agriculture toward the status of a graduate institution. By 1959, Tech already ranked 15th among schools of agriculture in undergraduate enrollment. But until the 1950's, the school had few graduate students although it had been granting the M.S. in certain fields since the 1930's. The number of graduate students began to grow during the fifties, and in 1958, Tech granted nineteen M.S. degrees in agricultural fields.[294]

293. News release by Adrian Vaughn, Department of Public Information at Texas Tech, *ca.* 1957, TTSAP, DF. Donald Ashdown, July 11, 1957, to W. L. Stangel, TTSAP, WLS.

294. *Texas Techsan*, vol. 9, no. 4 (1959):21.

FROM COLLEGE OF AGRICULTURE TO COLLEGE OF AGRICULTURAL SCIENCES

The only thing constant about Tech's College of Agricultural Sciences during the last fifteen years has been change itself. Responding to demands from its farmer and agri-business constituency as well as to new economic and social forces, programs and even objectives have changed. By 1965, agriculture was less a "way of life" and more of a business venture for the regional farmer. Farming on the High Plains was indeed "big" business. The number of farming units had continued to decline while growing larger since 1930. The average farm was now 940 acres and investment in land, machinery and buildings for that unit was more than $200,000. The average farmer grossed from $28,000 to $30,000 per year. The primary reason for the greatly increased capitalization and land valuation was the expansion of irrigation into more than 5 million acres, more irrigated acreage than any single state except California and, of course, Texas.[295]

The very definition of agriculture was changing to include all food and fiber processing industries, suppliers of production resources, and environmental endeavors such as landscape architecture and wildlife management. The common denominator which bound agri-business, the still extant family farm, and wildlife management together was man's relationship to the land. Thus the discipline of agriculture was becoming both more comprehensive and more complex. The new Dean of the College stated in 1962: "Using this broad concept of the industry, it becomes evident that *increased emphasis must be placed upon science and business training.*" Reflecting these changes, the College of Agriculture became the College of Agricultural Sciences in 1968, the year before Texas Technological College was renamed Texas Tech University.[296]

The faculty grew rapidly in the 1960's, including such additions as: Thad Box, Eric Bolen, Joe Schuster, Henry Wright, and Bill Dahl in Range and Wildlife Management; Ellis Huddleston and

295. J. Wayland Bennett, " 'Agribusiness'—A Major Texas Industry" and Gerald W. Thomas, "Comments on Water" (statements prepared for the Agricultural Committee of the Texas House of Representatives, March 1, 1966), W. L. Stangel Papers.

296. "Your Future in a Dynamic Agriculture," *Texas Techsan*, vol. 8, no. 7 (1962):3. For the controversy surrounding the name change for Texas Tech, see Rushing and Nall, *Evolution of a University*, 133-162.

Charles Ward (entomologists), James Kitchen, Thomas Musiak, and George Tereshkovich in the Department of Park Administration, Landscape Architecture, and Horticulture; R. M. Miller and R. L. Selman in Food Technology; Marvin Dvoracek, Walter Grub, Willie L. Ulich, and Joseph C. Newell in Agricultural Engineering; Lewis Eggenberger in Agricultural Education; James Graves, Herbert Grubb, Rex Kennedy, H. Y. Lee, James Osborn, Thomas Owens, Willard F. Williams, and S. K. Roy in Agricultural Economics; Robert Albin, Sam Curl, George Ellis, Dale Furr, Frank Hudson, Boyd Ramsey, Lloyd Sherrod, Leland Tribble, and Dale Zinn in Animal Science; and Harold Dregne, Raymond Meyer, Alfred Eugene Coleman, Bill Bennett, and B. L. Allen in Agronomy.

Other staff changes occurred through the inevitable turnover because of resignations and retirement. In addition to Dean W. L. Stangel (who retired in 1958), those who became professors emeritus were Arthur W. Young (Agronomy) in 1969, Ray C. Mowery (Animal Science) in 1960, Fred Harbaugh (Animal Science) in 1971, Ray L. Chappelle (Agricultural Education) in 1961, Warren W. Yocum (Horticulture) in 1963, J. J. Willingham (Food Technology) in 1971, Archie L. Leonard (Agricultural Economics) in 1972, and Elo Joe Urbanovsky (Park Administration, Landscape Architecture, and Horticulture) in 1975.

By 1975, the longest tenured members on the active faculty were George O. Elle of Agronomy who had joined the faculty in 1938, and T. L. Leach of Agricultural Education who had been teaching at Tech since 1937.

Modifications in curriculum were as noticeable as the additions to the staff. In 1962, the Department of Agronomy became the Department of Agronomy and Range Management. The first course in range management had been offered in 1939 by the Animal Husbandry Department when W. L. Stangel sent the six students in the new course, including later Tech faculty member J. H. Baumgardner, to study six different ranches in the region and gather materials on all phases of their operations. The old Department of Plant Industry began offering a course in range management in the early 1940's. Agronomy, its successor, began to expand its offerings in that area in the middle 1950's. Chester Jaynes, who came to the faculty in 1951, taught courses in range forage grasses, and John R. Hunter was added to the Department in 1958 to teach range management and later wildlife management. In the fall of 1961, the Department offered for the first time an introductory wildlife management course. And in 1962, a range ecology course was introduced. The

College had more than forty Range Management majors by the spring of 1962. The next year, the number had increased to sixty-three, giving Tech the third or fourth nationwide position in numbers of students in the discipline. Still another evidence of the growing strength of the Department's program was that its Range Plant Teams won first place at the annual meetings of the American Society of Range Management under coaches Joseph Schuster and Henry Wright from 1965 through 1969. Another indication of the growing popularity of Range and Wildlife Management was the hiring of Thadis W. Box in 1962 as the first Ph.D. (Texas A&M) in the field at Tech except for Gerald Thomas, the Dean. Box came to Tech on a three-quarter time basis while working one-quarter time for the Rob and Bessie Welder Wildlife Foundation of Sinton, Texas.[297]

Range and Wildlife Management split off from Agronomy to form its own department in 1968. With increased public awareness of environmental problems affecting wildlife, the new Department offered courses in wildlife management such as "The Ecology and Conservation of Natural Resources", "Upland Game Ecology", and "Wildlife Diseases", to name only a few. By 1975, the Department of Range and Wildlife Management, chaired by Donald F. Burzlaff, had a staff of ten.[298]

The name of the Department of Horticulture and Park Management was changed to the Department of Park Administration, Landscape Architecture and Horticulture, while Entomology was made a separate section in 1974, and was on its way to achieving departmental status. The importance of Elo J. Urbanovsky's program was emphasized by his election as President of the American Institute of Park Executives in 1961, his participation in the 1967 Third World Congress in Park and Recreation Administration in England, and his service as advisor to President Lyndon B. and "Lady Bird" Johnson's national beautification movement of the mid-sixties. Because of the growing national interest in furthering the quality of life

297. W. L. Stangel, April 3, 1939, to Virgil Parr, Manager of Pitch Fork Ranch, TTSAP, WLS. Gerald W. Thomas, September 30, 1961, to Thomas A. Booker; Arthur W. Young, August 14, 1962, to Wayne James; Thadis W. Box, May 28, 1962, to John Hunter; Thad W. Box, Logan, Utah, October 24, 1961, to Gerald W. Thomas; Clarence Cotton, Director Welder Wildlife Foundation, Sinton, Texas, January 15, 1962, to Gerald W. Thomas; typescript copy of Clark Hatcher, Leon Badeen, and Gerald W. Thomas, "Employment Outlook for Range Managers," *Occupation Outlook Quarterly*, 7 (1963); Texas Tech Division of Public Information Service News Release, February 13, 1969, Dean's Files, Texas Tech College of Agricultural Sciences, hereafter cited as DF, TTCAS.

298. W. L. Stangel, April 3, 1939, to Virgil Parr, Manager of Pitch Fork Ranch, TTSAP, WLS. *Bulletin of Texas Technological College*, vol. 21, no. 7 (1945): 87, 93; vol. 21, no. 4 (1955): 108, 110. *Bulletin of Texas Tech University*, vol. 50, no. 6 (1974): 124-125. Vitas from files of Dean of the College of Agricultural Sciences, 1975. Personal interview with Arthur W. Young, March 6, 1973, by Beth Schneider, Lubbock, Southwest Collection.

in the late sixties and early seventies, the Department not only expanded its offerings in park administration and landscape architecture, and was involved in more research, but also added a program in horticultural therapy. When Urbanovsky retired from the Department in 1975, he was succeeded by horticulturist George Tereshkovich as acting chairman.[299]

Other important changes in the College included the addition of a B.S. degree program in Mechanized Agriculture offered by the Department of Agricultural Engineering under its new head, Willie L. Ulich. The new program was designed to train students in sales, service, and management of agribusiness industries as well as in agricultural machinery technology. The Department of Dairy Industry (formerly Dairy Manufactures) was changed to the Department of Food Technology in 1970. Reflecting changes in American consumers' dietary habits, that Department was offering only one course in Dairy Products by 1975, but now had courses such as Food Microbiology, Processing Oilseeds and Cereal Grains for Foods, Fruit and Vegetable Processing, and an internship course in Food Processing. J. J. Willingham retired as head of the department in 1971 and Milton L. Peeples, a Tech graduate with a Ph.D. from Ohio State who had been in the Department since 1951, was named acting chairman.[300]

The College continued to expand its services to its agricultural constituency as well as for its students. In 1962, it was sponsoring or co-sponsoring eighteen conferences and short courses annually. That year, Agriculture furnished speakers for sixty-four meetings held off campus, more than thirty radio programs, and about a dozen television shows. By 1970, the number of conferences and short courses had grown to thirty, and one department alone was providing speakers for more than one hundred off-campus programs. Using private funds, the College also began to publish bulletins entitled *Reports on Agricultural Industry* with information on such subjects as improved grasses and results of livestock feeding experiments. The Dean commented in 1962 on the increased public pressure for services: "On campus, we are literally 'snowed under' at times with phone calls concerning everything from sick horses to rose bushes. It seems that this spring every Blue Bird, Cub Scout, and kindergarten group in Lubbock has asked for a special tour of

299. *Texas Techsan*, vol. 16, no. 1 (1965): 28; vol. 13, no. 4 (1962), 20; vol. 13, no. 7 (1962): 19. Vitas from files of Dean of the College of Agricultural Sciences, 1975. *Bulletin of Texas Tech University*, vol. 50, no. 6 (1974): 111-120. Rushing and Nall, *Evolution of a University*, 94.

300. *Ibid.*, 109-111. *Texas Techsan*, vol. 15, no. 7 (1964): 24-25.

our farm and livestock area. Whether we like it or not, we are one of the public service arms of the College."[301]

A significant new area of participation for the College of Agricultural Sciences was that of furnishing expertise to the emerging, economically underdeveloped nations of arid and semiarid regions. This new role was facilitated by the creation by the Board of Regents of the International Center for Arid and Semi-Arid Land Studies (ICASALS) in 1966. ICASALS was a broad, interdisciplinary approach for studying the problems and cultures, both common and unique, of those regions of low rainfall throughout the world. The idea for its creation came from Tech's new president, Grover E. Murray, who conceived the plan while working as a geological consultant for a major American oil company in North Africa. Thadis W. Box of Range and Wildlife Management was appointed the organizational director and served in that position until 1970 when he left Tech to become Dean of the College of Natural Resources at Utah State. He was succeeded by geologist Frank B. Conselman. The most important ICASALS related endeavor of the College was probably the agreement reached on March 19, 1970, with SONATRACH, the national petroleum company of Algeria, to supply that nation with agricultural expertise and help train Algerian technicians over a three-year period for the sum of $1,504,000. Emmanuel T. G. M. Van Nierop, Professor of Park Administration, was appointed project director.[302]

The appearance of foreign agricultural visitors on the Tech campus was nothing new. On December 13, 1930, N. I Vavilov, the famous geneticist, director of Soviet agricultural experiment stations and a member of the Institute of Applied Botany of Leningrad, arrived in Lubbock as the guest of Dean A. H. Leidigh. At the time, Vavilov was on a lecture tour of the United States and Mexico. He visited the Lubbock experiment substation and some area farms in order to see cotton harvesting sleds at work. Before leaving he spoke to the Tech Science Club on the rather broad topic of "The Origin of Cultivated Plants."[303]

The slow trickle of foreign dignitaries to Tech became a steady stream in the sixties and seventies. In a world of growing food short-

301. "Your Future in a Dynamic Agriculture," 5. Gerald W. Thomas, "Agricultural Sciences at Texas Tech," *Texas Techsan*, vol. 22, no. 2 (1970): 6-7.

302. *ICASALS Newsletter* (Texas Tech), 3 (March 1970); (July 1970). Rushing and Nall, *Evolution of a University*, 153.

303. *Lubbock Avalanche-Journal*, December 14, 1930, p. 1. H. H. Muller, Austin, October 27, 1930, to A. H. Leidigh; telegram, N. I. Vavilov, El Paso, Texas, December 12, 1930, to A. H. Leidigh, TTSAP, DF.

ages, they came from Africa, eastern and western Europe, Asia, and Australia seeking to use American agricultural technology to solve problems of production and marketing. A typical visit was that hosted by ICASALS and the College of Agricultural Sciences, for Vice President Quett K. J. Masire and Minister of Agriculture Amos M. Dambe of the semiarid African nation of Botswana. They came to the campus in October, 1972, to study advances in growing seed, feedlot operations, and experiments in producing food from grain sorghum and cottonseed flour. In another instance, a group of Hungarian agricultural experts which arrived in April, 1971, showed special interest in the heavy agricultural machinery of the High Plains.[304] The new relationship with foreign agriculture was a two-way street, and had been since Casey Fine took a leave of absence from the Department of Animal Husbandry in the mid-fifties to work for the U.S. Overseas Mission in Iraq. Instead of taking extended leaves of absences Tech agricultural professors now generally remained with the University while doing consultative work with various foreign nations and agricultural institutions.[305]

When Dean W. L. Stangel retired in 1958, he ended one-third of a century of work at Texas Tech. The genial cigar-smoking Dean, one of the most beloved men in southwestern agricultural circles, had done much to influence the cattle industry of the region. Two years before retirement, Texas A&M conferred an honorary doctorate degree upon him in recognition of his work.[306]

The new Dean was Gerald W. Thomas, a 39-year old native of Idaho with a Ph.D. from Texas A&M in range management. Thomas' experience included work with the Soil Conservation Service and a faculty appointment in range and forestry at Texas A&M. He had done a great deal of research in various aspects of range management-conservation, much of which had been published by the Texas Agricultural Experiment Station (TAES). Before accepting the position at Tech, he was the TAES research coordinator for West Texas during the period 1956-58 and played no small role in working out a long-term cooperative research agreement between Tech and the TAES.[307]

Agronomist Chester C. Jaynes, one of the late Dean Leidigh's students who came back to Tech in 1951 to teach courses in forage and

304. *ICASALS Newsletter*, 5 (January 1972); 4 (May 1971).

305. The *ICASALS Newsletter* furnishes a continuing flow of information about such work in any given year.

306. "West Texas' Favorite Dean Retires," *Texas Ranch and Farm* (August 10, 1958), 4.

307. *Texas Techsan*, vol. 13, no. 7 (1962): 1. *Bulletin of Texas Technological College*, Publications of the Faculty and Staff, 1956-1960, vol. 37, no. 1 (1961): 7-8.

pasture crops, and fellow agronomist Clark Harvey were two of the earliest faculty members to receive joint appointments to the TAES under the new program in 1957. Jaynes's research project was to evaluate both native and foreign range grasses for use in seedings in West Texas which was just emerging from the severe drouth of the 1950's. Working in a grass nursery established on campus, he and John R. Hunter found that from among the 3,000 strains of grass collected by the TAES during the dry cycle, Premier sideoats grama exhibited exceptional drouth-resistant qualities suitable for many of the soils of West Texas.[308]

Thomas guided the College of Agriculture into a new phase of accelerated research activities as Texas Tech advanced into the full role of a university. When he arrived in 1958, the only clearly earmarked research money aside from a few TAES cooperative ventures was $1,200 from the Texas Cottonseed Crushers Association for livestock feeding experiments, a program supported by that group since the late 1930's. Realizing that money was a vital key to building a research-oriented program, he led the College in pursuing new sources of aid coupled with projects of interest not only to West Texas, but to the state as well.[309]

One important new area of involvement was related to a problem threatening the irrigation-based agriculture of the High Plains—a sharply declining ground water table. With more than 5 million acres in irrigation by 1964, the economy was threatened by ground water levels falling as much as three feet or more per year. What earlier settlers and pioneer irrigation farmers had first termed an "inexhaustible" resource appeared to be dwindling as many six and eight-inch wells narrowed to three and four-inch streams while weaker wells became "drippers."[310]

In 1964, Governor John Connally, hoping to use federal money available under the new National Water Resources Act of 1964, instructed the Texas Water Commission to draw up a comprehensive, long-range plan to meet Texas's water needs into the next century. Responsibility for the study was vested in the new Texas Water Development Board on 1 September 1965.[311]

Dean Thomas, believing that High Plainsmen should have some input into the plan, wrote Joe D. Carter, Chairman of the Texas

308. Statement of Chester C. Jaynes, January, 1976. *Lubbock Avalanche-Journal* clipping, December 31, 1961, section F, p. 2. *Texas Agricultural Progress* (College Station), 11 (Winter 1965): 16-17, DF, TTCAS.

309. Telephone interview with President Gerald W. Thomas of New Mexico State University, by author, February 10, 1976, in possession of author.

310. Green, *Land of the Underground Rain*, 191-192.

311. *Ibid.*, 219-220.

Water Commission on September 28, 1964, to offer "the resources of the West Texas Water Institute and Texas Tech." The West Texas Water Institute which the Dean had helped to establish had been created in the early 1960's as a joint effort of Tech and its regional constituency, primarily through the West Texas Chamber of Commerce, "to develop and promote educational and research programs concerning the water resources of West Texas." The Institute, chaired by Thomas, held its annual program on the Tech campus.[312]

The Texas Water Commission accepted the Dean's offer and a memorandum of agreement was signed on January 14, 1965. At the suggestion of John J. Vandertulip, Chief Engineer of the Texas Water Commission, the Tech participants were to be primarily concerned with studies on the economic impact of High Plains irrigation, artificial recharge of the Ogallala formation (the aquifer of the High Plains) from playa lakes, relationship of public health and recreation to the playas, and the re-use of sewage effluent for agricultural and industrial purposes.[313]

Pursuant to this agreement, the College worked with the College of Engineering and obtained the support of the Tech Institute of Science and Engineering. A staff of six, including five members of the Agricultural Faculty, began work on the project in February, 1965. Included were Clark Harvey, agronomist; Ellis Huddleston, entomologist; William Schwiesow, agricultural engineer; James Osborn, agricultural economist; and Herbert W. Grubb, agricultural economist who also acted as project leader. George Whetstone, of the Tech Department of Civil Engineering was the sixth member of the team. Consultants for the project were John Bradford, Dean of the College of Engineering; Keith Marmion, Head of the Department of Civil Engineering; and Gerald Thomas.

Tech's input into the Texas Water Plan included studies by William Schwiesow on "Playa Lake Use and Modification in the High Plains," and Ellis Huddleston and Virginia C. Riggs (research assistant) on "Public Health Aspects of High Plains Water." The Schwiesow and Huddleston studies graphically demonstrated the kind of interdisciplinary work which the College of Agricultural

312. Gerald W. Thomas, September 28, 1964, to Joe D. Carter; Memorandum from Gerald W. Thomas, July 22, 1966, to Board of Directors, West Texas Water Institute, DF, TTCAS. Telephone interview with President Gerald Thomas.

313. John J. Vandertulip, Austin, Texas, October 14, 1964, to Gerald W. Thomas; Gerald W. Thomas, November 19, 1964, to Joe D. Carter; John J. Vandertulip, Austin, Texas, November 25, 1964, to Gerald W. Thomas; Gerald W. Thomas, December 16, 1964, to R. C. Goodwin, DF, TTCAS. When the Texas Water Development Board (TWDB) was given responsibility for the water plan in place of the Texas Water Commission by the Fifty-Ninth Texas Legislature, Tech signed a memorandum of agreement with the TWDB in September, 1965. Joe G. Moore, Jr., Austin, Texas, September 21, 1965, to R. C. Goodwin, DF, TTCAS.

Sciences could now produce. Whereas Schwiesow pointed out the possibilities and problems of recharging playa lake water into the declining Ogallala formation and the need for constructing deep lakebed sumps to conserve water for irrigation, Huddleston pointed out that the modification of lake beds for irrigation purposes would lead to a decline in encephalitis, long a health problem in the region, by destroying the shallow water breeding grounds of the mosquito carriers.[314]

The Texas Water Plan project stimulated the growth of other research activities within the College of Agriculture and on the Tech campus. In 1965, the Texas Tech Board of Directors approved the establishment of a Water Resources Center, largely a creation of Thomas who was already Chairman of the Board of Directors of the West Texas Water Institute.[315]

An even more ambitious, but abortive, plan was a proposed national groundwater research laboratory. That proposal came out of a luncheon meeting early in 1966 attended by Thomas, Tom McFarland, (General Manager of the High Plains Underground Water Conservation District, HPUWCD, headquartered in Lubbock), and a few other interested persons. McFarland, who had helped create the HPUWCD in 1951 and had long been involved in High Plains irrigation issues, threw the idea on the table for discussion. McFarland believed that such a laboratory was needed in order to develop technology and expertise for handling the proposed importation of water from other regions into West Texas contained in the Texas Water Plan. Thomas was enthusiastic about the idea, especially about the prospect of Tech obtaining the facility. Personnel of the HPUWCD visited the Saline Water Laboratory at Riverside, California to obtain ideas for its implementation and operation. A Tech committee headed by Dan M. Wells of the Department of Geosciences drew up the proposal and Congressman George Mahon of Lubbock showed it to W. T. Pecora, Director of the United States Geological Survey. Although Pecora appeared to like the idea, Mahon failed to generate support for it in Congress.[316]

314. Research proposal prepared by Gerald W. Thomas on "Preparation of Certain Aspects of a Comprehensive Water Plan with Projections to the Year 2000," (*ca.* 1965) in Texas Water Plan File, DF, TTCAS. Studies of William Schwiesow and Ellis Huddleston are in *Studies of Playa Lakes in the High Plains of Texas*, Texas Water Development Board Report No. 10 (Austin, 1966).

315. Memorandum, Gerald W. Thomas, April 13, 1965, to Department Heads on the subject of a Water Resources Center, DF, TTCAS.

316. Thomas G. McFarland, October 20, 1966, to Gerald W. Thomas; Dan M. Wells, "Proposal to Establish a National Groundwater Laboratory (preliminary draft)," (*ca.* 1965); George Mahon, Washington, D.C., February 26, 1966, to Gerald W. Thomas; various letters

The largest interdisciplinary project put together under Thomas's leadership was the Noxious Brush and Weed Control Project. An article in the *Dallas Times-Herald* of January 26, 1969, declared that noxious brush was "perhaps the biggest problem facing the livestock industry in the state at present." As early as 1966, the West Texas Chamber of Commerce asked that the Department of Range Management make a statement about the "brush problem" slowly engulfing the grasslands of much of West and South Texas, especially mesquite. A paper, presented on July 15, 1966, by Dean Thomas emphasized the need for a "crash" program to deal with the menace. After pointing out that ranchers had been trying to eradicate brush for more than two decades with various mechanical and chemical means, Thomas stated that they were "fighting a losing battle" as evidenced by those who had treated brush from two to four times only to have it return. The speaker declared: "We must strive to find out how nature kept brush from our virgin range lands. If we can truly understand the factors that kept brush from some areas, perhaps we can remove it from other ranges as well."[317]

In September 1967, the state legislature responded by appropriating $100,000 for the Brush Control Project. The program under the direction of Joseph L. Schuster was primarily vested in the Department of Range and Wildlife Management created the next year, but with liberal assistance from other departments. For example, Joseph C. Newell of Agricultural Engineering worked to combine chemical application equipment with a rotary shredder. Rex Kennedy of Agricultural Economics evaluated in economic terms the real cost of long range methods. Charles Ward and Ellis Huddleston, entomologists, traveled to Argentina to study mesquite-feeding insects and their possible introduction into the Southwest.

The greatest concentrated effort was, of course, in Range and Wildlife Management. Bill Dahl primarily directed his research toward grass reseeding and grazing practices after brush removal. Joseph L. Schuster studied treatment combinations at various times of the day and night, and the ecology of redberry juniper. Don Klebenow researched the impact of brush control on wildlife population, especially on quail and deer. Last, but certainly not least, was the work of Henry Wright who was studying the effects of man's oldest means of controlling brush—fire. In addition, Tech was coop-

and memoranda in Ground Water Laboratory file in DF, TTCAS. For information on the water importation movement for the High Plains, see Green, *Land of the Underground Rain*, 219-228.

317. [Gerald W. Thomas], "The Brush Problem in Texas" (address, July 15, 1966) typescript in Brush Control Project file, DF, TTCAS.

erating with the personnel of Texas A&M, the Texas Agricultural Experiment Station, Abilene Christian College, Midwestern University, and Southwest Texas State College in various other facets of brush control.

The project was strongly supported by the region's ranching constituency. The Post-Montgomery Estate provided six graduate student research grants per year for experimentation on their lands in addition to various studies done by faculty members. The Spade Ranch and the R. B. Masterson Ranch contributed land and equipment for research on their pastures while still others offered even more assistance.[318]

Another team effort was apparent in the swine research program centered in the Animal Science Department which the state legislature first funded at $30,000 for 1968-69 and subsequently augmented by contributions from various private sources. The program involved faculty members of Animal Science, Agricultural Engineering, Agricultural Economics, and Entomology as well as the Food and Nutrition Department of the College of Home Economics. The primary thrust of the program was toward solving problems of commercial hog production unique to the grain sorghum area of the Southwest in order to feed out the surplus of grain which remained even after the needs of the beef cattle feedlots were met. Those in the program such as Leland F. Tribble and Archie Max Lennon of the Animal Science Department hoped to pave the way for a future Texas hog production area to rival the corn-hog belt of the Middle West.[319]

By 1973, West Texas had become an important producer of vegetables, contributing 64 per cent of the potatoes, 25 per cent of the onions, 27 per cent of the lettuce, 22 per cent of the green peppers, and 19 per cent of the carrots harvested within the state. The region also grew cantaloupes, cabbage, and tomatoes for marketing. Reflecting this growing agricultural industry, Texas Tech also used the team approach in vegetable research utilizing members of the Agronomy, Food Technology, and Agricultural Economics Depart-

318. [Joseph L. Schuster], "Noxious Brush and Weed Control Research at Texas Technological College" (*ca.* 1969), and Joseph L. Schuster, "Brush Control and Grassland Restoration Research at Texas Technological College" (*ca.* 1968), in Brush Control Project file; Texas Tech Division of Information Services News Release, January 27, 1969; C. L. Lundell, "Agriculture Policy Defies Description," *Dallas Times-Herald*, January 26, 1969, section F, p. 6, clipping, DF, TTCAS.

319. Vitas of Leland F. Tribble and Archie Max Lennon; Form letter by Leland F. Tribble relative to swine research program, *ca.* 1968 or 1969; "Swine Research at Texas Tech," mimeographed (January 24, 1969), DF, TTCAS. College of Agricultural Sciences, *Swine Research, 1975: Proceedings of the 23rd Annual Swine Short Course*, Agricultural Sciences Technical Report No. T-5-111 (Lubbock, 1975).

ments as well as the newly formed Entomology Section. Building upon the pioneer work done by George O. Elle and Donald Ashdown in the 1950's, noted earlier, the program by the 1970's had produced a number of research reports on such subjects as weed control, suitable varieties, damage by sand storms, marketing, and cost-price studies, under the direction of John D. Downes who came to Tech in 1970.[320]

The Department of Agricultural Economics continued to be involved in matters of regional importance with state and national ramifications. Willard F. Williams came to the department as chairman in 1963. His major field of research and publication was in the theory of agricultural market structure and development. In 1967 he testified before the Senate Committee on Agriculture and Forestry at the request of Senator Walter Mondale of Minnesota on the subject of "farmer bargaining power." Herbert W. Grubb and James E. Osborn were very active in studies on the regional and state economic impact of High Plains agriculture. Grubb's pioneer work, *Importance of Irrigation Water to the Economy of the Texas High Plains* published in 1966, was a by-product of his work with the Texas Water Plan. In it he demonstrated in quantitative terms that irrigation accounted for 21 per cent of all High Plains income in 1959 and that the percentage could be expected to rise until 1980. Grubb left the department in 1972 in order to serve in the Governor's Office as project director of a comprehensive input-output model analysis of the Texas economy which was published in 1973 as *The Structure of the Texas Economy.* James Osborn contributed to the study and came out with a separate *The Structure of the Texas High Plains Economy* in 1972. Two years later, Osborn and a graduate research assistant did a study on *The Economic Impact of Crop and Feedlot Sectors on the Texas High Plains Economy.*[321]

320. Texas Tech University College of Agricultural Sciences, *Vegetable Research, 1972-1973,* Agricultural Sciences Technical Report No. T-4-114 (Lubbock, 1973); *Vegetable Research, 1973-1974,* Agricultural Sciences Technical Report No. T-4-117 (Lubbock, 1974); and T. M Bell, B. G. Freeman, D. L. True and G. B. Fish, *Crop Budgets [for] Major Vegetable Growing Areas [of the] Texas High Plains,* College of Agricultural Sciences Publication No. T-10138 (Lubbock, 1975).

321. Vita of Willard F. Williams; J. Wayland Bennett, letter of recommendation for Horn Professorship for Willard F. Williams, March 6, 1968; telegram, Walter F. Mondale, Washington, D.C., March 22, 1968, to Willard F. Williams; Willard F. Williams, April 15, 1968, to Grover E. Murray, DF, TTCAS.

Herbert W. Grubb, *Inportance of Irrigation Water to the Economy of the Texas High Plains,* Texas Water Development Board Report No. 11 (Austin, 1966). Herbert W. Grubb, *The Structure of the Texas Economy* (2 vols; Austin, 1973). James E. Osborn and William C. McCray, *The Structure of the Texas High Plains Economy,* Texas Tech College of Agricultural Sciences Technical Report No. T-1-108 (Lubbock, 1972). James E. Osborn and Jack D. Mason, *The Economic Impact of Crop and Feedlot Sectors on the Texas High Plains*

In a period of constant improvements in complex agricultural technology, the Department of Agricultural engineering faced challenging research possibilities. Agricultural power mechanization had become a fact of life as computers, large diesel tractors, and other expensive labor-saving machinery entered the High Plains, while the general public became ever more concerned about environmental quality. Willie L. Ulich, who served the department as chairman from 1961 to 1974, was particularly concerned about irrigation pump efficiency, soil mulch, and inexpensive agricultural building construction. Through his research he determined that smaller pumping plants could be more cheaply powered by electricity than by natural gas engines and that fiberglass shell structures with set-foam type insulation were the least expensive all-purpose type of construction for farms. Ulich also carried on experiments on the use of petroleum by-products as crop mulch, on chemical spray methods to decrease cattle feedlot odors, and on equipment to control air pollution from such agricultural processing plants as gins, feed mills, elevators, and dehydrating plants. Walter Grub came to Tech in 1966 from Auburn University where he had done much research on problems of poultry-house environment. At Tech, he turned his attention to the construction of air ventilation systems for swine buildings, and "the organic stabilization of beef feedlot waste by composting."[322]

In contrast to the earlier lean days, by 1970, the College of Agricultural Sciences had a research budget of $1,669,792, of which 79 per cent came from state and local funds while private donations and federal funds furnished slightly more than 10 per cent each. More than 260 research projects were being conducted in all departments ranging from studies of the High Plains Mexican-American labor force to experiments in artificial ground water recharge from playa lakes.[323]

As in the earlier period, the contribution of Tech to the livestock industry was of major importance. The emergence of the High Plains as the major grain sorghum producing region of the United States after World War II set the stage for new developments in the industry. Through irrigation the region was producing more than 60 per cent of all the grain sorghum in Texas by the sixties; moreover,

Economy, Texas Tech College of Agricultural Sciences Technical Report No. T-1-118 and ICASALS Contribution No. 112 (Lubbock, 1974).

322. Vita and list of publications of Willie L. Ulich and Walter Grub, DF, TTCAS.

323. *Research Projects and Publications, College of Agricultural Sciences, 1970*, ICASALS Special Report no. 35 (Texas Tech, 1970). Thomas, "Agricultural Sciences at Texas Tech," 6.

irrigation supplied large quantities of ensilage as well as cottonseed for feed. By 1958, grain sorghum with some 1.8 million acres was the single most extensively cultivated irrigated crop on the High Plains. Eleven years later, irrigation farmers planted 2.2 million acres of the reddish-brown grain.[324]

Since the twenties, as noted earlier, W. L. Stangel had continually stated that the High Plains possessed the resources for developing into one of the nation's most important livestock feeding areas. He never lost faith in that proposition. In an article written for *The Farmer-Stockman* in 1951 entitled "Cattle Feeding Potential of the South Plains," he envisioned Plains farmers, like their corn-belt brothers of the middlewest, fattening out twenty or so head per year on their local feedstuffs. If each of the 16,903 South Plains farms did that, Stangel predicted that the area could produce 338,000 fed cattle per year. The Dean echoed the same message at the annual Tech Cattle Feeders Day programs, at meetings of the West Texas Chamber of Commerce and at every other opportunity he had.[325]

Conditions for livestock feeding were unfavorable in the early and middle 1950's because of the sharp break in the cattle market in 1952 and the accompanying southwestern drouth which lasted from about 1950 to 1957. The drouth accelerated the movement of cattle from West Texas to East Texas which had been going on since the 1930's when the federal farm program had decreased cotton acreage in the latter region. The agricultural census of 1954 illustrated the trend and showed that the overwhelming majority of Texas cattle were now raised in counties east of the 100th meridian.[326]

By the late 1950's, the High Plains was shipping not only its cattle to middlewestern and California feedlots, but was also exporting much of its cheap grain sorghum to other regions. One of the very few large operations on the Plains at the time as the D. W. Lewter feedlot southwest of Lubbock which had a 30,000-head capacity by 1960. When a group of West Texans including Stangel visited a California feedlot in 1960, they saw West Texas cattle being fed

324. Green, *Land of the Underground Rain*, 156-157, 200-201.

325. See chapter 3 for Stangel's early work in livestock feeding. W. L. Stangel, "Cattle Feeding Potential of the South Plains," manuscript written for *The Farmer-Stockman*, November 15, 1951, in W. L. Stangel Papers. "Farm News," *Lubbock Avalanche-Journal*, December 16, 1956; Conrad L. Lohoefer, "Livestock Feeding Could Be New Income for Farmers," *Lubbock Avalanche-Journal*, May 12, 1957; C. L. Richart, "South Plains Held Ready to Compete with Corn Belt in Fattening of Cattle," *Fort Worth Star-Telegram*, no date, clipping file, W. L. Stangel Papers.

326. Roger B. Letz, "Changes in Texas Cattle Population," reprinted from *The Cattleman* (December 1955); *Agricultural News Letter* (Federal Reserve Bank of Dallas), 8 (July 15, 1953); *Armour's Analysis* (Armour's Livestock Bureau, Chicago), 1 (October 1952), W. L. Stangel Papers.

High Plains grain sorghum. If Californians could make money importing both cattle and grain, why could West Texans not make an even better profit by fattening out their own cattle on their own feed? In 1959, Dean Emeritus Stangel, chairman of the Farm and Ranch Committee of the West Texas Chamber of Commerce, and Sam Thomas, agricultural development manager for Southwestern Public Service Company, a regional electric utility concern, organized the first of several feedlot tours. Under Stangel's leadership, groups of farmers and businessmen toured feedlot facilities in the middlewest, California, and Arizona.[327]

The tours stimulated much interest and by 1967, a "beef bonanza" was in progress on the High Plains as super feedlots, each capable of carrying 10,000 to 70,000 animals began springing up. The South Plains alone fed out more than 800,000 head that year. Almost 3 million head were being fed out in the region by 1970, primarily by seventy-three highly automated super feedlots, using computers to formulate daily rations. The packing industry, once centralized in a few cities such as Chicago, Kansas City, Fort Worth, and Oklahoma City, followed the feedlots into the region. By 1971, there were eleven of the processing plants on the High Plains.[328]

A gadfly arrived on the Tech campus in 1959 to give the Department of Animal Husbandry (changed to Animal Science in 1968) new directions, to influence the regional livestock industry, and to stir up controversy. His name was Ralph M. "Bull" Durham. Durham had grown up on a ranch in southeastern Colorado. After obtaining a B.S. degree in animal husbandry from Colorado A&M, he went to the University of Wisconsin where he received the Ph.D. in genetics in 1951. His first position was at New Mexico A&M. Soon after his arrival there in 1951, a dwarf was born in the college's herd of registered Herefords. Dwarfism attracted Durham's attention for the next few years. Like many genetic flaws, dwarfism was transmitted through recessive genes and cropped out with alarming frequency because of purebred line-breeding. An agricultural scientist at the University of Wyoming estimated in 1952 that 15 per cent of all purebred Hereford calves were dwarfs. Hereford breeders, by and large, kept the subject quiet. Then in the spring of 1953, Durham spoke on dwarfism at the New Mexico Cattle Raisers Association in Albuquerque. He told commercial cattlemen that they

327. Garry Lynn Nall, "Agricultural History of the Texas Panhandle" Ph.D. dissertation, University of Oklahoma, 1972, pp. 222-224. Green, *Land of the Underground Rain*, 201-202. Dunn, "Agriculture Builds a City," 260-261.

328. *Ibid.*, 203-204. Duane Howell, "Survey Reveals Feedlot Growth," *Lubbock Avalanche-Journal*, May 7, 1967, clipping file, W. L. Stangel Papers.

should stop buying purebred Hereford bulls in order to protect their herds from the flaw. That fall large dispersal sales of Hereford bulls were held all over the state. In 1957, an animal scientist named John Lasley discovered that insulin could be used as a test to detect dwarf carriers, and breeders began to clean up their herds.[329]

Durham moved to the U.S. Department of Agriculture research station at Beltsville, Maryland, and in the fall of 1954, Iowa State hired him to work in a swine improvement research project. The program evolved into a testing station where boars were graded on three characteristics passed to offspring: backfat depth, rate of gain, and efficiency in feed utilization. Boars failing to make the grade were castrated before being returned to their owners. An early Tech graduate named L. N. Hazel, who had grown up at Spur and gotten interested in animal research by observing R. E. Dickson's work at the Spur Experiment Substation, was associated with Durham at the testing station. One Iowa newspaper, referring to Durham as the "fiery little extension swine specialist," labeled him as the man "who has sparked the fatback probe testing program in Iowa."[330]

While at Iowa State, Durham exhibited the characteristics which became his trademark: a boundless inquiring mind, bluntness in his attacks on status quo positions, and a certain flair for dramatizing his ideas through the media. The results of his boar-station were indisputable. In 1956 the all-breed average lean cuts in Iowa were 48.5 per cent. By 1959, the average had risen to 52.3 per cent. As Durham was preparing to leave Iowa for Texas Tech in the spring of 1959, the farm editor of the *Omaha World-Herald* wrote: "Bull Durham stepped on some important toes. He had to in trying to produce a better product in years when pork consumption nationally was dwindling."[331]

When Durham arrived at Tech in May, 1959, as the new head of Animal Husbandry, he set out to change the beef industry in much the same way he had tackled the hog business. He began by criticizing the emphasis upon livestock judging shows. Durham's criticism was aimed at the dichotomy which had developed between desirable commercial cattle characteristics and those of "show" cattle.

329. Personal interview with Ralph M. Durham, July 12, 1975, by David Murrah, Lubbock, Southwest Collection. Ralph M. Durham, February 15, 1961, to Henry Elder, Manager of Texas Hereford Association, Texas Tech School of Agriculture, Animal Husbandry Department Papers, Southwest Collection. Hereafter cited as TTSAP, AH. John T. Schlebecker, *Cattle Raising on the Plains, 1900-1961* (Lincoln: University of Nebraska Press, 1963), 219-220, 233.

330. Personal interview with Ralph M. Durham. *Sioux City* (Iowa) *Journal-tribune Farm Weekly*, March 3, 1958, TTSAP, AH.

331. " 'Bull' Durham Leaves Mark on Hogs," *Omaha World-Herald*, April 17, 1959, clipping, TTSAP, AH.

Show cattle, he said, were overly fat while packers, reflecting current consumer tastes, purchased commercial cattle primarily for their large percentage of dressed meat cutout, as well as "marbling." If the basic idea behind the show ring was to prepare youngsters for producing cattle for maximum profit, Durham believed that the standards for judging should be changed to reflect current commercial standards.

The animal scientist suggested to one county agent that because "kids of today are bombarded with science of some sort, but not too much science on agriculture," the 4H programs should be changed to emphasize science rather than the "art" of preparing a calf for showing. For 4H projects he suggested building model feedlots, or contests in nutrition, marketing, breeding, meats, and other such areas. In a 1963 speech before the Dallas Agricultural Club, he charged that "stock show politics" at the Fort Worth Fat Stock Show prevented the judges from giving high marks to a Charolais steer which later produced the best dressed carcass. Durham consequently directed the movement within his department to revise the curriculum by dropping livestock judging offerings altogether and to introduce courses emphasizing the relationships between animal production and finished meats.[332]

Durham used the annual Feeder's Day program in 1961 to publicize his concepts of meat production. Ninety-six Hereford and Angus steers in a feeding experiment were slaughtered just prior to the meeting. Each carcass was graded and halved. Half was boned and half left intact. Information about the breed, tenderness, cutout percentage, etc. was attached to each carcass for the sake of comparisons. Durham also froze a slaughtered whole steer in a standing position, stripped the fat off one side, and placed the animal on exhibit in the large new Meats Laboratory in order to emphasize his view of the uselessness of excess fat and rounded conformation.[333]

The animal scientist believed that some dairy cattle breeds, because they were excellent producers of both muscle and milk, came closer to meeting packer-consumer beef standards than the established Hereford and Aberdeen-Angus breeds. He was particularly

332. Duane Howell, "Tech Man Urges Feeding Change," *Lubbock Avalanche-Journal*, August 14, 1959, clipping file; Ralph M. Durham, June 1, 1959, to Ollie Liner; Newspaper clipping entitled, "Tech Prof Blasts Livestock Shows," no date or name, clipping file, TTSAP, AH. Comparison of animal husbandry offerings in *Bulletin of Texas Technological College*, vol. 40, no. 3 (1964), and vol. 31, no. 4 (1955). Personal interview with Ralph M. Durham. *Texas Techsan*, vol. 13, no. 7 (1962): 18.

333. Ralph M. Durham, March 13, 1961, to Dick Hanson, editor, *Successful Farming Magazine*; Ralph M. Durham, March 29, 1961, to William Zmolek, Extension Specialist in Livestock Marketing, Iowa State, TTSAP, AH.

interested in trying to upgrade beef herds by cross-breeding dairy cattle and beef breeds. This approach sprang from his having read the experiments of L. J. Cole at the University of Wisconsin. Cole's cross-breeding work at Wisconsin took place from about 1915 to 1920. Those experiments had long gathered dust until a professor at the University of Wisconsin had them printed in 1948. Durham read them at Wisconsin as a student, and appeared on the scene during the decade that a number of new "beefier" breeds began to appear. The Santa Gertrudis developed by the King Ranch earlier in the century appealed to some cattlemen as early as the 1940's. But it was in the 1950's that numerous livestock producers began to raise Beefmaster (a cross of Brahman, Hereford, and Shorthorn), Charolais, Charbray, Brangus, and various crosses. At Tech, the animal scientist cross-bred Aberdeen-Angus and Holstein to produce the "Holgus", as Durham called the animals. Although cattlemen did not go for "Holgus" herds, many began stocking their ranges and feedlots in the sixties with the more muscular breeds and crossbreeds.[334]

Durham's most important contribution to the cattle industry may very well have been his feeding experiments. By 1960, the U.S. Department of Agriculture reported that livestock producers were feeding their cattle 20 per cent more grain per head than in 1954. The reason was obvious. Farmers had cheap grain on their hands. Profits on cattle could be maximized by sending the grain to market on the hoof. At the time the report appeared, the Animal Husbandry Department at Tech was experimenting with more than four hundred cattle per year, feeding them a mixture of about 50 per cent grain and 50 per cent silage. In 1962, Durham took two Jersey calves and got "Doc" Fred Harbaugh to "tie off" the rumen of one. The no-rumen calf was fed an "all-concentrate" diet (straight feed grain with no roughage), while the other consumed a traditional grain and roughage mixture. The calf on all-concentrate gained about twice as fast as the other. But when both were dressed out, it was discovered that Harbaugh's sutures had torn loose. Actually, the calf's rumen had been intact through most of the experiment, proving that a ruminant could be fed an all-grain diet.

The department head then decided to feed all-concentrate to a lotfull that same year. One day he took a pen of thirty-seven head of cattle and put 900 pounds of milo and 100 pounds of cottonseed

334. Schlebecker, *Cattle Raising on the Plains*, 233. Personal interview with Ralph M. Durham. Personal interview with Fred G. Harbaugh, May 29, 1973, by David Murrah, Lubbock, Southwest Collection.

meal into their feed bunk. When Durham told the boys who unloaded the feedstuff that he intended to let the animals clean it up they replied, "It'll kill 'em!" He kept them on their feet, the cattle lived and began eating about 18 pounds per day with some added vitamin A. They were kept on the grain for about 40 days. In September, 1962, a large group of Holsteins of the same weight was divided into two lots. Half were put on all concentrate, and each consumed more than 40 pounds the first day. On the second day they were sick, but none died. The Holsteins remained on the grain diet for 140 days. But when butchered, it was discovered that more than 70 per cent had abcessed livers and some had ulcers. The average daily gain was significantly higher than those on roughage and grain. After further experiments, Durham got the number of abscessed livers down to 30 per cent and below by using antibiotics and additives. Although Durham converted few to his all-concentrate diet, by 1973 ratios of 90 per cent concentrate were common in regional feedlots.[335]

Among other experiments, Durham fed the manure from his all-concentrate cattle to other cattle, pigs, sheep, poultry, and even catfish and in 1961 he designed a multi-pronged needle to inject "marbling" of either animal or vegetable fat into lean meat. He even suggested that because bulls were more efficient producers of meat on less feed than steers, the feedlot industry should consider switching to bulls.[336]

Controversy followed Ralph Durham like his shadow. Some purebred Hereford and Aberdeen-Angus breeders attacked him. Because the Department no longer showed an interest in promoting the feed merits of cottonseed oil products, the Cottonseed Crushers Association dropped the annual grants to the Department for those experiments which had been carried on since the 1930's. The controversy, however, which attracted the most attention was that over the future of a purebred herd of Herefords which had been given to Tech by a

335. *Texas Tech School of Agriculture Reports on Agricultural Industry*, Animal Husbandry Research (1966): i-vi, 1-13. Paul Friggens, "Change Rides the Range," *Readers Digest* (August 1964): 185-186. Personal interview with Ralph M. Durham. Interview with Fred G. Harbaugh by David Murrah, May 29, 1973, Lubbock, Texas, Southwest Collection, Texas Tech University.

336. *Ibid.* Ralph M. Durham *et al.*, "Coprophagy and Use of Animal Waste in Livestock Feeds," *Management of Farm Animal Wastes*, Proceedings of National Symposium, May 5, 6, and 7, 1966 (St. Joseph, Michigan: American Society of Agricultural Engineers, 1966), 112-113. Ralph M. Durham, Henry Elliott, and Dale W. Zinn, "A Technique for Marbling Beef," *Texas Tech Reports on Agricultural Industry* (one-page mail-out, [1962]). Personal interview with Fred G. Harbaugh. Ralph M. Durham, October 20, 1961, to Bernard Collins, President, Iowa Swine Producers Association, TTSAP, AH. Elmer Kelton, "Cattlemen Are Told Bulls May Be Top Beef Animal," *San Angelo Standard-Times*, no date, clipping file, TTSAP, AH.

prominent Texas breeder a few years before Durham arrived. Even before he arrived, the department had made the decision to cull undesirable animals in the herd and those cows which had not "taken" the herd bull. When Durham became head of Animal Husbandry in May, 1959, he allowed the culling to be carried out. The purebred herd was left with some forty or so cows and a bull. Some of those remaining cows who did not "take" the herd bull were used for cross-breeding experiments, but the majority of the Herefords were bred to the herd bull with resulting small and blocky offspring. Durham used the herd to confirm his belief about the undesirable effects of purebred line-breeding. But the widespread belief arose that Durham was purposely liquidating the herd.[337]

As early as 1960, some alumni, members of the Block and Bridle Club, and friends of the College of Agriculture who sincerely believed that the controversial figure was ruining the Department and driving students away began to criticize him and press for his dismissal. Enrollment, however, actually increased during the early 1960's.[338] And Durham's students and supporters came to his aid. The manager of a prominent regional ranch wrote to Dean Thomas: "I think that Dr. Durham's outspoken criticism of livestock shows and the type animal that is bred in order to compete successfully in shows is well justified. I have heard the same opinions of livestock shows expressed by many practical livestock breeders and people in the livestock industry." A former member of a Tech livestock judging team stated: "Tech needs this type of man and more like him if we are to advance." A high school vocational agriculture teacher wrote to Durham, "I have hoped for a long time that someone in a responsible position would take such a stand as you have regarding our livestock shows."[339]

It is difficult, perhaps impossible at this early date, to assess fully the role of Durham in the Southwestern livestock industry. How much he actually either directly or indirectly influenced the industry toward crossbreeding and feeding higher concentrated livestock feeds is impossible to determine in quantitative terms, but his activities were well publicized. There is little doubt that Durham's ideas were ahead of his time, but some who sympathized with his views

337. Ralph M. Durham, May 26, 1959, to Leslie Johnson, Head, Department of Animal Husbandry, Iowa State College, TTSAP, AH. Personal interview with Ralph M. Durham. Personal interview with Fred G. Harbaugh.

338. Personal interview with Ralph M. Durham. Ralph M. Durham, February 14, 1961, to Carl Williams; Ralph M. Durham, April 12, 1961, to Carl Williams, TTSAP, AH.

339. O. J. Barron, Jr., Manager of Spur Ranch, Spur, Texas, December 10, 1960, to Gerald Thomas; Billy Joe Boyd, Crosbyton, Texas, April 6, [1961], to Gerald Thomas; Harold V. Eades, Crosbyton, Texas, August 17, 1959, to Ralph M. Durham, TTSAP, AH.

believe that he could have moved the meat industry toward new concepts faster had he been more tactful. Others, however, believe that his "shock and anger" approach was instrumental in accomplishing his goals. However one chooses to view his role, one thing is certain: the Animal Husbandry, (later Animal Science) Department was never quite the same after his arrival.[340]

There were others in the Department of Animal Science who made significant contributions to the livestock industry. J. H. Baumgardner, a native of West Texas who first came to Tech in 1934 as a student and had conducted feeding experiments which culminated in the first Annual Feeder's Day at Tech in 1940, aided the growth of the gigantic feedlot industry on the High Plains in several ways. In developing the "micronizing process" of cooking seeds for livestock and human consumption through experiments from 1966 to 1969, he acted as a consultant. His most important contribution may well have been the development by 1972 of "Rumen Feed," a force-feed treatment for "stressed" calves newly arrived in cattle feedlots, a condition which interfered with early weight gain after transit. He served as consultant for cattle and sheep feedlots and ranchers on animal nutrition. And since 1972 he has traveled extensively in Europe and Asia as special feedlot management consultant for the United States Feed Grains Council.[341] Samuel E. Curl, in still another emphasis, began research in 1961 directed toward the improvement of cattle and sheep fertility, especially in experiments of "induced twinning." And Coleman A. O'Brien by 1965 had developed a simplified fertility testing method for use on sheep and goat males.[342]

Today, more and more research takes place off campus because expansion has taken its toll of the original college farm. A new law school, museum, and huge medical school complex greatly strengthened the University, but took large chunks from the college farm. The movement of agricultural research from campus began when Tech acquired the U.S. government's Pantex Ordnance Plant north of Amarillo in 1947 and renamed it PanTex Farm. The name was later changed to PanTech, and renamed again in 1961. This time it was designated as Texas Technological College Research Farm.

340. Author's conversations with various Texas Tech faculty members and animal scientists at institutions other than Texas Tech.

341. Vita of John H. Baumgardner, DF, TTCAS.

342. *San Angelo Standard-Times*, March 2, 1965, clipping, DF, TTCAS. *Research Projects and Publications, College of Agricultural Sciences, 1970. Grain Sorghum Research, Agriculture and Home Economics, Texas Tech University*, ICASALS Special Report no. 34 (no date). "Study of Beef Cattle Estrus Gets More Aid," *Lubbock Avalanche-Journal*, May 7, 1967, clipping file, W. L. Stangel Papers.

Today, it is Texas Tech University Research Farm. J. P. Smith, an early Tech graduate who had worked as a vocational agriculture teacher and county agent, was the first manager serving in that capacity until 1963. From the beginning, the farm was a cooperative venture with the Texas Agricultural Experiment Station and the U.S. Department of Agriculture. The first research centered on determining the causes of wheat pasture poisoning of cattle.

No state or federal money was used at the Research Farm. Money for research and operation came from private donations and the farm's own profits. In 1963, ground was broken for the Killgore Beef Cattle Center at the Farm. This new expansion was made possible by a $530,000 grant from the Florence Lee and C. L. Killgore Foundation, created from the estate of an early Panhandle ranching family. The Beef Cattle Center was completed in 1964 and W. L. Stangel donated his private library to the facility the next year.[343]

Research at "PanTech" has been both varied and related directly to the needs of High Plains-Panhandle agriculturalists. Experiments have been conducted with cattle in such areas as feeding, additives, digestibility of feedstuffs, and crossbreeding. Other research has included work in forage sorghum variety trials, fertilizers, the use of sewage effluent for irrigation, soils, herbicide tests, seeding of rangeland grasses, the effects of fire on High Plains rangeland vegetation, economic studies of feedlot operations, and the control of greenbugs and various aphids.[344]

For cattlemen, the Research Farm's most important work may well be its bull performance testing. This work started in 1950 was primarily stimulated by the low prices of cattle coupled with rising costs of production. Its objective was to evaluate the growth rate and efficiency in feed utilization of young bulls. A group of about one hundred commercial cattlemen and breeders met at PanTech Farm on November 8, 1955, and formed the American Beef Cattle Performance Registry Association under the sponsorship of Texas Tech and Texas A&M. W. L. Stangel presided over the meeting and Colby Conkwright, a Panhandle Hereford breeder, was elected president. Purpose of the organization was "to take research results gained in beef cattle improvement investigations conducted by Texas A&M and Texas Tech and put it into use among cattle breeders to help them produce better cattle at lower costs." By 1969, more

343. *Texas Techsan*, vol. 10, no. 8 (1961):14:15; vol. 11, no. 7 (1962):16. *Twenty Years of Progress in Agricultural Research, Education and Public Service*, Texas Tech University Research Farm, Pantex, Texas, ICASALS Special Report No. 27 (Texas Tech, 1969): 5-6.

344. *Ibid.*, 15-23.

than 2,500 bulls of seven breeds had been evaluated by the service.[345] The two papers presented during the annual Field Day at the Research Farm in 1975 reflected that continuing interest. They were: "Genetics: A Practical Tool in Beef Production" by Gary Conley of Perryton, Texas, and "Carcass Composition, Animal Performance, and Production Efficiency" by C. Boyd Ramsey of the Department of Animal Science.[346]

Texas Tech also acquired another farm when the Ruth Baird Larrabee Estate willed a number of scattered farms to the University. The Texas Tech University Foundation sold the farms, and bought a 1,920-acre block of land near Brownfield with the proceeds. In addition, the county commissioners of Terry County gave Tech a 99-year lease on an additional 320 acres some distance west of the Brownfield facility in a more semi-arid part of the county. Present plans are to develop those lands into research and graduate teaching facilities. Moreover, another 983-acre farm for undergraduate teaching purposes has recently been acquired north of Lubbock near New Deal.[347]

A number of other major developments have strengthened the College of Agricultural Sciences within the last decade or so. In 1962, Tech was elected a member of the Association of State Universities and Land Grant Colleges, putting the institution into a more permanent relationship with the nation's major agricultural colleges and universities. Perhaps the best indication of the College's maturity is that in 1969, the Coordinating Board of the Texas College and University System approved a Ph.D. program for certain areas in agriculture. Thus Texas Tech became the first non-land grant institution in the nation, except for the agricultural economics programs at the University of Chicago and Harvard, to offer a Ph.D. in agricultural disciplines. In 1975, the degree was being offered in agricultural economics, agronomy, animal science, and range management. In addition, an interdisciplinary Ph.D. in land use planning, management, and design was also a part of the College of Agricultural Sciences' graduate program.[348]

345. *Ibid.*, 17. Conrad Lohoefer, "Cattlemen Hold Pantech Meet," *Lubbock Avalanche-Journal*, November 9, 1955, clipping file, W. L. Stangel Papers.

346. *Texas Tech University Center Reports, 1975*, Research Report no. 25, publication no. T-8-112 (March 1975).

347. Personal interview and conversation with Dean Anson R. Bertrand, June 2, 1975, by author, Lubbock, Southwest Collection.

348. *Texas Techsan*, vol. 14, no. I (1963): 8. Personal interview with Anson R. Bertrand "Tech Doctorate Sets Precedent," *Lubbock Avalanche-Journal*, October 23, 1969, clipping, School of Agriculture folder, Southwest Collection. *Bulletin of Texas Tech University*, Graduate School Catalog, vol. 51, no. 4 (1975): 63.

The first Ph.D. was awarded to Margaret Briley in 1974. Her work was in animal nutrition under the auspices of the Animal Science Department. In view of the traditional feeling that agriculture was a man's field, it is ironic that the first doctorate at Tech was awarded to a woman. But women agricultural majors at Tech were not new arrivals on the scene. As early as 1931, two were enrolled in different sections of the general freshman course in agriculture. At that time, J. O. Ellsworth expressed a rather old-fashioned view when he complained to Dean Leidigh: "Personally I find it inconvenient to have one lady in a course with a large group of men."[349] By 1939, the Division of Agriculture had awarded two degrees in agriculture to women, Elizabeth Montfort Brumbley and Ethel Brown.And that year, Yedda Flatow of Plainview was enrolled as the first woman graduate student in the Division.[350]

In Agricultural Education, L. M. Hargrave and T. L. Leach continued to be influential forces in vocational agriculture and in 4H circles in Texas. About 250 of their former students were teaching in Texas schools and some 50 in public schools of other states. Hargrave served as co-author of a number of workbooks and teaching manuals for vocational agriculture students and teachers, and on various state vocational agriculture and Future Farmers of America (FFA) committees. In addition, he served as superintendent of the market barrow show at the State Fair of Texas for more than two decades. By 1975, twenty-two of his FFA students had won the prestigious Texas State Farmer Award and four of those went on to receive the American Farmer Degree. That year, Hargrave was honored with a 40-year service award by the Texas Vocational Agriculture Teachers Association.[351]

In 1960, the College of Agriculture had 2,629 alumni scattered throughout Texas with the largest concentration in West Texas, but also found in eighteen other states and six foreign nations. That number had almost doubled by 1973 when the College of Agricultural Sciences counted a total of 5,155 degrees conferred since its beginnings. Counted among the alumni were the six sons of the late J. B. Baumgardner of Collingsworth County, a record for one family at Tech. (The two daughters, Barbara and Priscilla, also graduated from Tech, but took their degrees in other fields.) The sons were

349. J. O. Ellsworth, October 8, 1931, to A. H. Leidigh, TTSAP, DF. *ICASALS Newsletter*, 7 (January 1974): 2.

350. *Texas Tech Magazine*, vol. 3, no. 2 (1939): 17. Personal interview with Anson R. Bertrand.

351. Vita of Levi Marlin Hargrave; *Lubbock Avalanche-Journal*, July 30, 1975, clipping, DF, TTCAS.

J. H. of the Tech Animal Science Department; Forrest, who was involved in a dairy manufacturing company in Tulsa, Oklahoma; Haynes, who took his degree in animal husbandry but became a career officer in the U.S. Air Force; Marion, a professor of soil science at Purdue University; David, who farmed in Collingsworth County; and Robert, a Brownfield businessman.[352]

Today, the College of Agricultural Sciences has outgrown the original Dairy Barn and Livestock Judging Pavilion. The huge Tech campus has grown around them. The Department of Park Administration, Landscape Architecture, and Horticulture now utilizes the remodeled Pavilion. It was announced in early 1971 that the Dairy Barn, which had been unused for almost ten years, would be renovated into a campus entertainment center. It still stands idle but news of these plans reached rancher Raymond C. Reed of Mineola, Texas, an alumnus who had served as bookkeeper of the old Student Dairy Association. Reed recalled with nostalgia that W. L. Stangel and the Dairy Barn provided a means for him to attend Tech. When in the late 1960's he sold five of his Charolais heifers for $5,000 each at Kansas City, he recalled that forty years before he had been a member of a Tech livestock judging team at the American Royal in that same arena. For those like Reed and other early alumni, the Dairy Barn and Livestock Judging Pavilion would remain fitting symbols of the impact made upon young rural students and Texas agriculture by Texas Tech, and of the hard work of the early West Texans to build their own "West Texas A&M."[353]

352. Conversation with J. H. Baumgardner by author, July 22, 1974, Lubbock. Edith L. Williams, "It's All In The Family," *Texas Techsan*, 1 (March 1950): 3, 16.

353. Perry Flippin, "Dairy Barn Due New Bag?" *Lubbock Avalanche-Journal*, March 1, 1971, clipping, School of Agriculture folder, Southwest Collection. "Highlights of Barn Relived," *University Daily* (Texas Tech), April 15, 1971, clipping file, W. L. Stangel Papers.

THE CONTEMPORARY COLLEGE OF AGRICULTURAL SCIENCES

Gerald Thomas resigned as Dean in 1970 to become President of New Mexico State University. Anson R. Bertrand was appointed to the position the same year. Dean Bertrand had grown up on a central Texas cotton farm near Gatesville. He graduated from Texas A&M, received the M.S. degree in agronomy from the University of Illinois, and was awarded the Ph.D. in soil physics from Purdue in 1955. Included in his experience was his role as: Director of the Southern Piedmont Soil and Water Conservation Center at Watkinsville, Georgia, Chief of the Southern Branch of Soil and Water Conservation of the U.S. Department of Agriculture Research Station at Athens, Georgia, and head of the Agronomy Department of the University of Georgia. Bertrand's special interests and research were (and are) in soils and water conservation. He is a Fellow of both the American Society of Agronomy and the Soil Conservation Society of America.[354]

In 1975, the College of Agricultural Sciences offers students sixteen different degree programs with thirty-one options. Dean Bertrand, aided by Associate Dean William F. Bennett, an agronomist, and Assistant Dean James E. Osborn, has a faculty of seventy-eight members teaching 1,646 students including 176 graduates, the largest enrollment in the history of the College. Students can take courses ranging from Beef Cattle Feedlot Management, to Environmental Analysis and Planning, to Commodity Futures Trading and Analysis. The new student, by and large, no longer comes almost exclusively from a farm or ranch background. Almost 60 per cent today come from a town or city environment.[355]

The continuing service of the faculty to High Plains and West Texas agriculture, despite lack of a specific budget for that purpose, is observable today on many fronts. For example, when the Federal Power Commission held a hearing in Lubbock in May, 1975, relative to its unfavorable natural gas priority ruling for irrigation users, James Osborn of Agricultural Economics testified that conversion

354. Personal interview with Dean Anson R. Bertrand by author, June 2, 1975, Lubbock, Southwest Collection. *Texas Techsan*, vol. 22, no. 4 (1970): 22. Vita of Anson R. Bertrand, DF, TTCAS.

355. *Bulletin of Texas Tech University*, vol. 50, no. 6 (1974): 78-125. Personal interview with Anson R. Bertrand. Anson R. Bertrand, "The College of Agricultural Sciences," (statement, May 11, 1975), DF, TTCAS.

of irrigation engines from natural gas to gasoline or propane would be virtually prohibitive because of greatly increased costs.[356]

The research budget reflects the maturity of the institution. In 1974-75, a total of $1,585,906 was provided for 132 research projects. Those activities in brush control, vegetable research, and swine research were "line item" appropriations by the Texas Legislature. Out of a faculty of seventy-eight, 55 per cent were directly involved in research projects, aided by seventy-nine graduate students holding research assistantships.

A number of recent developments should be noted. A large new west wing addition to the Agricultural Building was completed, the new Goddard Range and Wildlife Building was opened and now houses not only the Range and Wildlife Management Department, but also the Dean's offices. Proposals have been made to the State Higher Education Coordinating Board to change the name of the Agronomy Department to the Department of Plant and Soil Science, to combine Agricultural Engineering and Food Technology into a Department of Agricultural Engineering and Technology, and to give the Entomology Section departmental status. A Division of Agricultural Services was organized to assume control of all the College's field laboratories except the Killgore Beef Center. The first director was Dale Zinn of Animal Science; present director is Rex Kennedy of Agricultural Economics. A field unit of the Economic Research Service of the U.S. Department of Agriculture with two specialists in marketing is now housed on campus to research marketing in cotton, wool, and mohair.

Harold Dregne came to Tech in 1969 to become Chairman of the Agronomy Department upon the retirement of Arthur W. Young. Today Dregne serves as a member of the State Seed and Plant Board, Chairman of the Committee on Arid Lands for the American Association for the Advancement of Science, Consultant to the United Nations Desertification Conference and a member of the National Academy of Sciences Advisory Panel on the Sub-Saharan Drouth. Moreover, he has recently been appointed the Director of Tech's International Center for Arid and Semi-Arid Land Studies (ICASALS).

In other personnel developments, Max Lennon was made Chairman of the Animal Science Department and now serves on the Board of Directors of the American Society of Animal Science. Willie Ulich of Agricultural Engineering was appointed to the Air

356. Keith Henley, "Farmers Tell FPC Natural Gas Vital," *Lubbock Avalanche-Journal*, May 15, 1975, 1, 14.

Pollution Control Board of Texas. John Hunter serves as President of the Texas Section of the American Society of Range Management. Bill Bennett was named Chairman of a committee of the Texas State Higher Education Coordinating Board to study curricular standards for agricultural disciplines. Dean Anson Bertrand was elected President of the Soil Science Society for America in 1974-75. And James Osborn became Chairman of the Agricultural Economics Department while he continued to serve as Assistant Dean for Research.[357]

The primary thread running through the history of the College of Agricultural Sciences has been service to West Texas agriculture, although spinoffs have also aided agriculture in Texas and in other regions. But the basic thrust has been in meeting the needs of its own region. The College originated in the demands of West Texans, who were isolated by distance from the state land grant college, for their own "A&M." Once established, the constituency of the rapidly developing agricultural region looked upon the institution for leadership in meeting its own unique needs.

Service to the region has taken many forms. In the early period, the institution aided in such matters as the development of the infant dairy and dairy manufacturing industries, helped to publicize High Plains agricultural innovations, made Tech the center of professional horticultural training in West Texas, pioneered early feedlot practices, aided the certified seed business on the High Plains, introduced better farm management and soil conservation to numbers of Plains farmers, furnished most of the expertise for the Ropesville Resettlement experiment and much of the personnel for the new Soil Conservation Service in West Texas, provided better educated young farmers, and filled the classrooms of West Texas high schools with vocational agriculture teachers. All this, and more, was accomplished without state appropriations for either extension work or research.

World War II and President Clifford B. Jones furnished the opportunity for the beginnings of research. The acquisition of the Research Farm at Pantex from the U.S. government after the war, and President E. N. Jones's leadership in making Texas Tech a research and graduate institution offered more opportunities in the fifties. In the sixties, the College emerged as a research-oriented institution furnishing leadership for such varied fields as the massive emerging livestock feedlot and recreational industries of the Southwest and

357. The Dean's Report, College of Agricultural Sciences, September 1, 1974-August 31, 1975; Enrollment statistics supplied by Associate Dean William F. Bennett, DF, TTCAS.

significant research projects ranging from brush control to vegetable production.

Beginning with a skeleton staff and almost nonexistent facilities, the College has grown into one of the largest in the nation, and the largest College of Agricultural Sciences on the Great Plains. Its thousands of graduates are found in virtually every aspect of agriculture and agri-business today.

Although the scope of service has been enlarged to an international scale, West Texas farmers, ranchers, and agri-businessmen still look upon the College as primarily theirs. And it is. Men with ruddy, windburned faces, wearing wide brim hats or seed-company caps and overalls not only send their sons and daughters to the institution, but still find their way to the office of one professor or another with their problems.

And what of the future? The increasing world food shortage, declining ground water level of the High Plains, the energy crisis, annual increases in operating costs for agriculture, and the public demands for enriching the quality of life offer even greater challenges for tomorrow. Texas Tech has already emerged as a world leader in problems of arid and semi-arid environments. Its future work, if it is given the resources and flexibility to meet the challenge, may have an impact not only upon the High Plains region, but upon other regions of the world as well.

BIBLIOGRAPHY

A Note on Primary Sources

It is fortunate for those who are interested in the institutional history of Texas Tech University that so much of the "raw" materials dealing with its past has been preserved by the Southwest Collection of Texas Tech through the cooperative efforts of the institution's Colleges. This has certainly been true of the materials used by the author. Much thanks for this must go to those who preserved the correspondence and record files of the College of Agricultural Sciences, primarily to Dean Emeritus W. L. Stangel, Professor Emeritus Arthur W. Young, and the family of the late Dean Arthur H. Leidigh.

The primary sources for this book are found in the sixty or so file boxes containing the papers, records, correspondence, reports, and publications of the College of Agricultural Sciences located in the Southwest Collection. This material consists of the School of Agriculture Papers, Dean's Files; the School of Agriculture Papers, W. L. Stangel Files; the School of Agriculture Papers, Animal Husbandry Department; and the W. L. Stangel Papers.

The Southwest Collection also has a number of taped interviews with key personnel, such as W. L. Stangel, Arthur W. Young, Fred G. Harbaugh, J. H. Baumgardner, Ralph M. Durham, Donald Ashdown, and Anson R. Bertrand.

In addition, the author is indebted to Dean Anson R. Bertrand for access and use of the Dean's files in the College of Agricultural Sciences for the contemporary period, and to invaluable conversations with various faculty members.

In addition, I have used the *Texas Tech Magazine* and its successor the *Texas Techsan*, the *Bulletins of Texas Tech University*, publications of Texas Tech's International Center for Arid and Semi-Arid Land Studies (ICASALS), scores of newspaper clippings from regional newspapers (especially the *Lubbock Avalanche-Journal*), and news releases of the Texas Tech News Service.

Secondary Works

Andrews, Ruth Horn. *The First Thirty Years: A History of Texas Technological College, 1925-1955.* Lubbock: Texas Tech Press, 1956.

Bishop, Morris. *A History of Cornell.* Ithaca: Cornell University Press, 1962.

Bowers, William L. *The Country Life Movement in America, 1900-1920.* Port Washington, New York: Kennikat Press, 1974.

Connor, Seymour V., ed. *Builders of the Southwest.* Lubbock: Southwest Collection of Texas Tech, 1959.

———. *Texas: A History.* New York: Thomas Y. Crowell, 1971.

Curti, Merle, and Vernon Carstensen. *The University of Wisconsin, 1848-1925: A History.* 2 vols. Madison: University of Wisconsin Press, 1949.

David, Henry *et al.*, eds. *The Economic History of the United States.* Vol. 3, *The Farmer's Age: Agriculture, 1815-1860,* Paul W. Gates. New York: Harper and Row, 1960.

Dillon, Merton L.. "Religion in Lubbock." Pp. 449-516 in *A History of Lubbock,* edited by Lawrence L. Graves. Lubbock: West Texas Museum Association, 1962.

Dunn, Roy Sylvan. "Agriculture Builds a City." Pp. 239-299 in *A History of Lubbock,* edited by Lawrence L. Graves. Lubbock: West Texas Museum Assiociation, 1962.

Fite, Gilbert C. "The Farmers' Dilemma, 1919-1929." Pp. 67-102 in *Change and Continuity in Twentieth Century America, The 1920's*, edited by John Braeman. Columbus: Ohio State University Press, 1968.

———. *The Farmers Frontier, 1865-1900.* New York: Holt, Rinehart and Winston, 1966.

Gibbs, Clifford L. "The Establishment of Texas Technological College." M.A. thesis, Texas Technological College, 1939.

Graves, Lawrence L. "Education, Welfare, and Recreation." Pp. 517-609 in *A History of Lubbock*, edited by Lawrence L. Graves. Lubbock: West Texas Museum Association, 1962.

Green, Donald E. *Land of the Underground Rain: Irrigation on the Texas High Plains, 1910-1970.* Austin: University of Texas Press, 1973.

Hayter, Earl W. *The Troubled Farmer.* DeKalb: Northern Illinois University Press, 1968.

Johnstone, Paul H. "Old Ideals Versus New Ideas in Farm Life." Pp. 111-170 in *Farmers in a Changing World*, United States Department of Agriculture Yearbook, 1940. Washington, D.C.: Government Printing Office, 1940.

Jones, C. Clyde. "An Agricultural College's Response to a Changing World." *Agricultural History*, 42 (October 1968): 283-295.

Marti, Donald B. "The Purposes of Agricultural Education: Ideas and Projects in New York State, 1819-1865." *Agricultural History*, 45 (October 1971): 271-283.

Nall, Garry Lynn. "Agricultural History of the Texas Panhandle, 1880-1965." Ph.D. dissertation. University of Oklahoma, 1972.

———. "Panhandle Farming in the 'Golden Era' of American Agriculture." *Panhandle-Plains Historical Review*, 46 (1973): 68-93.

Perry, George Sessions. *The Story of Texas A and M.* New York: McGraw-Hill, 1951.

Prothero, Roland E. (Lord Ernle). *English Farming: Past and Present.* 4th ed. London: Longmans, Green, 1927.

Rosenberg, Charles E. "Science, Technology, and Economic Growth: The Case of the Agricultural Experiment Station Scientist, 1875-1914." *Agricultural History*, 45 (January 1971): 6-13.

Rushing, June Gilmore, and Kline A. Nall. *Evolution of a University: Texas Tech's First Fifty Years.* Austin: Madrona Press, 1975.

Schlebecker, John T. *Cattle Raising on the Plains, 1900-1961.* Lincoln: University of Nebraska Press, 1963.

Smith, Wilson. " 'Cow College' Mythology and Social History: A View of Some Centennial Literature." *Agricultural History*, 45 (July 1970): 299-310.

Solberg, Winton U. *The University of Illinois, 1867-1894: An Intellectual and Cultural History.* Urbana: University of Illinois Press, 1968.

Stadtman, Verne A. *The University of California, 1868-1968.* New York: McGraw-Hill, 1970.

Stafford, Vernon C. "The Ropesville Resettlement Project." *West Texas Historical Association Year Book*, 25 (October 1949): 87-100.

True, Alfred Charles. *A History of Agricultural Education in the United States, 1787-1925.* Washington, D.C.: Government Printing Office, 1929.

Wade, Homer Dale. *Establishment of Texas Technological College.* Lubbock: Texas Tech Press, 1956.

Warren, George F. "The Origin and Development of Farm Economics in the United States." *Journal of Farm Economics*, 14 (January 1932): 2-9.

Wilson, N. James. "The Farmers' Search for Order, 1880-1910." Ph.D. dissertation. University of Oklahoma, 1974.

Wright, Hamilton. *The Winning of the West Texas College*. Amarillo: privately printed, 1926.

FACULTY: 1925-1975

Deans

Arthur H. Leidigh	1925-1945
W. L. Stangel	1945-1958
Gerald W. Thomas	1958-1970
Anson R. Bertrand	1970-

*Agricultural Economics**

Leander D. Howell	1926-1928
John O. Ellsworth[1]	1928-1937
Elmer L. McBride	1935-1960
Marshall B. Harrison	1936-1947
Archie L. Leonard	1947-1972
Don A. Marshall	1947-1950
J. Wayland Bennett	1948-
Jack O. Ashworth	1949-1956
David H. Pinson	1950-1953
Ray V. Billingsley	1956-1963
John W. Thomas	1957-1960
Walter B. Rogers	1958-1965
Harold L. Mathes	1960-1962
James W. Graves	1961-
Herbert W. Grubb	1963-1972
Hong Y. Lee	1963-
David G. Moorman	1963-1971
Robert G. Welch	1963-1967
Willard F. Williams	1963-
Gerhard H. Newfeld	1965-1967
James E. Osborn	1965-
Thomas R. Owens	1965-
M. L. Fowler	1966-
Raymond A. Dietrich	1967-
Rex P. Kennedy	1967-
Richard J. Foote	1968-1972
Sujit K. Roy	1968-
William R. Flint	1970-1971
Kenneth B. Young	1971-
Thomas M. Bell	1973-
Billy G. Freeman	1973-

*Organized in 1927 and originally designated the Department of Agricultural Economics and Farm Management; the name was expanded in 1933 to the Department of Agricultural Economics, Farm Management, and Rural Sociology as a gesture to the new President Bradford Knapp who subsequently taught a course in rural sociology for the Department. In 1947, "farm management and rural sociology" were deleted from the name.

1. Left the Department in 1937 to become head of the new Department of Economics and Business Administration. He later became the first Dean of the School of Business Administration.

*Agricultural Education**

Cyril Luker	1933-1936
Robert L. Burdette	1935-1937
Ray L. Chappelle	1936-1961
Oscar T. Ryan	1936-1947
T. L. Leach	1937-
L. M. Hargrave	1946-
T. Euel Liner	1947-1951
Jack R. Tinney	1948-1951
U. Lewis Eggenberger	1961-
Marcus L. Juby[1]	1972-1973
Leonard Sigler[1]	1973-1974
Jerry Don Stockton[1]	1975-

*First organized in 1933 as the Department of Vocational Agriculture Education; the name was changed in 1938.

1. Joint appointment with Agricultural Engineering Department.

*Agricultural Engineering**

Arthur W. Young (Acting Head)[1]	1951-1953
Herman F. Williams[2]	1951-1952
Archie W. Sullivan[2]	1951-1952
Howard Keck	1951-1952
Eldred A. Jordan	1952-1955
Ira L. Williams	1952-1974
Charles T. Bourns	1953-1955
Eschol A. Crook	1955-1957
Billy R. Stewart	1955-1956
Victor L. Hauser	1956-1957
William F. Schwiesow	1957-1967
Donald L. Day	1957-1958
Douglas C. Rattan	1960-1961
Ivan Kirk	1961-1964
Willie L. Ulich	1961-
Martin J. Dvoracek	1962-
Donald F. Wanjura	1965-1967
Walter Grub	1966-
Ronald Wheaton	1966-1969
Alan D. Brashears	1967-
Joseph C. Newell	1967-1973
Eugene P. Foerster	1969-
Leonard L. Keeton	1969-1973
Thomas G. Carpenter	1970-1974
William M. Lyle	1970-1973
Marcus L. Juby[4]	1972-1973
John P. Ford	1973-1974
Leonard Sigler[4]	1973-1974
J. Wayland Bennett (Acting Head)[3]	1974-
Jerry Don Stockton[4]	1975-

*Organized in 1951 from Plant Industry Department

1. Also Head and member of Agronomy Department.
2. In Plant Industry Department prior to organization of Agricultural Engineering Department in 1951.
3. Joint appointment with the Agricultural Economics Department.
4. Joint appointment with the Agricultural Education Department.

Animal Science[*]

Wenzel Louis Stangel	1925-1958
Ray C. Mowery	1926-1960
Fred G. Harbaugh	1927-1971
Neil Casey Fine	1935-1942, 1945-1958
J. D. Strickland	1939-1945
Jamie Caviness	1942
John H. Baumgardner	1945-
Delvert L. Devin	1946-1948
Coleman A. O'Brien	1947-
Hubert L. Mathews	1948-1950
Harry R. Burkhart	1948-1954
Kirk B. Turner	1948-1970
Stanley E. Anderson	1948-1962
Waymond T. Miller	1948-1949
Koy L. Neeley	1948-1961
Ray T. Crane	1949-1950
Fred W. Boren	1950-1955
Nathan J. Allen, Jr.	1951-1954
William H. Cloninger	1953-1954
Robert H. Black	1954-1956
Herbert R. Crookshank	1954-1960
Ralph M. Durham	1959-
Frank A. Hudson	1960-
Samuel E. Curl	1961-
Dale W. Zinn	1961-1975
James G. Cloyd	1962
Ronald L. Davenport	1962-1963
George F. Ellis	1963-
Robert C. Albin	1964-
Richard Dale Furr	1965-
Blaine B. Breidenstein	1966-1968
Lloyd B. Sherrod	1967-
Leland F. Tribble	1967-
Allen F. Parr	1968-1969
Clovis Boyd Ramsey	1968-
Raymond H. Klett	1969-1973
Keith D. Lind	1969-1971
Charles T. Gaskins	1970-1975
Archie Max Lennon	1970-
Henry W. Wohler, Jr.	1970-1973
Leif Harry Thompson	1972-
John W. Allen	1973-
Charles E. Sasse	1973-
Donald E. Orr	1975-

[*]Organized originally as the Department of Animal Husbandry; the name was changed to Animal Science in 1968.

Entomology Section[*]

Donald Ashdown[1]	1953-
Ellis W. Huddleston	1960-1975
Charles R. Ward	1967-1975
Darrell N. Ueckert	1969-1970
Charles W. O'Brien	1970-1972
David E. Foster	1973-
John C. Owens	1975-
James K. Wangberg	1975-

[*]Prior to 1974, Entomology was in the Department of Park Administration, Horticulture, and Entomology.

1. Employed exclusively in entomological research at the PanTech Farm from 1952 to 1953. Received faculty appointment in 1953.

Food Technology[*]

Kenneth M. Renner	1927-1948
Mart G. Pederson	1932-1944
Arthur Prichard	1933-1936
Laurence G. Harmon	1936-1954
James W. Huffman	1939-1942
William H. Tinney	1947-1951
Joe T. Cardwell	1947-1951
J. J. Willingham	1948-1971
Kenneth Robert Renner	1950-1954
Milton L. Peeples	1951-
Kenneth T. Scott	1954-1955
Edgar R. Jarman	1955-1960
John N. Morgan	1958-1960
Ronald M. Miller	1960-
R. L. Selman	1968-1971
Lee Blakely	1971-1973
Linda Stokley	1973-1974
E. D. Maxson	1974-

*First organized as the Department of Dairy Manufactures in 1927; the name was changed to the Department of Dairy Industry in 1955 and to the Department of Food Technology in 1970.

*Park Administration, Landscape Architecture, and Horticulture**

Elo J. Urbanovsky	1951-1975
Warren W. Yocum[1]	1951-1964
George O. Elle[1]	1951-1970
Charles R. Rouse	1951-1953
Edward W. Zukauckas, Jr.	1952-
William M. Gosdin	1953-1964
Robert H. Rucker	1956-1962
Robert R. Reed	1957-
Donnie Joe Johnson	1960-1966
Bill A. Chevalier	1964-1970
James W. Kitchen	1964-
Charles C. Doell	1965-1974
Arvil C. Hamilton	1965-1968
Thomas A. Musiak	1965-
Glen M. Rydl	1966-1968
Malcolm George Bishop	1968-1969
L. B. Houston	1968-1973
George Tereshkovich	1968-
Emmanuel T. Van Nierop	1968-1973
Conrad Wirth	1968-1975
John Mark Gosdin	1969-1972
Pat Dwayne Taylor	1969-1973
Arthur N. Glick	1970-
James D. Mertes	1970-
Robert Marlett	1972-
Ernest B. Fish	1973-
Robert L. Frazer	1973-1974
Joe Thomas Verdoorn	1974-
James B. Harris	1975-

*Originally in the Plant Industry Department, it was first organized as the Department of Horticulture and Park Management in 1951. The name was changed in 1963 to the Department of Park Administration, Horticulture, and Entomology. When Entomology became a separate Section in 1974, the Department was given the present name. To avoid duplication, entomologists are included in Entomology Section.

1. In Plant Industry Department prior to organization of Department of Horticulture and Park Management.

*Plant Industry**

Arthur H. Leidigh (Agron.)	1925-1950
Charles H. Mahoney (Hort.)	1925-1931
Harley J. Bower (Agron.)	1926-1932
Harold J. Brodrick (Hort.)	1927-1928
Hershel M. Bell (Agron.)	1927-1935
Clive E. Russell (Hort.)	1929-1937
George W. Woodbury (Hort.)	1931-1935
Eugene C. Buie (Ag. Eng.)	1934-1935
Claude E. Hope (Hort.)	1935-1936
Orville B. Howell (Hort.)	1935-1943
Henry P. Clay (Ag. Eng.)	1935-1946
Arthur W. Young (Agron.)	1935-1951
Warren W. Yocum (Hort.)	1937-1951
Earl T. Duke (Agron.)	1937-1942
Darrell D. Morey (Agron.)	1938-1939
Ernest Mader (Agron.)	1939-1947
George O. Elle (Hort.)	1941-1942, 1946-1951
Cecil I. Ayers (Agron.)	1942-1951
Herman F. Williams (Ag. Eng.)	1946-1951
Naud Burnett (Agron.)	1947-1950
Goah A. Lynch (Hort.)	1948-1950
Archie W. Sullivan (Ag. Eng.)	1948-1951
Alfred B. La Gasse (Hort.)	1948-1950
Judd Morrow (Agron.)	1948-1951
Elo J. Urbanovsky (Park Mgmt.)	1949-1951
Noble K. Peterson (Agron.)	1950-1951
Aral B. Gwin (Park Mgmt.)	1950-1951
Michael A. Samchok (Park Mgmt.)	1950-1951

*This Department was established in 1932 by combining the Departments of Agronomy and Horticulture which had been organized in 1925. Agricultural Engineering was added to its curriculum in 1934. The Park Management area was added in 1949. The Department passed out of existence in 1951 when it was split into the Departments of Agronomy, Agricultural Engineering, and Horticulture and Park Management.

Plant and Soil Science (Agronomy)[*]

Arthur W. Young[1]	1951-1969
Cecil I. Ayers[1]	1951-
Noble K. Peterson[1]	1951-1953
Gordon E. Gatherum	1951-1953
Chester C. Jaynes	1951-
Coleman Y. Ward	1952-1954
Samuel N. Little	1953-1957
John E. McCaleb	1953-1954
Clark Harvey	1954-
Gene L. Spain	1955-1958
William H. Kelly	1957-1960
Charles W. Wendt	1957-1964
John R. Hunter[2]	1957-1968
Gerald W. Thomas[2]	1958-1968
B. L. Allen	1959-
Jack G. King	1960-1961
Thadis Box	1962-1968
Alfred Eugene Coleman	1963-1966, 1967-1973
Douglas F. Owen	1963-1966
Kenneth C. Killian	1963-1967
Joseph L. Schuster[2]	1964-1968
Raymond E. Meyer	1965-1973
Eric G. Bolen[2]	1967-1968
Henry Wright[2]	1967-1968
William F. Bennett	1968-
Harold E. Dregne	1969-
Anson R. Bertrand	1970-
John D. Downes	1970-
George O. Elle[3]	1970-
Daniel R. Krieg	1970-
Robert G. Stevens	1971-
David L. Stamp	1974-1975
Richard E. Zartman	1974-

[*]Organized in 1951 from Plant Industry Department, expanded into the Department of Agronomy and Range Management in 1962, and reverted to Department of Agronomy when Range and Wildlife Management split off in 1968; the name was changed to Plant and Soil Science in 1975.

1. In Plant Industry Department prior to organization of Agronomy Department.
2. Left Department in 1968 to form the Range and Wildlife Department.
3. Member of the Department of Park Administration, Landscape Architecture, and Horticulture prior to 1970.

*Range and Wildlife**

John R. Hunter	1968-
Gerald W. Thomas[1]	1968-1970
Thadis Box[1]	1968
Joseph L. Schuster[1]	1968-1973
Eric G. Bolen[1]	1968-1973
Henry Wright[1]	1968-
Billie E. Dahl	1968-
Donald Klebenow	1968-1971
Russell D. Pettit	1969-
Ronald E. Sosebee	1969-
Darrell N. Ueckert	1970-
Jerran T. Flinders[2]	1971-1972, 1973-1974
Emmanuel Van Nierop[3]	1971
Donald F. Burzlaff	1973-
Dee A. Quinton	1973-1975
John D. Garcia	1973-
C. David Simpson	1975-
Kenneth L. Stromborg	1975-

*Originally a part of the Agronomy Department; organized into a separate department in 1968.

1. Members of Agronomy Department prior to organization of Range and Wildlife Department.
2. In Entomology Section from 1969 to 1970.
3. Joint appointment with the Department of Park Administration, Horticulture, and Entomology.

INDEX